PRAISE FOR LINDA GILLIAM,
THE SEVEN STEPS TO HELP BOYS ___ ___ ___

"Linda Gilliam has the unique talent of bringing out the best in every student in which she comes in contact. She has made major contributions to our students, staff, and community over the many years she has taught. She truly is an exemplary educator, 'master teacher,' and model for all." —*Linda Hauser, retired principal of Nelson Elementary School, Clovis, CA*

"Linda Gilliam has a real talent for meeting the needs of the students and adjusting her curriculum accordingly. She knows how to utilize whole language, thematic teaching, and language experience methods." —*A. H. Petersen, retired principal, Gettysburg Elementary School, Clovis, CA*

"Linda Gilliam makes learning a fun, positive experience for her children, and I wish every child could start their education with a loving and competent teacher like Linda, as she is one in a million!" —*Erla Stanley, retired vice-principal, Nelson Elementary School, Clovis, CA*

"Linda Gilliam's students are well prepared, and her classroom environment is bright and interesting; showing her talent for creative endeavors." —*Julia R. Hollenbeck, retired mentor teacher, career development and employment service, California State University, Fresno, CA*

"Linda Gilliam has many teaching strengths, but her number one strength is the positive-feeling tone she creates in the classroom for her students. Linda works well with all students, but she is truly outstanding with our minority, bilingual, and low-income students." —*Carl R. Campbell, assistant superintendent, King's Canyon Schools, Fresno and Tulare, CA*

"Linda Gilliam was one of the finest elementary teachers I have observed. Her classroom learning environment was positive, interesting, and creative. Her colleagues often looked up to her for professional, educational, curricular, and instructional help and expertise." —*Bob Kamph, principal, Friant Elementary School, Friant, CA*

"Linda Gilliam is a teacher who really cares about her students. Her students loved her, as she worked to make learning fun and exciting for all of her students. I was often in the room when she was teaching and loved to watch her work her 'magic.' It was so enjoyable to watch her students get involved with hands-on activities and see them get excited about learning." —*Cheris Meek, retired teacher of thirty years*

"Linda Gilliam's ever-positive personality sets the classroom in a learning environment like no other! She used teaching Spanish, poems, and music/songs daily to keep the students engaged in participating in activities. Learning was fun, challenging, and exciting!" *—Sandra DeLuca Hendrichs, elementary teacher for twenty-eight years*

"The majority of my students whom I serve are boys who are ELL as well and require specially designed instruction to meet their academic, social, and language deficits. I have so much respect for Linda Gilliam and am thankful for her early influences in my life! She showed me what it looks like in a very practical way how to teach to the multiple intelligences and how to engage the whole student in a positive, fun, and engaging way." *—Barb Blakeslee, special education teacher and creator of "My Choice ePortfolio System," Seattle, WA*

The Seven Steps to Help Boys Love School

Teaching to Their Passion for Less Frustration

Linda Marie Gilliam

ROWMAN & LITTLEFIELD
Lanham · Boulder · New York · London

Published by Rowman & Littlefield
A wholly owned subsidiary of The Rowman & Littlefield Publishing Group, Inc.
4501 Forbes Boulevard, Suite 200, Lanham, Maryland 20706
www.rowman.com

Unit A, Whitacre Mews, 26-34 Stannary Street, London SE11 4AB

British Library Cataloguing in Publication Information Available

Library of Congress Cataloging-in-Publication Data Available

ISBN 978-1-4758-1578-8 (hardcover)
ISBN 978-1-4758-1579-5 (paperback)
ISBN 978-1-4758-1580-1 (e-book)

∞™ The paper used in this publication meets the minimum requirements of
American National Standard for Information Sciences—Permanence of Paper
for Printed Library Materials, ANSI/NISO Z39.48-1992.

Printed in the United States of America

Contents

Acknowledgments

First and foremost, I thank Mrs. Oden, a wonderful lady with whom I worked at Modesto Junior College in California, the one who encouraged me to become a teacher. Sadly, she recently passed away, and I was so wishing to present this book to her as a gift of appreciation. Hopefully, she knows the tremendous impact she had and the valuable seed she planted in me. I encourage and challenge everyone to do the same with some child, helping him or her to pursue his or her own passionate dreams.

Mrs. Oden was supportive, encouraging, and enthusiastic in her belief that I would make a wonderful teacher; she took the time to listen carefully to learn that I loved camp counseling and teaching children. I never dreamed that "her choice for me" would become my passion. By discovering this passion, every day of "work" was a joy and almost seemed like a hobby rather than an occupation. We should all be so lucky.

My wish is that all children, especially boys, will be allowed to find their own passions early in life and supported in doing so, with more time to enjoy living their dreams. I thank all the parents, teachers, coaches, administrators, and anyone leading the fight for our children to be taught at their developmental level and in the way in which years of brain research show us they learn best.

Finally, thanks are given to all the teachers, administrators, and parents sharing thought-provoking comments in my book. Unending appreciation is given especially to Mr. Ralph Marston, a wonderful author and the publisher of *The Daily Motivator* (www.greatday.com), who allowed me to use so many of his excellent quotes of positive advice and encouragement for young and old alike.

Preface

Over the course of my forty years in the field of education, teaching children, helping teachers, counseling parents, and giving presentations at various workshops, I've learned that the most significant reason for children *not* liking school—boys in particular—is the lack of the educational system finding a successful template to use. In addition, boys learn differently than girls and develop slower when it comes to literacy.

Numerous studies have proven this fact over and over, yet classes are taught the same way to everyone. Girls like sitting and listening for long periods of time, while many boys feel tortured. Boys need more hands-on activities, with movement and exploration, for their learning to flourish. Medication may be necessary for some, but it is not the answer for boys who are just "acting like boys."

In my opinion, we as educators and parents, early on, need to encourage children to discover their own strengths through finding a child's true passion or interest, no matter what it might be. Those interests will *change, but then so must our teaching. My heart goes out to those children lost in the shuffle of schools trying to "shove children through the educational mill" of reading, writing, and math, hoping only that they will do well on an upcoming mandated test. Our curriculum leaves little time for much creativity by teachers or children.*

There is no time for learning foreign languages or any other subject not directly tied to the Common Core Standards or tests given. It is obvious that little has changed over the century to solve the many problems prevalent in our schools today. To further substantiate this, we have heard of how a number of our best-known Nobel Prize winners and other well-known men truly hated school. Many of them even thought that school was boring, confining, prison-like, and frustrating at best. Consequently, a large number of brilliant men dropped out of school, choosing homeschooling and learning on their own.

The time is now if we want to close the widening educational gap between boys and girls as well as the increasing achievement gap between the United States and other countries. My theory is that if we do not change our "antiquated" school system soon, children's frustration will lead to the serious epidemic of aggressive behaviors and a general feeling of failure found mainly in boys. We may be doomed to the mediocrity that our country will accomplish in the future, not to mention what it is doing to our society as a whole. School shootings and stabbings, bullying, fighting, gang activities, bomb threats, and even suicides are constantly in the news, much to our dismay. To even think that many schools are now eliminating recess to give more time for "teaching" is ludicrous.

In *The Seven Steps to Help Boys Love School: Teaching to Their Passion for Less Frustration*, I spell out simple, exciting ways we can motivate children at home as well as in the classroom. We must help them become focused on their passions or interests early on, or many will come to hate school by the tender age of five.

Participating in hundreds of conferences with parents, giving workshops, and coaching teachers, I was constantly asked how to help children love or even like school, again boys in particular. They wanted to know how their children could learn to enjoy reading, writing, and math in the classroom as well as at home. During my ten years as a literacy specialist, I tried a "new approach of teaching" to a child's passion or interest. This program was developmentally appropriate as well as individualized. Observation portfolios were available to parents and other teachers. These folders became a valuable resource during our conferences—for students to see their newest improvement and for parents to evaluate progress. We did not simply focus on the current core curriculum offered by the school district; more important, we made sure all that we taught was "developmentally appropriate" for each student, as mentioned repeatedly in this book. This is the key to successful learning.

The results were truly amazing, showing that if we can discover that passion or interest early, a child can learn to love school and even enjoy reading, writing, and math but, more important, to love oneself. Over the years, while using this new system, the child's self-esteem flourished. With my new program, children saw literature as a "necessary tool" to find out more about their curiosity. The students could finally see how reading and writing were relevant. School was more fun and more interactive and, naturally, was less stressful for everyone.

I am proud to say I was recognized for my efforts by receiving a "Teacher of the Year" award for the Vancouver School District in 1997. In addition, I was published in the *Who's Who of Teachers* for two consecutive years and again in the book *Poets Speak Out*.

Introduction

Causes for Concern

WHY SO SLOW FOR CHANGES TO HAPPEN?

In order for us to even come close to closing the nation's educational gap, the future of America depends on creating successful students by the third or fourth grade. Reading, writing, and math are the major subjects assessed. Talk about pressure. Isn't it odd that science appears not to be as important as the other subject areas because it might be the key to our survival in the future?

Now with many students coming to America from different countries and having different languages and cultures, our educational system is ripe for a drastic change. And if not now, when? Many talk about this necessary change—year after year—but that change never really comes to fruition. There seem to be many changes, but are they the ones we need to make our children succeed in learning? We need to succeed.

Producing successful students, boys in particular, will lead to less frustration, less bullying, fewer dropouts and suicides, and, most important, a happy, confident, productive human being. Today, not only are many little boys frustrated, but teachers and parents are becoming the same. They all question *why* our educational system is so bent on repeating the same antiquated techniques for learning.

There are many boys who do really well in school. They are bright and attentive; they enjoy school and get the most out of it. Studies have shown that there are more boy geniuses than there are girl geniuses and that there are more boys at the top of the IQ scale than there are girls as well. Unfortunately, many boys lack the concentration that is required to thrive in school and do *not* enjoy being there. Others are extremely bright but lack the focus that it takes to really progress educationally, and school is ill-fitted for them, leading them to perform below their potential.

It is hard for many kids to sit still all day and listen to lectures from teachers, but it is especially hard for boys. They have tremendous energy, but they do not get to expend it while they are in class. This can lead to poor performance because they cannot sit still and focus on the task at hand. The U.S. Department of Education states that two-thirds of special education students are boys and that they are five times more likely to be considered hyperactive than their female counterparts.[1]

Over the past forty years of teaching, there has been very little change in the way we teach and the way children learn. Most of what has changed is the earlier emphasis on reading and writing in hopes that the children will be better prepared for the mandated tests. Expectations for boys who are struggling developmentally are too high.

Why does the educational system of today keep trying to understand all the "problems" it observes in boys? Perhaps those problems are really the problems of the educational system, ignoring the needed fix for what and how boys should learn best. By trying to fix middle school or high school, the administrators are waiting until it is too late. The changes need to begin at the very beginning of schooling, not in the middle or when those in high school drop out. The mistake that everyone is ignoring is huge.

> Never allow the fear of doing it wrong prevent you from doing it at all. If you are not making mistakes you are not trying anything new.
>
> —R. E. Shockley

By beginning in kindergarten and using engaging strategies that excite boys, we can build a stable, solid structure, similar to a pyramid of skills, required to be learned for success in education.

Our children dread test time, as do many teachers, parents, and even administrators. This continual testing can cause undue stress for all and make teaching and learning tedious and often uncreative. There is no time for impromptu teaching. So when a child asks about something that is more interesting to him and that may be off topic, there is no time left for questioning. There are few productive discussions or hands-on activities with exciting exploration for the very young.

"WHAT, NO MORE RECESS?"

The worst mistake the educational system is doing to children, again boys in particular, is cutting back on recess time. This fun break is one thing all children need and look forward to. A boy needs to let off some steam and feel ready to come back into the classroom to try to absorb more information. Sadly, he is not really engaged in the lesson he has to come in for.

This exclusion of recess might seem like a form of punishment when taken away. This "punishment" is even worse when the boy comes to the realization that his recess interferes with reading and writing, perhaps math as well. He begins to dislike those subjects even more, thinking recess is not as important to the teachers.

A rare male teacher, teaching second grade at the age of fifty-two several years ago, had this to say:

Teaching second grade was wonderful! A classroom full of seven- and eight-year-olds who are curious about life in general made it easy to teach and enjoy the school day. And the more enjoyment I had, the more it reflected on them and allowed a happy experience in school for the whole class. Taking them out for physical education on a daily basis was a highlight for all the students, and to this day I still hear that playing kickball and beating the fourth graders was something they will remember for a long time.

That type of learning environment is beneficial in their studies as well and clearly showed by the academic progress that was made throughout the school year.

Don Campbell, now a pilot instructor, was obviously a perceptive teacher and the type we need now more than ever. So why can't we recruit more male teachers at the elementary level? We must find more hiring incentives to lure exceptional male instructors to help us with struggling boys.

This valuable time spent at recess time is used for socialization, playing games, and competing with others and is a good form of healthy exercise. Recess may become a thing of the past if we do not complain more—and soon. All I want to know is, when do teachers go to the bathroom? In addition, without recess time, there must be more interruptions in the classroom for children having to go to the bathroom. Going to the bathroom can become their only escape from the unending lessons they do not totally understand.

It may be argued that physical education fills in now for recess, but we have to agree they are two totally different activities. Recess is monitored by adults with whistles, but the choices of what children want to do are usually their own. Physical education is structured, with children being told what to do, how to do it, and when to do it, whether the child feels competent in certain skills or not. Many underdeveloped boys even soon hate the activity and become embarrassed with how they do unless they are lucky enough to have had a teacher like Don Campbell.

Subsequently, boys dread the thought of even participating in physical education due to their lagging growth spurt or lack of coordination in performing various skills. The only thing recess and physical education have in common is a loud, annoying whistle.

Sadly, recess has now become an anticipated but missed freedom for thousands of schools and children across the nation. Can you imagine kindergarten without recess? Seems like "cruel and unusual punishment"— certainly for the little boys who have trouble sitting still for more than half an hour at best.

EVEN CREATIVE TEACHING
IS BEING SLOWLY ELIMINATED

Unfortunately, many excellent veteran teachers are dropping out of education for many of the reasons stated above, while as many boys are dropping out of high school. Boys are not seeing any relevance to what they are required to learn or any connection to the areas of learning they want to know more about. Other boys feel frustrated, trying to keep up with the unending assignments given. It can be overwhelming when a child is below grade level in reading, writing, or math. Testing often only validates their fears of failure.

In many schools, the real joy of teaching and learning is not there for either teachers or students. We all can remember taking classes, studying hard for test grades, and then never using that information again in real life. How ridiculous is that—consequently becoming such a waste of everyone's time and effort?

Teachers all over the country got into the teaching profession hoping they could make a difference in a child's life. They had hoped to use their special creative talents and skills to make learning more meaningful and especially exciting for each and every student they worked with. Low salaries were never a huge deciding factor when a person wanted to be a teacher. The rumors of low pay had circulated often and were certainly known.

Many of these underpaid and underappreciated teachers still are spending much of their hard-earned dollars making their teaching more hands-on and interesting for their students. They all need a big hug for all that they are expected to do now. Today, they still spend their money but mostly on dull charts for facts that need to be memorized by the young students. These skills are now mandatory for children being able to pass assessments given and core standards required by the states.

In reality, the child would learn these skills much faster with lessons out of doors, playing games, singing songs, and learning poems that make learning fun. More importantly, that active learning would be retained much longer by the student. This type of interactive learning comes naturally to children and does not have to be forced.

What if you discovered a program that addresses a successful way to reach most children by teaching "basic skills" through whatever passion that child has at the time? By basic skills, we mean speaking, reading, writing, math, and even science.

To further clarify, when you read the word "passion," the word "interest" can be also used in its place. Passion is usually much stronger and develops later, but an interest can easily turn into a passion through learning more about that particular interest. Everyone finds an interest eventually, and they can change to something else just as quickly. However, sometimes it is in the child's best interest to find another passion.

BRAIN DIFFERENCES IN BOYS AND GIRLS

If we are to make our improved teaching fit the child, we cannot ignore the differences between girls and boys when it comes to learning. Studies have shown that the brains of girls deal with language much differently than those of boys. Girls seem to have more connections between the parts of the brain that handle emotion (the amygdala) and the parts of the brain that handle language.

While boys have bigger brains, on the average, brain research is showing more complex connections between the parts of the brain in girls. Bigger is not always better: it is just different. Research shows that the large tract of neural fibers connecting both brain hemispheres (the corpus callosum) is larger in girls than in boys.[2]

Some scientists have even found that the brains of girls process verbal language simultaneously in the two hemispheres of the frontal lobe, while boys tend to process it in the left side only. Furthermore, these connections, as well as their greater use of both hemispheres of the brain, may explain why women lose fewer language capabilities than men after suffering a left-hemisphere stroke.[3]

Additionally, this could have some bearing on why so many boys suffer from dyslexia. Who knows for sure, but maybe having more areas of their brain involved in language allows girls to compensate for weaknesses in their brains more readily than boys if one area is not working in an optimal way.

These structural differences may be related to a greater tendency for females to sense emotional states and use language to describe those feelings. Often this continual sharing of feelings is to the chagrin of their husbands, boyfriends, or boys who are just friends. No wonder it is so much easier for females to share how we feel regardless of whether it is desired or appreciated by the male.

Most of us have certainly noticed that the brains of girls generally mature earlier than those of boys. From as early as the age of six months, girls show more electrical activity in the left hemisphere than the right. The left hemisphere is dominant for language in most people. Even in the classroom, the maturity of girls is usually evident and can continue for a long time, leaving boys in the dust.

In contrast, levels of testosterone have been shown to be related to increased development of the right hemisphere, which usually is dominant for spatial skills in most boys. Brain-imaging studies have shown that when faced with emotional issues, boys process these issues in the brain stem, causing their "fight-or-flight" response.[4]

Girls' brains appear to move emotional information into the brain's cortex. This makes them more likely to process emotions and to get help from others. Girls' development is also faster in the prefrontal cortex, which helps in executive decision making. This adds to a girl's ability to control impulsive behavior and to be able to be more empathetic to others. On the other hand, boys' brains are set up for systemizing.[5]

So are your eyes glazing over while thinking, "Too much information?" However, we needed to discuss these discoveries related to the differences between the brains of boys and girls to emphasize how these differences clearly have an impact on school performance. We cannot continue teaching all children in the same ways.

You might observe most girls speaking sooner than boys; by first grade, girls are approximately one year ahead of boys in language development. Research is showing that girls' speech is more cooperative, reciprocal, and collaborative and that they verbalize their feelings more readily. They perform better in speech discrimination, word reading and spelling, reading comprehension skills, verbal memory, accurate speech, and fluent speech. Girls have better communication skills, eye contact, and social skills.

No wonder boys hate school. Perhaps they may notice some of their shortcomings. Boys have twice the risk of having language disorders. But now let's hear about their strengths for a change. Boys are better in many aspects of spatial learning and superior at navigation. They excel in geography and building activities. Boys also have high-level abstract logic and math reasoning.

It is obvious that most boys have better ability in movement activities, such as throwing and catching objects, as well as aiming. However, new studies find that while the girl's eye has better perception of color and texture, the boy's eye had better perception of movement.[6]

Many say that the early learning years of children or students are for teaching them to read. Yet when older, children must read to learn. Often we need to read this last statement over and over for it to be of consequence; here is where it gets sticky for many frustrated boys trying to keep up. If a child is not ready to read or if, for his age, reading is not developmentally appropriate, the snowball effect of becoming a poor or nonexistent reader starts by first grade.

Think of how the pressure to read, when children are not developmentally ready, could easily affect how they feel about themselves as learners and about school. Just trying to sound out letters or words will take away any comprehension of what they are struggling to read. In a way, it would be like trying to learn algebra, but you never learned number sense or relationships of simple addition and subtraction.

Boys' frustration levels go sky high—and understandably so when this pressure and frustration build year after year. Perhaps this sad situation is leading to the need for this book. Hopefully, many can still be saved: SOS—Save Our Students!

BULLIES ARE EVERYWHERE; JUST ASK THE TEACHER

Many (but not all) children have to act out in class one way or another. What can be observed in various behaviors is seen daily in school. A bored or frustrated child can just tune out, while others have to be class clowns. The latter is harmless but can be distracting to others, including to the teacher trying to teach.

However, other children turn their frustration into anger and become more aggressive, a much greater and serious concern. Such behavior is naturally worse and should be more of a concern to everyone. Many teachers and parents may even find those same frustrated children turn to bullying. A bully can feel powerful and more in control of his environment.

These same young children can grow larger and more aggressive as they become older. Frustrated in their lack of success in school, combined with low self-esteem as a result, these bullies can cause real harm to others. Often joining up with gangs is an option that makes them feel even more powerful and more in control.

In conclusion, we can see why boys need more movement, more variety, and certainly more stimulation in school. The movement not only helps boys manage boredom and being impulsive but also stimulates their brains. This leads to better learning. As concerned parents, teachers, and administrators, better learning should be our constant goal.

We see that boys tend to want to test the rules and are usually more motivated by competition. Sadly, many of our schools are not taking these important differences into account when it comes to differentiated instruction with children. This book gives strategies that use these strengths in boys to help change this situation in our educational system. For boys to feel successful, competition with self is the best kind of competition.

WHAT MUST BE DONE FOR EDUCATIONAL CHANGE TO HELP BOYS?

No one should blame the teachers or the schools since now their curriculum is not their own. Creativity is often taken away, with no time left for music, art, or physical education except in very structured settings. Teachers are now under the pressure of programs and core competencies dictated mostly by the state. Collaboration among teachers is at a minimum while they teach with the apprehension of how their students will perform on the mandated tests given. Too much time and effort is spent on guessing what might be on the all-important test.

THE SEVEN ES OF EXCELLENT EDUCATION

Either passion or interest is what drives children to further explore, investigate, question, and become excited about learning. Doesn't that fit adults as well?

This book also emphasizes using the "seven Es of excellent education" during teaching. *These seven characteristics are meant to provide excitement, enthusiasm, entertaining lessons, engaging lessons, exploration, and evaluation. So what is the last "E"? You counted only six, right?*

Encouragement, the seventh "E," is probably the most important "E" and one we should share with every child on a daily basis. This seven-step program is highly individualized for every student and evaluated daily. The exciting lessons, with age-appropriate grade-level reading, are constantly changing to fit the learning style and interest of students, be they girls or boys.

Ralph Marston, an author and publisher, is an excellent motivational speaker. He expresses this book's goals for teachers, parents, caregivers, coaches, and administrators and also, more importantly, for the boys who struggle with school. His words of comfort, wisdom, and advice would make anyone feel better:

> Expecting the youngest child to stay on task, sit quietly, while trying to learn how to read and write too early . . . are unrealistic goals! Education presented in constant structure, with so many "inappropriate for their age" required tasks, bullies everywhere, and all the other things that diminish the child's self-confidence and self-esteem need to be changed. We wish for boys to Love School, or at the very least, like it.

We are fortunate to have Ralph Marston's most generous permission to use some of his passages in each chapter, as they fit so perfectly with our philosophy of learning and life—in children as well as adults. *The Daily Motivator*, written and published by Ralph, is an amazing resource for anyone, with hundreds of themes and interesting topics fitting just about any problem or scenario. When you have some time, check out his wonderful website (www .greatday.com); you will feel more powerful and full of purpose.

YOU GET TO BE YOU

> Today you get to be you. Today you get to be immersed in the *abundant richness* that is your life.
>
> Today you get to *grow stronger* by dealing with new and unique challenges. Today you have the immense good fortune of being *able to create joy* where none existed before.
>
> On this day that's one of a kind, you get to experience the wonders of the universe from *your own unique perspective*. Today you can envision a dream and then immediately start working to bring that dream to life.
>
> What's truly wonderful is that even in the midst of the most frustrating frustrations, you can *make a difference*. In your world, in your life and in the lives of others, you can make a positive difference.
>
> Today, in a new and fulfilling way, you get to be you. And even the setbacks, shortcomings and obstacles *make your life richer* and more meaningful.
>
> *So here it is, and here you are. Stand up, step forward and live the grand adventure that now stretches out in front of you.*[7]

Some of the lessons in this book will be not only exciting but also entertaining, fostering engagement of all students. There will be lots of exploration of study inside and outside the classroom, resulting in more movement and enthusiasm by boys. Girls will like it, too. This type of learning is refreshing for parents and teachers as well. The payoff is evident for everyone involved in providing a happier, healthier learning environment at school or at home. Who would not be in favor of that? The following quote by Rock Christopher is pretty basic but for some boys is hard to attain: "The keys to a happy life: Have something to do, have someone to love, have something to look forward to." Perhaps with our help, we can make this happy life more within reach, especially for struggling boys who seem to need it the most. Naturally, for those who can discover a passion, the part of finding "something to do" is addressed. When it comes to love, certainly parents, teachers, coaches, and friends can provide that.

While directing the Reading Clubhouse, as elementary literacy specialist, our children displayed more self-confidence and self-motivation by the end of the year. These children became happier in school, were all given love and caring daily, and were willing to work very hard on their own for a change.

This change was due mainly to the students finally seeing a reason to learn—in an exciting, new way to find out more about what they were interested in knowing. The material they read was at their developmental skill level, not grade level, as that was too difficult for them. They looked forward to coming each day. We all tried our hardest constantly to make the Reading Clubhouse an exciting and loving environment, individualized for every unique child we had coming there.

Many students were sent to our clubhouse with severe discipline problems, reading difficulties, and low self-esteem and most of them having a general dislike of school. By using the seven steps, children saw a way to be successful that was developmentally appropriate for them. Learning about their interests made them eager to return each day as they started realizing how much they could easily read and finally understand. The teachers, aides, and "coaches of reading" loved working with those "misfits," as many would unfairly call them. Enthusiasm for learning began to build day by day.

Research has shown that children from the ages of five to eight have to be taught differently than older children. Young children love learning and learn best from active, hands-on teaching methods. By using games, storytelling, pretend play, and exploration of objects, they become engaged. They don't have to be taught to learn and at first come to school with joy and excitement to learn more. They expect to know how to read on their first day of school but soon see how difficult it is.

Then, years later, some of these same children changed. We heard that for many of them, the excitement and joy had decreased and that their previous love for learning had faded away. Boys were fidgeting, tapping their pencils, or totally checking out, looking out the windows. Why? It might be that the educational experience was inappropriate for their developmental stage once again, and soon they felt that they were less-than-capable learners. Think of their feelings of defeat. Could it be they are lost in the high-level expectations of middle schools everywhere?

Now the same struggling boys became just one of so many other students attending larger schools. The teachers usually could not take the time to individualize their programs like we could on a smaller scale; their curriculum was dictated by the administration and the laws of their state. Creativity was lost in this rigid, structured curriculum for children who needed much more. We felt all our hard work had been in vain since it was not continued with the children who grew older. Now we felt as defeated as the older children did.

WHY IS "DEVELOPMENTALLY APPROPRIATE LEARNING" IGNORED?

Curricular and instructional programs can be designed so that they are appropriate to the whole child, reflecting the student's level of development, age, and cultural, linguistic, and ethnic diversity. Not only boys but many girls as well will benefit when "boy-friendly" strategies are introduced into our classrooms.

There are obviously many differences between and among boys. The problems and solutions are found to be true for most boys, but naturally we cannot say that it will be the same for all boys. We hope that educators and parents will look at children as individuals, each one unique with different learning styles, to see what is currently true for them. This book provides better solutions that may be a good fit for the boys in your life—at least that is our goal.

One thing is certain: on the whole, in poor neighborhoods with decrepit schools, in elite schools that serve the very rich, and in many middle-class suburban schools around the country, boys are doing less well than girls. Referrals to special education are increasing for both girls and boys. However, referrals of boys outnumber those of girls by at least two to one. Some children display the results of drug abuse, child neglect or abuse, or teenage pregnancies, with more children living in poverty. Children might be raised by caretakers much of the day or come home to an empty house. Often there are breakdowns in the traditional family structure and in supports for these children.

We see critical social and health conditions resulting in an increasing number of infants and preschools requiring early intervention services. Additionally, boys are much more likely to be labeled with having a variety of school problems. Boys make up a majority of both students identified as having learning disabilities and those identified with emotional disturbance. The news lately is focusing more on poor mental health, too, unfortunately sometimes ending in violence.

WHY SO MANY MORE ADHD DIAGNOSES NOW?

Special education programs are overpopulated with boys. Boys are three times more likely than girls to be diagnosed with the attention-deficit/hyperactivity disorder (ADHD).[8] In reality, there are no definitive tests for ADHD—you can't do a blood panel or a brain scan to reach a diagnosis. Instead, experts rely on observation, self-reporting, and various psychoeducational assessments.

A child only suspected of having ADHD might take a long, tedious exam on a computer to evaluate a number of different ADHD indicators that still might be wrong. What is a parent to do? According to a *New York Times* article, it is disturbing to know that "about two-thirds of those with a current [ADHD] diagnosis receive prescriptions for stimulants like Ritalin or Adderall, which can drastically improve the lives of those with ADHD but can also lead to addiction, anxiety and occasionally psychosis."

A comment by psychiatrist and ADHD researcher James Swanson hit home: "There's no way that one in five high school boys has ADHD. If we start treating children who do not have the disorder with stimulants, a certain percentage are going to have problems that are predictable—some of them are going to end up with abuse and dependence." This is a dilemma for parents, teachers, and children—to say the least.

Maybe some boys are just more active than others. Are medications absolutely necessary? Medications are probably required by some so they can study better; others simply need more tolerance and understanding. Some children were raised in a totally different environment than others, naturally causing differences in behaviors.

One study found that exercise boosts "executive control," that is, the ability to resist distraction and stay on task. Another study found that kids who participated in physical activity for thirty minutes before school every day exhibited significantly lower inattention and moodiness both at school and at home.

Physical activity is particularly important for kids who have trouble staying focused, but it benefits every child, says Harvard psychiatrist and author John Ratey, an expert on the brain-boosting benefits of exercise. "Kids with ADHD and other learning issues may get a bigger bang for the buck from vigorous exercise, but science shows that it boosts tests scores for *all* kids," Ratey says. "And it reduces discipline problems significantly, too."

So it's ironic that as a society, we're heading in the opposite direction. As writer James Hamblin observed in *The Atlantic*, the cautious calls for additional research on the benefits of exercise stand out in stark contrast to the exuberant—and growing—distribution of ADHD drugs to children. Between 2007 and 2011, ADHD prescriptions increased from 34.8 million to 48.4 million. "The pharmaceutical market around the disorder has grown to several billion dollars in recent years, while school exercise initiatives have enjoyed no such spoils of entrepreneurialism," he writes.

Hamblin also notes the illogical inverse relationship between mounting evidence of exercise benefits on health and learning—and languishing investments in school exercise programs. Many districts and schools around the country have cut both physical education and recess for budgetary reasons and to increase time for back-to-basics academics, according to a report by the Institute of Medicine.

There are many factors to consider when comparing boys to boys, boys to girls, and girls to girls. What does this tell us? We should never try to compare children to children, as even within families they are all unique human beings, changing and growing daily.

UNFULFILLED MALE EDUCATIONAL POTENTIAL

As Tom Mortenson, who has done extensive research about boys and young men, states, "Because males make up roughly half the nation's population, unfulfilled male educational potential diminishes national economic, social, political, mental and spiritual health."[9] This statement definitely shows the consequences of young boys and men not reaching their educational potential, reinforcing that changes in education are needed now and certainly not down the road.

Of course, we want our nation to do well, but the destruction done to a boy's self-esteem has to be devastating and certainly more concerning. This will affect every aspect of their lives. We must avert low self-esteem at all costs. We cannot tolerate more of the same strategies when it comes to educating boys and with the gender gap increasing. Boys are the ones losing in the end.

The underlying causes of the problems associated with boys, like almost everything else, cannot be attributed solely to their heredity or their environment. Clearly, it is a combination of both the characteristics making up the current status of boys in education.

The combination of both the characteristics that boys are born with and the way that various societal factors shape them can affect how they do in school. Many of these conditions have a direct impact on the schooling of young boys and must be considered today.

Are you thinking that this book is just a downer, filled with doom and gloom? We can look at everything as a crisis with no hope, but remember what John F. Kennedy said: "When written in Chinese, the word 'crisis' is composed

of two characters. One represents danger and the other represents opportunity."
This is a serious situation and is a wake-up call for everyone who cares about
children and their future. Hopefully, you can use this book to help your son not
become one of the statistics. If you at least give the strategies and lessons a try,
you might change your son's life and his love for learning.

Of course, there will be challenges and frustration in most of our lives, but
that is what living is all about. The following quote from Ralph Marston puts
productive meaning to this challenge and frustration:

Challenges and Frustrations

The moment you were born you were faced with the serious, life-threatening
challenge of a lack of oxygen. So with only the slightest hesitation you figured
out how to breathe and have been doing so ever since.

A year or so later you had become extremely frustrated at not being able to
move quickly from place to place. So you figured out, largely through trial and
error, and with incredible persistence, how to walk.

But the people around you didn't understand you very well, and you longed to
improve the situation. So you listened very carefully, and learned the *subtleties
and enormous complexities of language.*

It sounds like an empty, high-minded platitude to say that the challenges and
frustrations are blessings in disguise. Yet when you look back and think about it,
which has been precisely your experience since the day you were born.

Even to this day, the challenges and frustrations continue. Yet you have already overcome some of the most serious, difficult and complicated ones imag-
inable, and there's every reason to be confident that you'll continue to do so.

The fact is that the challenges have indeed *made you stronger*; the frustrations
have most certainly *motivated you* to reach ever higher. *And as you confidently
work your way through each new challenge and frustration, you'll continue to
receive the valuable blessings they have to offer.*[10]

Many of these daily conditions and challenges have a direct impact on the
schooling of young boys and must be considered even more today. Growing
numbers of working parents, along with the increased number of children in
poverty, establish the need for more quality preschool and child care programs that are affordable.

Studies indicate that the preschool experience can be of great value for
children, especially those who are economically disadvantaged. Several studies have documented the short-term benefits for preschool children as they
move into kindergarten and first grade. Other, long-term studies indicate
that certain types of preschool experiences can begin to help break the ter-
rible cycle of poverty. These studies have found children better prepared for
school intellectually and socially. They were also less likely to be retained
or to be placed in special education classes. Given these changing conditions

and the benefits of early education, the need for continuing improvement of the educational system—and the extent to which the system meets the needs of our children—is huge.

Years ago, kindergarten and first-grade classrooms had children required to sit passively for long periods of time while working on ditto sheets or in workbooks. The children had to sit quietly listening or trying to learn by rote memorization. These instructional strategies not only are inappropriate to the children but also can be torture for boys trying to focus and keep on task. In addition, these types of strategies are certain to convince many boys that they cannot be successful in school.

Now academic programs in the elementary grades have been pushed down into some kindergarten and even preschool programs. This should be a critical concern to educators of young children due to how inappropriate it is. Many children are not ready to read yet and cannot hear phonics or letter sounds.

Time is of the essence, even if that sounds cliché. The years roll by, and many more boys are losing interest in education, especially at the higher levels. We want our children to become productive and happy when they grow up. It is also important to note that we are becoming less and less competitive in the world. As a rich, industrialized country, this should not be the case. Why are other nations passing us by or even "leaving us in the dust" when it comes to educational testing results?

WHAT MUST BE DONE

Studies show that young children do not learn in the same way as older children and adults. Since the world of things, people, and language is so new to infants and young children, they learn best through direct encounters with their world rather than through formal education.

Given the well-established fact that young children learn differently, the conclusion that educators must draw is a straightforward one: the education of young children must be in keeping with their unique modes of learning, or learning styles. In too many preschools and kindergartens today, being a perfectly normal, loud, enthusiastic, and active boy is not acceptable to the teacher. The child's boisterous learning style disrupts the desired quiet environment of many classrooms. Unfortunately, too many boys end up in special education or on medication by being misdiagnosed. This book tries to expose and explain the crisis that many boys experience in our educational system today. Our antiquated institutionalized educational template is often a mismatch with the way boys naturally learn (discussed more in chapter 1).

Both boys and girls deserve to feel successful, gain self-esteem, and be happy and productive in pursuing their education. However, the primary focus of the seven steps concentrates on boys who struggle with learning in a structured school environment. You will also see these steps work for all children, not only struggling boys.

As stated before, much of the joy of learning and teaching has been taken away in the past thirty or more years. If our schools kept up with other countries, then this book would have never been written. In addition, if young boys were doing just fine in school, changes would not be needed. Who knows if it might not be too late to make a difference even now?

On a happier note, this teacher and author has witnessed preschools already doing the perfect thing for children, even the boys. Laurie Cornelius, head coordinator of Clark College's Early Childhood Center in Vancouver, Washington, wisely summed up what a preschool today should look like:

Imagine a classroom where you were required to participate depending on subjects chosen by the teacher, and where you sit and receive information as defined as important by the *teacher*. On the other hand, what does a classroom look like where *you* can choose your own questions, exploring topics of *interest* to you, leaving the classroom if you need to follow your inquiry, designing your *own* experiments, conducting your *own* research and documenting your observations?

Your teacher *encourages you* to try out new ideas, to take risks, to explore your environment and to follow your curiosity. In these two environments, who would feel *passionate* about learning? Who would be innovative? Who would be social, confident and empathic?

Children are so *incredibly capable* at questioning and investigating their world around them. Their very ideas and thoughts must be the source for curriculum along with family interests, emergent sources and staff plans. Children aren't vessels to be filled. The natural childhood environment for investigation is in *play*. I've never figured out why play must be separated from the concept of work. So many creative innovations or contributions to society come from sources of intrinsic motivation and the merging of *work and play*. How can children love to learn without this element in their day?

Young children *can be citizens* at very early ages. They can accept responsibilities, explore social issues and find creative solutions in their world to problems. By participating with adults, asking questions, and conducting research, they learn their actions can create change with positive outcomes, a foundational skill necessary for living in a democratic society. *Child voice* must be present in the daily operations of programs.

I believe schools should be "collaborative learning communities" where families, staff and the broader community partner together in building exceptional environments that are both nurturing and support investigative exploration. Outdoor and indoor environments as well as curriculum will only be as creative as the adults who prepare them. In partnership, teachers and families become guides when they develop the keen art of observation. Children can study topics in-depth for deeper understandings of their world.

I believe we should ask the questions, "Is everybody here? Is everyone safe and warm inside?" This speaks to our ability to ask difficult questions, to have open and honest conversations and to individualize to the *divergent needs* in our community. Our obsession with metrics and performance is *threatening the passion* and creativity that would carry our nation's future generation into a rapidly changing world requiring adaptation, good judgment, teamwork and innovation. We must harness the "magic of childhood" and nurture the natural impulse toward exploration and inquiry. I want to see children run through our door eager to learn and play.[11]

Here is a woman and progressive educator who "gets it" and needs to train others to do this transformation in our schools today. Time is running short for us to Save Our Students—SOS!

Additionally, many have observed excellent and progressive grade schools squeezing in the same active strategies and engaging techniques for boys—in between mandated testing. We give them kudos for sure. Now if we can just convince the others, mainly our administrators, to try those strategies as well. Pass along this book to someone who needs help, but do not mention that part. As R. E. Shockley wisely states, "It's a new day, time for new beginnings, remain positive and affect those things that you can control."

One never knows who might decide they will seriously consider changing their thoughts about how we teach children. Hopefully, they will try doing this more progressive and developmentally appropriate teaching in the best way possible for each individually unique child.

STRUCTURE OF THE SEVEN STEPS TO HELP BOYS LOVE SCHOOL: CHAPTERS 1 TO 7

Chapters 1 and 2 explain the extreme importance of discovering what a child wants to know more about and the best ways to teach him. It does not matter whether it is dinosaurs, bats, bugs, snakes, rats, drawing, music, or sports. There will be simple ways explained of finding out a child's interests or passion and then doing something constructive about it.

We believe that the opportune time for learning is when a boy first begins school. In addition, it is extremely important to understand how boys and girls learn differently and how to teach to their strengths or modalities, both addressed in chapters 1 and 2.

We all know interests and passions can change, but they need to be grabbed when we discover what they are. A weekly calendar of suggestions is given, explaining how to make each day of the week an Adventure in Learning, but this time the learning pertains to students' interests and passions.

There is a step-by-step summary of ideas a parent or teacher can use to encourage this learning while exploring how the seven steps should be used successfully at home or in the classroom. Learning about the way children use different learning styles or modalities is continued in chapter 2.

Chapter 3 emphasizes the importance of working in conjunction with your child's present teacher. Especially now, with the state core standards, there needs to be collaborative work between the parent and teacher. For the seven steps to succeed with the child, the teacher needs to know what you are doing at home and how he or she can reinforce and encourage your child's interests and passions in the classroom.

Chapter 3 also lets the parent know that most teachers appreciate any and all help given at home. For example, weekly spelling words can be easily incorporated into any subject. But how much more fun it could be for the child if the spelling list were used in the context of stories or sentences made by using interesting material taught to that child. The power of passion cannot be overestimated. The discussion of how important it is to try to volunteer in some way at your child's school is also emphasized, with a call to all dads as well.

It stands to reason that all of us should be working toward the same goals for children. However, the primary goal we all want is for the child to love learning in school and, if homeschooled, just loving to learn—period.

Chapter 4 really gets into the fun ways children can report to others about what they have learned by creatively using video, tape-recording stories, illustrating and writing simple stories, taking photos of experiments, and making games to share with others. As teachers at home or in school, we need to reinforce what is learned through various means. By using videos, photos, tape recordings of their voices, and simple writings and making games to share with classmates or family, the child discovers excellent ways to build his own self-confidence and to share his passion with peers and adults. The importance of puppetry is also emphasized for learning and sharing.

Techniques are discussed that were used in kindergarten and first- through third-grade classrooms. These same techniques were replicated by the author in our Reading Clubhouse as primary literacy specialist. The children attending were boys and girls in kindergarten through fifth grade. Witnessing these children who were once frustrated by reading now making huge gains validated this program even more. The benefits were rewarding to observe. All the steps can be easily done at home with success, but these steps must be done day after day with consistency. You must also incorporate the seven Es of education previously discussed.

The best benefit of all was seeing these same frustrated children blossoming into "role models" for others to emulate on returning to their primary classroom. Now *they* became the "expert" in their field, loving to share with others all that they discovered about their passion by research done in the library or in the Reading Clubhouse. Their peers loved the game "Try to Trick the Expert," asking various questions made up by the "expert." Naturally, this becomes a win-win situation for all involved. The homeroom students learn more, the expert practices his verbal skills, and self-confidence soars.

When reading chapter 5, keep in mind that writing is probably the most difficult skill for all children but for boys in particular. Writing is perhaps dreaded the most over the course of the school years. This chapter gives teachers and parents step-by-step instructions on how to help a child enjoy writing a simple book for peers, parents, teachers, and relatives. And yes, even their own book can be read to pets and stuffed animals. Children lose all inhibitions when reading to their pets. Most pets are more patient than adults, too. Stuffed animals are definitely more patient—who knew?

Many libraries welcome these student-made books to their shelves. To become "an author" is exciting to a young child. The child develops the desire to write another and then another. No longer is writing dreaded or too tedious to even be attempted by the student. Once learned correctly, education in the upper grades becomes a breeze.

Obviously, this writing must encompass their area of interest and passion and at the same time should incorporate the weekly spelling list used in the classroom. Chapter 5 reiterates how working closely with the classroom teacher further develops a child's self-esteem and also keeps the child on track with assignments given. Most important, the goal of a young writer is not to be letter perfect but rather to be able to communicate ideas to others. Perfect spelling comes with time and practice, but it can also limit ideas when writing short words only.

By allowing inventive spelling, the written material can still be read, while bigger, more descriptive words can be used to convey ideas. Even with more time and practice, those hard words will come to be spelled easily anyway and will not frustrate the writer in his first years of writing. Teachers need to allow this inventive spelling, with an early explanation to the parents of the subsequent "benefits" that are added to the child's writing more and more.

Chapter 6 discusses how important it is for a child to feel success in his early years of learning, when concentrating on his passion or interest. Without this much-needed success, there will be a lack of self-confidence, leading to frustration. Severe frustration often leads to aggressive behavior or bullying.

As most of us already know, any attention is better than no attention. Class clowns, obnoxious boys, loud noises, bad behavior, and boys bothering others need better direction. It is important to concentrate on those boys with displaced anger who need their behaviors addressed and redirected from the very beginning. Hopefully, boys can become more on task by engaging these students more at their level of ability as well.

Teaching for over forty years has allowed this author to witness all types of behaviors, even ones you may not want to know about. Parents, teachers, and coaches soon realize that a young child learns early on how to get that wanted attention, whether that attention is positive or negative. Many times, both types of behavior can become reinforced without our realizing it or expecting that to happen. Children do not seem to realize that the negative behaviors are not the good kind. If a child is starving for attention, he soon learns that scolding is still a form of attention. No one wants to become invisible, not even adults.

Finally, chapter 7 deals more with what we can do to help change the "love of power" to the desired "power of love for learning and life." This final chapter ties the book together by suggesting the additional benefit of a child discovering his passion early, turning it into a truly positive power for living a full, happy, productive life. The world is an open door to success if the right tools are secured.

You're not what you think you are. You are, what you THINK.

—Nancy Huffman

The successful child will see the positive consequences of learning, all of us carefully guiding them in the years to come. We now know that even if those interests or passions change, it really does not matter. The engaged child is already on his journey of learning and enjoying the trip. The basic skills necessary for literacy will have been established by the end of third grade, a pivotal point for success in school.

By feeling successful and worthwhile during his school years, that same child would hopefully grow up to be a productive, happy human being. Through this productive passion, we as parents and teachers could help produce children who love what they do as adults. Whoever said, "If you find a job doing something you love to do anyway, you will never work a day in your life"?

We all know many people who dread each and every day of work, and it does not have to be that way. Wouldn't it make sense that those same motivated children, as adults, would also be happier in their jobs and more peaceful in the workplace or society in general? Life should hold a long future of exciting learning and fulfilling productivity for all.

Witnessing our test scores so far below those of other countries in reading, math, and science is discouraging to all of us. Seeing these low scores only reinforces my hopeful vision for a new and improved curriculum for pre-kindergarten through fifth grade. We must have an invigorating curriculum that will get teachers, students, and parents finally excited.

No more playing the "blame game," as it is time wasted, and we must use that time in taking responsibility and then making the changes that are vital to our society. All educators, teachers, and parents, in addition to coaches, would be teaching what is developmentally appropriate, seeing students engaged at their own levels. They would be teaching with meaningful activities of the child's interest. There would be more hands-on lessons that fulfill their curiosity and that are coordinated with meaningful technology.

This new curriculum would help all children with different learning modalities. To better understand how children learn best, modalities are discussed in chapter 1. To review, the word "modality" refers to a student's *best* learning style and would be especially helpful, as brain research validates large differences between the brains of boys and girls. These studies should help all of us know how to better reach out to boys. We must teach in ways that help those boys learn at their own levels of ability to become the best they can be.

PUTTING STUDENTS FIRST IN EDUCATION POLICY: "STUDENTSFIRST": WHAT IS IT?

You might have already come across this national movement, which is gaining momentum every year:

StudentsFirst is a national movement of more than two million parents, teachers, students, administrators and concerned citizens mobilizing for one purpose: to make sure every child in America attends a great school with great teachers. Driven by the power of our members, we have already helped pass more than 100 student-centered policies in states across the nation. Get involved today and help us put students first.

At StudentsFirst, we believe that every child from every background can learn and *excel if* put in the right school environment. That's why we created this annual *State Policy Report Card*. This is a different kind of report card. Rather than rank states based on current *student achievement* levels, it evaluates whether your state has the right *policy environment* in place to best raise academic levels from where they are today.

We focus on *three* areas fundamental to student achievement: *teacher quality*, *empowering parents with choice and information*, and *spending school dollars efficiently and effectively.*

Michele Rhee, founder of StudentsFirst, made these comments about the *State Policy Report Card*:

As you read through this report, you will see that over the last 12 months some progress has been made. The overall nationwide GPA ticked up slightly, and several states showed very strong individual growth. However, a tremendous amount of work still remains. Only 14 states, for example, received a *C grade* or better, leaving millions of kids in systems *not* designed to give them the tools needed to achieve their full potential.

We don't accept mediocrity from students, and we shouldn't from adults either. In an increasingly global and competitive economy, we *cannot* sit back and let our kids fall further behind peers in China, Western Europe, South America and elsewhere. That's why we encourage you to use the SPRC, State Policy Report Card as a resource to *demand* and compel change. You have the power to make a difference. So see how your state stacks up, and then spread the word. Together, we can create an education system that puts *students first*.[12]

The people who serve on our school boards have a thankless job but can also initiate change when enough people demand it. As said before, the time is now.

Michelle Rhee is doing her part, and now it is up to all of us to support her efforts and get others to take a look at StudentsFirst. According to school board member Joe Tommarello, "Unfortunately, state laws sometimes get in the way of what is best for kids, and the StudentsFirst State Policy Report Card (SPRC) highlights these issues clearly for the public." Rhee goes on to say,

Students in the United States face an uncertain future. In our increasingly globalized, dynamic economy, they will be forced to compete for jobs with peers from around the world. As a result, a high quality, modern education is more important than ever.

Unfortunately, our schools are falling short. On the Program for International Assessment—an exam given to students in 34 developed countries—the United States scored right in the middle of the pack, finishing 17th in reading, 21st in science, and 26th in math. By the time this book is published we will bet the statistics will be the same disappointing ones you see . . . or even worse. This puts us behind such countries and regions as Hong Kong, Singapore, Estonia, and Poland. As our students enter the global workforce, they'll have to overcome this significant disadvantage.

Yet the *problems* with our education system run deeper. Indeed, our schools are marred by tragic *inequity*. While nearly half of white fourth graders scored proficient in reading on the National Assessment of Educational Progress, fewer than one in five African-American students did. Furthermore, just 64 percent of African-American students graduate high school on time, compared to 82 percent of white students. This combination of *mediocrity and inequity* is intolerable. We can do better.

Some education observers suggest that this is simply a matter of low funding. But that isn't necessarily the case: our students achieve at the same level as in the Slovak Republic, though we spend t*wice as much per-pupil.* In many states, spending per child has gone up dramatically while student achievement has *not.* Nor is poverty the culprit, as both our poor and rich kids scored worse than their global counterparts.

Instead, the crux of the problem is a *failure of policy* and robust implementation. And while much of the public discussion on education policy focuses on national programs—including *No Child Left Behind* and *Race to the Top*— Washington has a relatively *tiny role* in our schools. In fact, only a *small fraction* of our education expenditures come from the federal government. Most policies that affect our schools are actually made at the *state and local level,* often keeping the big picture out of the view of the broader public.

Unfortunately, these policies frequently work *against* the interests of students. Across the country, states have laws on the books that cheapen and *devalue* the teaching profession, deny *parents* choices and information, and force districts to make false choices or allow them to perpetuate *bad* investments. Continuing to prop up these systems is a *disservice* to taxpayers, teachers, parents, and—most importantly—students. If we are serious about guaranteeing an excellent education to all students, *major changes* are necessary.[13]

Reading this makes it evident that our states are moving very slowly to implement change to improve our educational systems—all the more reason for parents, teachers, and administrators to look at what is happening and decide to do something about it. Our state policies for education need revamping, as does the curriculum.

Finally, and of utmost importance, this book can and will help our boys if given a chance. We have seen that policy changes in education will take much longer to become a reality in our schools. On a more hopeful note, we know that, with effort, we can try harder to change instruction with our own children and schools than with the seemingly impossible red tape involved with policy change

> Chains of habit are too light to be felt until they are too heavy to be broken.
>
> —Author unknown

Now the policymakers will be the ones lagging behind, while our boys will consistently move ahead despite all that red tape. We know there will be many challenges, but anything worth doing right will always present big challenges in life. Hopefully, with our changed attitudes and new strategies to help our boys, all will not be lost.

The work of Ralph Marston is read by many people all over the world, encouraging everyone to move on progressively forward no matter what the challenges might be. We have to start somewhere, and even if it seems like baby steps, at least the effort is being made. This next quote discusses how to face our challenges and why they are important:

When the Challenges Are Great

When the challenges are great, so are the rewards. If the journey is long, there is much value to be gained in making it.

When people criticize what you're doing, it means you're making a *difference*. When you keep encountering obstacles, it means you're moving *forward*.

Just because you experience life's difficulties is *not* a reason to be dismayed. Keep in mind that the more solidly you're making progress the more resistance you'll feel.

Feel the resistance, and realize that the very fact you're feeling it push against you means you're pushing forward through it. Feel the palpable sense of *progress*, and keep going. Just on the other side of challenge is *achievement*.

Just on the other side of the obstacle you're facing is your next step on the path forward. Persist through one challenge, and another, and another. *You'll emerge as a much stronger person, having created great new value in your world.*[14]

AGAIN, CHANGE IS NEEDED NOW

Seeing our country slipping further and further behind other countries is not only disturbing but also unacceptable. Change has to start with saving the sanity of our children as well as the sanity of teachers and parents. This change needs to begin now and in the early years of our precious children, who are so curious and eager to learn. The first experiences of education and learning in a child is where initiating change is possible. As educators of our unique children, boys and girls alike, we need to do our due diligence to find a curriculum that is individualized, exciting, and engaging and that fits each and every child, not just some.

> To be successful you must accept all challenges that come your way. You can't just accept the ones you like.
>
> —Mike Gafka

We hate to toot our own horn, but many people have expressed concern, as much as this book does, about our current educational system. The following quote is from Yvonne Schappell, West Coast production planner for Chevron Corporation:

> Being a granny to two eleven year old boys I find your assessments to be brilliant! If only the bureaucracy of education had your insight. I once met another

educator that said we *lose boys by the fourth grade.* I truly hope someone *listens* to your expertise and acts. Everyone should realize this is *the future of our country.*

If you want a great country you need a great public education system.

In conclusion, it would stand to reason that our public education system needs to be not only great but in the future characterized by excellence. First the excellence must come from our policymakers in changing education to fit our boys, thus helping students to desire the same from themselves, as Ralph Marston explains:

Insist On Excellence

Insist on excellence from yourself and your efforts. Don't settle for anything less.

Excellence is not quick or easy, but that doesn't mean it is out of reach. You know when you're doing your very best, so don't let up until you're doing it.

If you're going to make the effort, make it all the way. You can learn, and improve, and learn some more, and make use of your experience to make your way toward excellence.

The energy you put into doing it right is energy that's well invested. Instead of wasting your time on half-hearted efforts, you can transform your time into real, lasting value.[15]

Chapters 1 through 7 will help us discover what we can do—"When the Challenges Are Great."

NOTES

1. U.S. Department of Education, National Center for Education Statistics, *The Nation's Report Card: Reading Highlights* (Washington, DC: U.S. Department of Education, 2013).

2. Katherine M. Bishop and David Wahlsten, "Sex Differences in the Human Corpus Callosum: Myth or Reality?" *Neuroscience and Biobehavioural Reviews* 21 (1997): 581–601.

3. Doreen Kimura, "Sex Differences in the Brain," *Scientific American* 267 (1992): 119–25.

4. Shelly E. Taylor, Laura C. Klein, Brian P. Lewis, Tara L. Gruenewald, Regan A. Gurung, and John A. Upderaff, "Biobehavioral Responses to Stress in Females: Tend-and-Befriend, Not Fight-or-Flight." *Psychological Review* 107 (2000): 411–29.

5. S. Simon Baron-Cohen, *The Essential Difference: The Truth about the Male and Female Brain* (New York: Perseus, 2003).

6. Leonard Sax, *Why Gender Matters: What Parents and Teachers Need to Know about the Emerging Science of Sex Differences* (New York: Doubleday, 2005).

7. Ralph Marston, "You Get to Be You," *The Daily Motivator*, May 9, 2011 (www.greatday.com).

8. Centers for Disease Control, "ADHD: A Public Health Perspective Conference," retrieved March 30, 2006, from www.cdc.gov/ncbddd/adhd/dadabepi.htm.

9. Tom Mortenson, "What's Still Wrong with the Guys?," retrieved June 2, 2014, from www.postsecondary.org/last12/152guys/pdf.

10. Ralph Marston, "Challenges and Frustrations," *The Daily Motivator*, November 4, 2002 (www.greatday.com).

11. Laurie S. Cornelius, Director of Child & Family Services, Chair of Child Ed & Family Studies, ECE/Family Life Faculty, Clark College EST. 1933, Vancouver, WA (www.clark.edu).

12. Michelle Rhee, retrieved July 12, 2014, from www.StudentsFirst.org.

13. Rhee, retrieved July 13, 2014, from www.StudentsFirst.org.

14. Ralph Marston, "When the Challenges Are Great," *The Daily Motivator*, January 28, 2014 (www.greatday.com).

15. Ralph Marston, "Insist on Excellence," *The Daily Motivator*, January 29, 2015 (www.greatday.com).

1

Finding a Child's Passion in the Early Years

Be Amazing!

You're *not* here today to just get by. You're here to *be amazing*!

There are a lot of *challenges and obstacles*, yet there is no reason to be anything less than amazing.

Feel the *true passion* that lives in you, and let the passion push you to do something amazing. Look around, and see *how beautiful* and filled with wonder the world is.

You are part of an amazing universe, and can be just as amazing in your own unique way.

Today is not just a couple dozen hours to struggle through.

Today represents *your opportunity* to express your amazing nature in new ways.

Focus your *attention and energy* on what *you love* and treasure most.

In that *love is the power* to be authentically and uniquely amazing.

This is a *one-of-a-kind*, amazing day.

You're here to make it even more so, so starting right now; do it![1]

Children need to know the reality that they could even become president if they work hard enough in school and life. At the same time, you might be thinking, "Who would want that demanding and stressful job for their child's future?" We could probably agree with you in this age of unending wars, new diseases, and economic strife for many. The point is that there are no limits placed on children who dream big and who work diligently to accomplish what they set out to do—obstacles, yes; limits, no.

Children's dreams, passions, and interests can be developed by their parents, teachers, coaches, or caregivers as they grow, allowing them to be more engaged with learning. Naturally, they will stay happier through this passionate pursuit, hopefully becoming very productive adults and the very best they can be. Keep in mind the following quote:

> There has never been a statue erected to the memory of someone who let well enough alone!

> —Jules Ellinger

SO WHY IS PASSION SO IMPORTANT?

You will see later in this chapter that with larger numbers of boys dropping out of high school, fewer numbers of young men attending college, and even more boys at the elementary level not liking school, there is a big problem in our current educational system. We must find better ways to address these issues by getting boys engaged in learning as early as kindergarten or even preschool. "Besides trailing in academic performance, boys are *more* likely to drop out of high school than girls and *less* likely to graduate from high school, to attend college, and to go on for graduate degrees."[2]

Evidence has shown that, when reviewing a variety of statistics from almost any state, any school district, and nearly every school, problems with boys are prevalent. When looking at any grade level, any socioeconomic group, and any race, we will also show that boys are not performing as well as girls. Not surprisingly, statistics from other countries show the same type of results. Maybe boys are similar everywhere.

"When looking at boys' participation in honors and Advanced Placement classes, we can see that a *smaller* percentage of boys than girls are participating in these advanced courses, providing additional evidence that boys are *not* doing well in our schools today. Although boys historically have performed better than their female peers, the last 30 years have seen the *reversal* of that trend."[3]

It would seem that our society always has to assess by means of a test; however, with passions or interests, a parent or teacher can learn much by simply observing the behaviors of the child and listening to what the child asks questions about.

Asking simple questions can also show where a child's interests lie. Watch to see the choices that children make in learning new things. Try to predict what topics he will become passionate about as he grows older. There are many clues to help us if we take the time to care and watch daily.

We have a natural instinct to teach our children to succeed, but when we show up to do the intense listening, ask the hard questions, and make the choices, instead of expecting our students or children to do these things for themselves, it teaches them precisely nothing. However, it does teach them something: that we will always be there to live their lives for them. Then the next reality is that none of us can be there or really want to "live their lives."

HOW DO WE FIND THAT PASSION OR INTEREST?

Observe your child at play. Really pay attention to the themes he is drawn to and the activities that make him happy. As stated before, these will change. Trucks, trains, or tools may excite your youngest child but will be replaced by sports, reading, science, and so on, by kindergarten. However, many five-year-olds still prefer trucks, trains, and tools if given the choice. Try to expose your child or student to cultural events, sports activities, and museums.

It is important to always keep in mind the individual strengths or weaknesses of children and the enthusiasm they show about special things they like most. Do not forget to take notes as you observe. Keep an "observation notebook" where all entries are recorded and dated for future reference and guidance.

One of the easiest ways to find out interests is to ask the child what he would like to learn more about at home or in school. Perhaps the child has a favorite book or an exciting activity he likes doing. How about taking him to the library for Story Hour and then showing what the library has to offer? Many still think that libraries have only books. Psychologist Madeline Levine says,

> Every kid has something that interests them, so don't give up on a kid who checks out or *appears lazy*. Parents can help by encouraging kids to develop their interests and talents—whatever they may be.
>
> You know people say "oh my kid is bored" or "my kid is lazy." I've been a psychologist treating kids and teens for 30 years; I don't see it that way. I see kids who are not engaged because the platter that is being offered to them does not include the kind of things that interest them. But if we had a broader curriculum for kids, then I think every kid has something that really does interest them. And it's our failure to understand how a broad skill set can be *useful* in life.
>
> So every once in a while somebody will say to me, "You know I don't know what my kid is going to be. All she can do is talking to her friends all the time. She's always solving their problems." And it's like "oh so she can be a psychologist."
>
> So I have a short story. When my oldest kid played softball, there was that one kid in the back of the field—who always got put out in the back of the field cause he would wander off. Hit a ball and where's Tony? Nobody could find Tony. And Tony was always off in the woods finding plants. So Tony was like the weird kid, right?

Well actually, Tony is now the *head of botany* at a major university. So it's just understanding that there's a lot more in life, and that so many of these skills that we're quick to dismiss, actually are particularly useful given the needs of the global economy in the 21st century—creativity and collaboration, communication skills. These are the things that business after business after business is saying we are looking for in our new hires.[4]

CHILDREN MUST READ EVERY DAY IN SOME WAY

Children usually will select books that have a strong interest, whether you read it to them, they read it with you, they read it to others, or they listen to a tape or audio recording while reading the book. All of these are excellent ways to learn about interests in individuals and to show the empowering value of books and reading. Again, make certain that notes are taken in your observation notebook for your quick reference. This will help you discover what your child's interest or passion might be.

IMPORTANCE OF READING TO DISCOVERING PASSION

Reading cannot be underestimated when it comes to the relationship and importance it has for children exploring new things. Children must be exposed to all types of reading as soon as possible. Then, hopefully, the act of any type of reading becomes ingrained in them as an integral way to find answers to their questions. Reading can also serve as a relaxing way to be entertained and the key to success down the road.

Sadly, prisons everywhere are filled with people who were possibly not read to as children. We see lost-looking, homeless souls on the street in various cities of our nation, leading us to question if someone ever read to them when they were young. The answer is probably not. Did anyone show them how to "travel" anywhere in their imagination by reading a great book? Was there anyone caring enough to spark their interest when they were growing up and to nurture all their budding passions? Did the person see all that can benefit us from reading?

Once that spark is established from reading, it never goes away. This is fortunate for their learning of new things. The interest in life, its surroundings, and the environment around us opens up a brand-new world when discovering books. Technology is great, but in order to enjoy a full, productive life with an opportunity to succeed, one must be able to read. It then makes more sense that the ability to read and comprehend what was read begins with being read to as a child.

According to author and entrepreneur Tom Harken, the value of reading is priceless. He advises parents, caregivers of children, grandparents, future parents, and even teachers to make reading a real experience that will be remembered for a lifetime: "So pop some popcorn, create comfortable surroundings for a few quiet moments, and take that child on a journey that begins wherever you are and becomes an everlasting experience." This is such great advice, and reading is the one most important thing adults can do for children or students.

This suggestion goes for teachers as well. Maybe just on Friday, this special day can be your exciting Popcorn/Reading Day, although, of course, reading will happen daily. Years from now, students will look back and remember that magic moment when you revealed the world in an unexpected but delightful way. Children will look forward to that special reading time. In that gesture of reaching out, you will have helped provide all of us with a better world.

Harken firmly believes that by reading to a child on a regular basis, an adult can help point that child in the right direction. Furthermore, this reading will place him on a course that leads away from the pitfalls experienced by many who grow up "unread to," as he calls it. And it follows that those who cannot read are unable to view distant horizons or dream big dreams. We believe that all children have the right to read and that, by reading every day, they can be led to a better life.

Scholastic Magazine has developed a global literacy campaign to share its "Reading Bill of Rights" with you, your family, friends, and colleagues on Facebook, Twitter, or through a personalized e-mail:

Reading Bill of Rights

A Child's Right to Read

Today we live in a world full of digital information. Yet reading has never been more important, for we know that for young people the ability to read is the *door opener* to the 21st century: to hold a job, to understand their world, and to know themselves. That is why we are asking you to join our Global Literacy Call to Action. We call this campaign: "Read Every Day. Lead a Better Life." We are asking parents, teachers, school and business leaders, and the general public to support their *children's right to read for a better life* in the digital world of the 21st century.

Here is what we believe about reading in the second decade of the 21st century. We call this *The Reading Bill of Rights:*

1. **WE BELIEVE** that literacy—*the ability to read, write and understand*—is the birthright of every child in the *world* as well as the pathway to succeed in school and to realize a complete life. Young people need to read *nonfiction* for *information* to understand their world, and *literature* for *imagination* to understand for themselves.

2. **WE BELIEVE** that the massive amounts of digital information and images now transmitted daily make it even more important for a young person to know how to analyze, interpret and understand information, to separate fact from opinion, and to have deep respect for *logical thinking*.
3. **WE BELIEVE** *that literature and drama*, whether on printed pages, screens, on stage or film, help young people experience the great stories of emotion and action, leading to a deeper understanding of what it means to be truly human. Without this literacy heritage, life lacks meaning, coherence and soul.
4. **WE BELIEVE** every child has a right to a "textual lineage"—a reading and writing autobiography which shows that who you are is in part developed through the stories and information you've experienced. This textual lineage will enable all young people to have a *reading and writing identity* which helps them understand who they are and how they can make their lives better. In short, "You Are What You Read."
5. **WE BELIEVE** every child should have *access to books*, *magazines*, *newspapers*, *computers*, *e-readers*, and *text on phones*. Whatever way you read, you will need to figure out what the facts are or what the story tells you. No matter how and where you get access to ideas, you will *need the skills of reading* to understand yourself and your world.
6. **WE BELIEVE** that reading widely and reading fluently will give children the reading stamina to deal with *more challenging texts* they will meet in college, at work and in everyday life. And every child should be able to choose and own the books they want to read, for that choice builds literacy confidence—the ability to read, write and speak about what they know, what they feel, and who they are.
7. **WE BELIEVE** that every child has the *right to a great teacher* who will help them learn to read and love to read. Children need teachers who provide intentional, focused instruction to give young people the skills to read and interpret information or understand great stories they will encounter throughout life.
8. **WE BELIEVE** that in the 21st century, the ability to read is necessary not only to succeed *but to survive*—for the ability to understand information and the power of stories is the key to a life of purpose and meaning.[5]

So rather than our magical number of seven steps that you will find throughout this book, *Scholastic* found an additional one.

HOW CHILDREN GROW AND CHANGE:
FOR BETTER OR FOR WORSE

As babies grow, children are driven from within to learn, focus, practice, and accomplish personal goals. Their excitement and enthusiasm increases as they get more encouragement and praise from their parents or teachers. Unfortunately, in many of our classrooms today, we may wonder what happened to that interest and see more children disliking school tasks. Perhaps if those children discovered their "flow," they would continue to love school from the first day to the last. In reality, learning and education for people should *never* really end. Are you asking, "What is 'flow'?"

The Hungarian psychologist and researcher Mihaly Csikszentmihalyi shows us that the pursuit of passion usually leads to personal happiness. True happiness, Csikszentmihalyi argues, comes from your being completely absorbed in some activity: you are completely "in the zone," and time slips by unnoticed. Csikszentmihalyi was credited with naming this state of complete absorption "flow." After interviewing many people, all of whom had one thing in common (they pursued an activity for its own sake, not for the money or status but simply for the joy of it), he came to label these experiences as "flow" activities.[6]

Csikszentmihalyi says that creativity is a central source of meaning in our lives. A leading researcher in positive psychology, he has devoted his life to studying what makes people truly happy: "When we are involved in [creativity], we feel that we are living more fully than during the rest of life."

Csikszentmihalyi teaches psychology and management at Claremont Graduate University, focusing on human strengths, such as optimism, motivation, and responsibility, and is the director of the Quality of Life Research Center there, having written numerous books and papers about the search for joy and fulfillment.

Csikszentmihalyi, author of the acclaimed book *Flow*, studied why some adults as well as adolescents, rather than give up, pursue their passions at great personal cost. His research reveals a direct link between the pursuit of a passionate interest and personal happiness.

Writer Adam Gopnik finds happiness in being vigilantly absorbed in some activity of his choosing. He goes on to say,

> "You will like Happiness Experiment no. 11 because it involves doing more of what you love to do. It sounds so simple, surely attaining happiness should be more complicated and involve more of an effort? How can you be happy just by doing what you love to do? Simple as the idea sounds, most of us forget to do the things we love to do. We get more involved in the daily 9 to 5, the things we ought to do; the daily must do, should do and need to do lists instead.
>
> We all have different activities that put us in a state of flow, and this can vary from individual to individual. So how can you tell if you are in flow? If you are experiencing most of these seven characteristics while performing a task, then "flow" is prevalent:
>
> 1. You experience oneness and ecstasy (you lose sense of self).
> 2. You are completely involved and concentrated.

3. You experience the task as highly challenging and requiring a high level of skill.
4. You have a wonderful sense of serenity.
5. You experience a distorted sense of time.
6. You are intrinsically motivated.
7. You have a sense of control.

Happiness Experiment no. 11 is therefore to become aware of which activities are flow activities for you. Make sure you set aside time for these flow activities this week rather than telling yourself you are too busy. Make more time in your life for doing the things that you love. It sounds a simple experiment but is a remarkably effective way of increasing your happiness."[7]

As we now know, Csikszentmihalyi calls this single-mindedness "flow," and he equates it with happiness. Furthermore, they do their passion because they love doing it. So, above all, for flow to occur, the activity needs to be personally gratifying. Finally, the skills taught have to be slightly above one's current skills. This provides just enough challenge to occupy attention without overloading the person or child.

HOW CAN WE HELP MIDDLE SCHOOL BOYS FIND "FLOW"?

By making the conscience decision to keep fewer thoughts active at any given time, you allow a different kind of intelligence to take over . . . one that doesn't require as much effort. You might call it wisdom.

—Author unknown

A retired teacher we know taught middle school years ago and took the time to make the learning in her classroom exciting, engaging, enthusiastic, and, more important, "boy friendly." We are certain there are many others, but she serves as our example of a desired result for middle schools in the future. She proved that with more effort in planning, boy-friendly activities can be provided. The rewards were tremendous for all.

This is the grade level where we begin to lose many boys who tune out. Again, this only substantiates the importance of what we are saying about finding a child's interest or passion when he is younger.

Shirley Anderson states the following:

My 6th graders at Mac Middle School LOVED coming to class EVERY DAY!! I had many parents tell me that was their child's 1st year they ever loved school! I had KINESTHETIC learning going on CONSTANTLY, with both my boys & girls! Hands-on learning seemed to work for everyone. For instance, fractions were easily understood when food was involved . . . especially when team members were measuring and computing to create food from their own recipes.

I often individualized and encouraged decision-making skills (they CHOSE . . . what a concept, right?). I also encouraged cooperative team-building where the goal was *always to work together* to help one another be successful in their learning processes. Always fun! Never stressing over "incorrect" outcomes, just going forward and feeling good about what they had accomplished. They learned to enjoy setting realistic goals and we were constantly inventing new learning games.

I knew how transient that student population could be in our area. Often I would hear fellow 6th grade teachers talk about how frustrating it was, that their kids were constantly moving in or out to another school, to the point that they had to constantly redo their grade books. Often only half or less of the students who began the year in their classes were still present at the end of the school year. Not so with my class of 37.

The students were adamant about *not* moving to an area where they'd have to change schools, so although there was quite a bit of moving to another apt building or home, parents would often volunteer. They did everything they could to make sure their child would continue in our class because they had never seen them so excited about going to school every single day.

We did not lose ANY of those 37 students from Sept until March. But in March one girl whose parents had done everything to try to stay until June, finally had to move north to the Quinault area (involved a divorce situation and she had to move back to her original Indian reservation). Our entire class was so sad that Shannon had to move but we embraced her and many students still kept in touch with her.

Back to boys and girls learning, I developed most of my teaching techniques based on the *needs of the boys* in my class, and it worked for the girls too. Yes, we had a few quiet or silent times, but there was usually *body movement* involved in most of our learning, whether it was quick stand up/sit down actions during spelling (the vowel and consonant game), or standing up to stretch, or copy a student leader's pose that resembled yoga.

Friday's learning games were marathons with pathways all over the room leading to different *learning stations*, sometimes involving quick movements, physical skills, or even producing sounds or rhythms. *No sitting at desks* because the desks were grouped inward (no access) to form learning stations. Oh how I miss that fun. It was a lot of work coming up with all these creative ways to teach, but well worth it in many ways.

Testing at the beginning and end of the school year showed remarkable gains in both *reading and math* scores (MUCH higher gains than any of the other 11 6th grade classes at our school), and I NEVER taught to any tests. There were *huge gains in self-esteem, socialization skills as well as academic learning*—they learned empathy, there was NO bullying, and each student developed a sense of pride & non-arrogant confidence; traits that many future employers would probably have at the top of their list when interviewing potential employees.

How encouraging to see that what we are trying to emphasize in this book really does work with children, even in middle school. We must look at children differently and teach them differently, and then we might see different positive results at the end of the year. In Shirley Anderson's case, taking more time for planning her lessons for the individual needs of each unique student, making her class more active, and using hands-on and engaging activities, with boy-friendly techniques, all nurtured the positive attitude of children wanting to learn more each day. She provided them with exciting lessons that worked for each child, stressing again the importance of instructional change necessary in today's curriculum.

HOW HAPPY IS YOUR CHILD IN SCHOOL?

The flow of happiness relates to a quote by Hugh Downs: "A happy person is not a person in a certain set of circumstances, but rather a person with a certain set of attitudes." This happiness can relate to children as well as parents, teachers, coaches, and certainly administrators. Attitude is everything when it comes to embracing change for the better. Teachers and parents need to realize that everyone's positive or negative attitude of how they teach to a child can make all the difference when it comes to worthwhile, engaged learning.

Young children may have fleeting passions and interests, but they are not able to fight with adults in order to keep those passions alive at such a young age. From babyhood, children are driven from within to learn, focus, practice, and accomplish personal goals. It all begins with a type of passion. Healthy young children show intense determination to accomplish their goals, and their urge for mastery thrives with our encouragement and respect. We should note that the most intriguing activities for young children are not passive. Just watch how a child gets totally involved with music by listening, dancing, clapping, and singing.

Around ages two to three, children begin to love spontaneous pretend play, such as when building a tower or baking a cake, playing house, or becoming make-believe policemen, firemen, pirates, ballerinas, supermen, and even mommies and daddies. Preschoolers are as intensely concentrated on their pretend games as they once were with peekaboo as babies.

As they get older, the content becomes richer and more revealing of preschoolers' individual interests, thinking styles, and desires. One might think it would be hard work to stay so focused on their play, but it is not—because they love what they are doing. This is the true essence of passion.

But what happens to a young boy's passion for learning and exploring over time? Later on, in formal learning settings, we may wonder what has become of this early eagerness to get it right. So what can we do to prevent our children from losing interest in or giving up on what they love to do? Findings from Csikszentmihalyi's research might offer some clues and help us preserve the drive for mastery seen in healthy young children.

To reiterate, Csikszentmihalyi revealed a direct link between the pursuit of a passionate interest and personal happiness. Early on, he studied adult artists' strong determination to pursue their art despite difficult personal circumstances, and he found that each one experienced a total absorption in the activity of painting or sculpting, again pointing out the single-mindedness of "flow" and equating it with happiness.

This researcher's descriptions of those artists' intense focus, pleasure in involvement, and hard-won mastery is similar to the persistence of young children when they are learning to walk, talk, and make sense of the world through rich, imaginative play. Csikszentmihalyi concluded that at any age, the most dedicated people in arts, sports, business, science, or any endeavor are drawn to the activity for its own sake. To further explain, people or children do their thing because they love doing it. So, above all, for flow to occur, the activity needs to be personally gratifying:

> The best moments in our lives are not the passive, receptive, relaxing times. . . . The best moments usually occur if a person's body or mind is stretched to its limits in a voluntary effort to accomplish something difficult and worthwhile. . . .
>
> The implications for parents and teachers seem clear: We would be wise to tune in to our children's individual interests and temperaments from birth on. That doesn't mean that children's tastes may not change; they will evolve . . . all the more reason to stay tuned in. Know that the interests and passions expressed in a preschooler's pretend play are likely to be transitory. What really matters is that young children thrive on the pursuit of their own passions, bolstered by the gentle encouragement of parents who wisely show interest, resisting any urge to take charge. The key is to tune in to and accept your child's uniqueness and enthusiasm. Doing so promises the rewards of a life enriched by the happy pursuit of genuine passions and meaningful accomplishments.[8]

Often parents try to discourage particular interests or encourage their children to like the same things they like. Remember that imposing your own dreams on your children can take the magic out of their personal discovery, creativity, and learning. A child's enthusiastic focus cannot last if his parents' expectations are at odds with his own interests and abilities. Pushing our own passions can compromise the foremost goal that most parents have for their children: happiness.

However, if our schools and parents could help children discover what their children's own interests are and then guide the child with the skills necessary for literacy, the child should see the importance of school, reading, and learning. The child will begin to realize that these will become the tools he needs to pursue his interests further. Here is another great quote by Ralph Marston:

Without Compromise

Don't just go through the motions. Go through life with *passion* and purpose.

This day is yours to live, so make something truly meaningful and beautiful out of it.

Get curious, get interested, get involved, get active, and bring your life to life.

This is your *one* chance to live this moment, so make the very most of it. You can create great, rich, meaningful value, so do it now and do it often.

Let yourself be amazed and enthusiastic about the possibilities. Let yourself be joyful and purposeful and filled with *love* for all the goodness that surrounds you. Choose what to do and then follow through. *Dream* your best dreams and then bring them to life.

The amazing gift of life is yours, so do something truly amazing with it. Live fully and richly now, without compromise and with a *passion* that is uniquely yours.[9]

Note that writing is not mentioned since most teachers have discovered that writing is the most difficult skill of all, certainly for boys. That is why this book devotes an entire chapter to writing, with the realization that it is definitely a difficult skill. Learning to write takes lots of practice and guidance. Writing is not simply a skill; writing is a process that takes time and much effort, especially for boys. We love this quote from Abraham Lincoln: "Most folks are about as happy as they make up their minds to be." It is evident that it is mostly our attitudes that dictate our happiness. Happiness can be more of our mental state and ability, but certainly it is more likely to occur when the child is happy in his learning environment.

Seeing our students' test scores so far below those of students in other countries in reading, math, and science is discouraging to all. Seeing such low scores reinforces the hopeful vision of a new and improved prekindergarten through third-grade curriculum. Our educational system cannot wait until the children are older and have already tuned out. Children must have an invigorating curriculum that will get teachers, students, and parents finally excited.

No more playing the blame game, as it is time for all of us to take responsibility and make changes now. There is enough blame to go around, and it is counterproductive. All educators—teachers and parents alike—would be teaching what is developmentally appropriate. They would see students engaged at their own levels with meaningful activities of their interest. There would be more engaging, hands-on lessons, fulfilling children's curiosity and being coordinated with meaningful technology.

This new curriculum would help all children with different learning modalities. We are referring to the best learning style of students, discussed in more detail in chapter 2. The use of our seven steps would be particularly helpful with boys and the unique ways they learn. Schools and even homeschooling would become more exciting, practical, and engaging and produce a great foundation for all learning after third grade.

Marston sums up this teacher's beliefs perfectly. What he says is not only for boys but for girls, adults, and the elderly as well. One's dreams or passions can be achieved at any age, but if these passions are found earlier, the child can have more years to love life and fulfill one's dreams. We cannot let so many of our children continue to flounder through life. They need our help and guidance while they are still young to find the secret to success.

> The secret to success is to do common things uncommonly well.
>
> —John D. Rockefeller

Suppose that someone starts a business that is nearly identical to another and that it becomes more successful than the other. Why does this happen? Because they took a simple idea and found a way to make it much better, causing us to ask, "Why didn't I think of doing that?"

NOW WHO IS NOW LEFT BEHIND WITH NO CHILD LEFT BEHIND LEGISLATION?

When we take a long, hard look at where our education is headed, many are more confused than ever and seem to stick their heads in the sand like an ostrich. They are beginning to observe goals that are unattainable for many children and for boys in particular.

> When it is obvious that the goals cannot be reached, don't adjust the goals, adjust the action steps.
>
> —Confucius

Many of our politicians, administrators, and teachers need to read this famous quote over and over. Goals are paramount, but they have to be achievable. Due to the No Child Left Behind (NCLB) legislation, our schools are involved in some of the most dramatic efforts at school reform we have ever seen.

Principals are now responsible for showing the steady achievement of every student and from every racial and ethnic subgroup. We can already predict what the results show, especially for many boys. Maybe this will raise a "red flag" to those principals sooner rather than later. But why is it taking so long to do something about it?

> Even if you are on the right track, you will get run over if you just sit there!

> —Will Rogers

The NCLB was passed by Congress in 2001 (becoming effective January 8, 2002). Here we are, many years later, and the frustration over the NCLB legislation is evident, yet it is still stagnant with regard to necessary change. It even passed with bipartisan support. The NCLB is a reauthorization of the Elementary and Secondary Education Act, which included Title 1, the government's flagship aid program for disadvantaged students. The NCLB supports standards-based education reform based on the premise that setting high standards and establishing measurable goals can improve individual outcomes in education. On the surface, who would not agree with this?

This act requires states to develop assessments in basic skills. To receive federal school funding, states must give these assessments to all students at select grade levels. The act does not assert a national achievement standard. Therefore, each individual state develops its own standards. The NCLB expanded the federal role in public education through annual testing, annual academic progress, report cards, teacher qualifications, and funding changes.[10]

Across the nation, most educators acknowledge that impoverished black and Latino boys are lagging badly behind white boys and all girls in school. Now we are finding white boys lagging more each year. Doesn't anybody notice or care? Every group needs nurturing to become the best they can be.

WHY IS THERE A GENDER GAP AS WELL?

Even more confusing is that boys and girls perform about the same on aptitude and IQ tests. What is causing boys, in general, to keep falling further and further behind? This gender gap in education is due to the way boys are taught—or maybe not taught. Why are so many boys turned off by education by fourth grade or earlier? Why do so many boys hate to read and write or even attend school?

The research has been out there for decades about how boys learn differently than girls. If you are interested to see how boys in your state, school district, and school are performing, you can see data on the performance of the boys in your area. Sources for collecting this information might include your state department of education's website, your school district's website, your school's Parent-Teacher Association, and your school's administrators.

One question to ask is, "What standardized tests and assessments results are available regarding my school, my school district, and my state?" A second is, "How are *boys* performing on these assessments?" Go to www. nces.ed.gov/nationsreportcard and look at the results by gender for your state. If you see that assessment results are not already being reported by gender for your school and school district, ask for the results to be broken out for boys and girls. Get ready for some shocking results, especially between boys and girls.[11]

We may have the "new and improved" curriculum from time to time, spending endless money and demanding more teacher's learning time, but does this help boys like school any better? For struggling students, it does not. In fact, by trying to fit boys into the mold of what is called the "educational box," it is clear that one size does not fit all for children—boys and girls alike. Rather than changing the boys to fit our schools, schools might change to capitalize and expand on the strengths of boys. Doesn't that make more sense?

Maybe you have a son who is smart and capable yet struggling in school. When he talks about his classroom, does he seem fearful, bored or frustrated, or even disengaged with learning and school activities? Does he dread going to school in the morning by having a stomachache or headache? Does he hate doing his homework? You wonder, "What is going on? Joshua was always so eager to learn and showed curiosity about many different things at home."

You read to Joshua about frogs, turtles, snakes, and dinosaurs—all his interests of passion. He could not wait to be a kindergarten student like Tiffanie. His sister had been enrolled in school two years ago. Joshua hoped he would learn to read as soon as kindergarten began. Now he finds any reason not to catch the bus.

Odd, you think, as Tiffanie still loves school and talks incessantly about her teacher and fun assignments in second grade. She loves to read and write. Tiffanie would not miss a day of school if she could help it. All her girlfriends feel the same and even play "school" at home on the weekends. They look forward to Monday and "real school" again. The only thing different is that Tiffanie is a girl. Why should that matter? From preschool days, your son showed just as much interest and ability as Tiffanie did.

As you will see in this book, boys and their learning styles are entirely different from girls and their learning styles. Programs for boys must be adapted to their styles of learning. They have to be developmentally appropriate, but mainly they must involve active, hands-on lessons in order for real learning and the retention of information to occur.

We realize that, as a parent, your time is at a premium, so taking the time to read this book shows that you really do care. If you are an educator, your days are jam-packed and stretched to the limit already, trying to learn ways to teach your students better. Finally, if you are an administrator looking for better answers to the dilemma with boys, we salute you. Pass along this book to other administrators who you think might sway educators and politicians to do something to help our boys. Time is of the essence.

So here is the answer to that very important question: Why is finding a child's interest or passion so important? Teachers and parents must find a child's interest or passion at the beginning of the educational process in order for the child to see a reason for reading, writing, spelling, and even math. When this passion is discovered, whether it be for dinosaurs or digging up worms, learning will become more natural, and the skills will be retained much more readily. Now learning is relevant to attaining the information that is wanted.

When there is more passion or interest, boys will have less fidgeting, scattered attention, and problems in reading and might learn to focus more on their homework. They will easily become engaged and enthusiastic about what they are learning. Teachers and parents will feel satisfied that they are doing their very best for their children. Everyone is less frustrated.

In addition to finding that passion, school instruction must change as well. By the way, you need not worry that your child will become a dinosaur vet or a worm collector, but who knows for sure? There are no guarantees in life.

There are related vocabulary words, books to explore, and games you can make, supporting those interests while the child is still learning basic skills. Even math skills can be changed to counting dinosaurs or worms. With a little hunting, there is also plenty of fun science to learn about dinosaurs and worm digging, still building literacy skills. The spelling word list for the week can be easily incorporated into their interests.

Although girls have interests and passions, they can still enjoy learning whatever the school decides is appropriate for their grade level. Most girls love to sit in a reading circle, do the daily calendar routine, and eagerly answer questions asked of them. Just walk into most classrooms and notice who has their hands in the air; it's not the boys. For girls, school is something they played for years, even before attending it. You might think it was in their DNA to "play teacher and school" with everyone who would sit still.

We even see that boys get expelled from preschool five times the rate of girls. In elementary schools, they are diagnosed as having attention problems or learning disorders four times as much as girls and are two times as likely to repeat a year of school.

Girls used to lag behind in science and math but lately have all but closed the gap. Boys continue to lag badly behind girls in reading and writing, and this gap is growing and getting bigger, not smaller, every year. Doesn't anyone question why? To complicate things further, many bright boys are just very creative. Perhaps you have a son with many of the following seven characteristics:

Characteristics of Very Creative Boys

1. They can become easily bored.
2. They are often risk takers.
3. They color outside the lines and hate the rules.
4. They would rather work independently.
5. They can change their minds often and make lots of mistakes.
6. They think with their hearts.
7. They love to dream big.

So why is it important to treat creative boys differently? It is because their unique characteristics may be misdiagnosed as bad behavior when they simply need to be taught in a different way. If these bright boys are stifled early and labeled as "problem children," there will be many missed opportunities to make a real difference in the life of one of these boys. Worse, some of these boys might mistakenly fall into the category of needing to be tested for a learning disability. This happens way too often.

In relation to finding a passion or even specific interests, these creative boys may change their interests often, as you see in item 5 above. This is fine since the parent or teacher can learn how to address these changes of mind in a proactive manner, allow for changing their teaching strategy, and select new topics of interest. Boys have to stay engaged in learning in their early years, even if it may not be as easy or convenient for us. If we do not make that small effort, these children can tune out and be lost boys forever.

An excellent librarian in Vancouver, Washington, Kay Ellison, has watched struggling boys trying to be engaged in various activities over the years. She not only runs the library at an elementary school but also heads up Read Week and the yearly Science Fair. She is wonderful with children and takes the time to care about each and every one she works with. Kay realizes that it is nearly impossible for some active boys to sit still, even for the best stories she reads. She has a child at this school whom she is observing with frustration, yet she has a real desire to help him. Kay says,

> As I watch boys in elementary school who are struggling, I have no single cat-
> egory in which to place them. It often seems that boys that are *very intelligent*
> seem to struggle the most. I don't believe all of their struggles are due to being
> bored because they are smart. Perhaps it is. But it is possible that a boy who is
> already bored when met with *another big challenge* finds that being in trouble

meets some need. Currently there is a smart young man at our school who has family problems. He acts out almost constantly now. I wonder if it is to get attention that he doesn't seem to get in any other way. I've tried catching him doing something "good" in order to give him attention for that, but right now it is hard to find him doing anything positive. And even the good things he is doing seem surrounded by so much negative they are hard to praise or connect with.

Mostly, it seems that boys that struggle seem to respond to real needs. Studying and advocating for an issue that he cares about seems to help with struggles. Last year our fourth graders showed an interest in animal rights, and as a group interviewed stakeholders and researched newspapers and magazines. This actual issue seemed to grab boys. I believe *making schooling as practical and meaningful* as possible helps children in their struggles to learn.

How perceptive of Mrs. Ellison to note what we have reiterated often in this book: boys need attention; whether it is positive or negative, one or the other is craved regardless. We often observe that any attention is always better than no attention, realizing that they have the need to be noticed and not invisible.

As boys grow older, their grades are usually worse than those of girls. Boys are more likely to report being the victims of violent crimes. Sadly, they even commit suicide in far greater numbers than girls. These facts can be found in many books, but it seems that nothing is being done about this crisis to help bring about real change for the better.

Moreover, in high school, girls take harder classes, do better in them, and dominate all extracurricular activities with the exception of sports. We see more boys dropping out of high school than girls year after year. Currently, the achievement gap in college is even more apparent, with more girls than boys attending college. Why all this male underachievement?

Unfortunately, for many reasons, there haven't been many educators willing to openly discuss boys' underachievement. For the most part, "boy problems" have not become part of the national conversation when it comes to fitting education to their needs. Much research has been done to prove that the problems exist, but somewhere the ball gets dropped, and now it is rolling out of control, like a snowball going downhill, cruelly collecting our boys along the way.

TEACHERS SHOULD NOT BE BLAMED

Teachers now have to teach subject areas dictated by their state. Reading, writing, math, and science fill their days, weeks, and months. The core standards have to be addressed. There is less time for music, art, and physical education. Now many districts are cutting out recess, even with so many children needing to lose some weight.

Now we have "dictators of education" telling teachers what to teach, how long to spend on each subject, and how it must be incorporated into the day. Many of these administrators have never taught young children and have worked only in administrative capacities. You wonder if any of them were ever little boys feeling that school was boring or too hard. If they were or could remember how they felt, might things change?

In addition to the problem above, teachers today have students with a wide variety of abilities, as well as cultural differences, all in one classroom. Class sizes are so overwhelming for teachers that they can't even think about individualized teaching. Controlling the students and keeping the peace in the classroom and on the playground often needs a referee. Many teachers are asked to be nurses, psychologists, and coaches in some schools, simply to fill in for those absent.

This dilemma sounds familiar and makes sense, having been a teacher for over forty years. Still, this book suggests some simple strategies you can use with any struggling child. Some of the strategies are directed to the strugglers and even those who seemingly are bored. Any small change can make huge differences—ones that cost nothing and that are easy to administer wherever you are. There are stretches, movements, and brain exercises that are even good for the teacher at the same time.

For instance, before doing any structured activity, do a few jumping jacks, hops, or waving of the arms to get the blood flowing to the brain. You will see children settling down to business, calmer and with more enthusiasm. Choose different students to lead this activity each day who have demonstrated good behavior in some way the day before. Soon you will have an incentive for many "rowdy or boisterous" boys now wanting to be the leader of the pack.

The power of being the leader seems silly to us, but children feel extremely important if the teacher selects them for any leadership role. An easy reminder to a child with unwanted behavior, such as "Oh, I am really sorry, I was just considering you for my exercise leader, too" will get instant results in younger children. Behaviors can change.

The playing of quiet music as you read to them after physical education or recess makes for a much smoother transition to a subject coming up, especially if it is a subject they may not enjoy. Breathing exercises or simple yoga help not only the brain but also muscle stiffness from sitting so long. "Magical meditation" is always a crowd pleaser, and the teacher can collect his or her thoughts as well after the students learn there can be no talking, only thinking of fun thoughts. Silence can be golden.

Always use one of these simple strategies before a spelling test, math exam, or assessment of any kind. You will call it a miracle, and the children will love you even more. The small time taken for movement can save your sanity and everyone's frustration. You will receive the healthy benefit as much as the children do.

From kindergarten to even fifth grade, for some teachers the unending basic knowledge and performance skills must be taught to many boys simply to become good readers. Starting with phonemic awareness, phonics, fluency, comprehension, and vocabulary, these five domains of reading involve many lessons and reteaching of those skills. And this is only for the subject of reading. We have not yet delved into writing, math, or science.

Often the achievement of boys is confused as related to standardized test data.

When taking this into consideration, combined with the fact that multiple factors contribute to children becoming confident and lifelong lovers of reading, we may need to focus on the broader notion of reading outcomes. Reading outcomes usually consist of two components: reading engagement and reading achievement. Both are different.[12]

As mentioned earlier, many teachers have extraordinary creative talents and knowledge that now have to be put on the back burner. Their super skills are put away so that their classes are better prepared for testing and meeting the NCLB regulations. As teachers, we used to joke and say, "We should be getting combat pay for all we have to do." But we can be pretty sure our soldiers do not get paid enough either for all they have to endure.

WE ALL NEED TO DEMAND CHANGE NOW

It would seem that everyone is being "left behind"—not only the students but also the teachers, the parents or caregivers, or any instructor working diligently with our children. Unfortunately, we are noticing more lagging behind in all subject areas, our boys being left behind more and more. Naturally, the stakes are high at all levels. Hopefully, education will begin to change from the lower grades on up. This change will occur only with help from everyone. We all need to demand it—and now.

Parents, teachers, and administrators must start the conversation of instructional changes for boys. Our common goal has to be that we want excellent education available to all children to learn in the ways that fit them best, even if it does get a little noisy. Productive noise is much different than disruptive noise; we have to learn how to allow the first kind in our classrooms. Children need to learn together cooperatively.

Across the nation, most educators acknowledge that impoverished black and Latino boys are lagging badly behind white boys and all girls in school. Now we are finding white boys lagging more and more each year. The lag problem is universal.

Is there a way we can head off so many high school dropouts? Are there better strategies we can use to help all children learn better? What should we all do to help them?

Our boys need to love or at least like school. By attending schools that demonstrate the best possible methods of teaching boys, as well as girls, both genders will soar to be the best they can be, whether they choose to attend college or not. We should all want our children to grow up to be happy and productive members of society, whether they go beyond high school or decide not to.

SUPPOSE THIS EDUCATIONAL CHANGE DOES HAPPEN

Once that "foundation of literacy" is established, education becomes less difficult and can even be fun as well as meaningful. Naturally, as with all of us, passions and interests can change, but by grabbing them when they are discovered, the joy of learning can unfold more quickly. More time will be spent reading, researching, and producing writing.

Another issue we seem to be ignoring is that children are born with natural curiosity, hoping to see, touch, smell, taste, and hear anything in their immediate environment by learning through different modalities. (Modalities are discussed in chapter 2.)

With very young children, any object that comes across their path has to be figured out. Children learn in different ways and modalities, while some use a combination of all learning styles. Regardless of how they learn, wouldn't it make more sense to teach to their strengths, or modality of learning, and not have only one recipe of lessons for all?

In the child's earliest years, much time of their life is spent exploring their world in pursuit of new information and experiences. Children's imaginations are exciting and endless, being continually intrigued by their surroundings. They love learning and life.

So how is it that some children come to hate school by the age of five? Easy. Now they have to be force-fed information that they are not as interested in learning. Memorizing letterforms, letter sounds, names of numbers, days of the week, months of the year, and how to write their names correctly (not in all capital letters the way they first learned) can be overwhelming and stressful to a young child.

Coloring within the lines is tedious, and trying even to write on a line is difficult at best, certainly being harder for boys with poor fine motor skills. Filling in worksheets in class day after day is not the way for children to learn to love or even like school.

Sitting for long stretches is almost impossible for young boys and some girls as well. Maybe both could still learn what is being taught in the classroom but through observation of activities and hands-on exploration. Active learning can accomplish the same goal. The natural way to learn is how they first did so before even starting school.

Many schools are focusing too much on becoming prevention-oriented and trying not to have errors in children's classroom work. There is no time for the exciting curiosity of children's interests and passions. As educators, parents, and teachers, we must be more flexible to nurture this natural curiosity; in fact, it should be mandatory.

Concentrating on rules, being inflexible with time, and having children sit still curbs enthusiasm for learning. Think about the times you have had to sit through a boring lecture or dull movie. New learning material needs to be presented in unique ways that will energize kids to learn more quickly and internalize that information. When children are excited about what they are learning, the obedience issue mostly resolves itself. A happy, productive student or child does not need to act out. He now is engaged in something motivating to him, and he forgets about behaving badly.

Why is this approach important for preparing kids for the jobs of the twenty-first century? They are going to enter a world where they won't know what the problems are, and there won't be any single answer. We need people to be able to think more flexibly. These are not the skills that are being targeted in education today. Culture is evolving at a rapid rate, and it's odd that our educational system has not evolved in a similar way.

We, as parents and teachers, need to build creative activities around the children's interest with a sense of challenge that is developmentally appropriate for the age of the child, always remembering if the activity is too challenging, the child will lose interest and feel unsuccessful. Conversely, if the activity is too easy, the child becomes quickly bored and tunes out.

In both cases, the learning is lost.

We must find ways to focus on what boys do well and provide them with opportunities to develop these natural tendencies and strengths. We should reverse the current trend to provide a one-size-fits-all school system that focuses on remediation of certain weaknesses while ignoring other strengths. We could find ways to increase the connection that boys feel when they are in school, or we will lose more of them by high school.

If your child is lucky enough to have natural talent or strength in certain areas or skills, you must nurture them: Dale Lovett made this eye-opening statement about talent: "Natural talent will only get you so far. It's dedication to perfecting your strengths and improving your weaknesses which will allow you to be great."

Children in today's rushing society cannot do this alone but will need encouragement and guidance as they grow. We, as teachers, parents, coaches, and administrators, must find new and engaging techniques in their learning skills to allow our children to be great. Furthermore, ways for boys to feel safe from bullying at school must be well established and enforced constantly. Boys need to know they have the opportunity and encouragement to discuss their feelings, good or bad. They need to realize that there are adults in their lives whom they can trust will provide leadership and caring. Real boys are not afraid to cry or show emotion. It means only that they are human.

Additionally, and especially important, is for young boys to learn early that there are many ways to be a successful male that go beyond the traditional concept of what is acceptable male behavior when they grow up. Money does not always measure success. How many times do we see wealthy people still very unhappy?

Better teaching methods—by using learning games, storytelling, pretend play, and exploration of objects in their environment—lead to better learning, more participation, and more fulfillment in the early years of education. These active learning strategies are required in today's fast-paced society. Teachers, parents, coaches, and administrators need to heed the following quote by Richard Parkes: "*Persistence* is not willpower, and it is much stronger and is grounded in belief, passion and desire." Let's be persistent in improving our schools so that children's passion and desire thrive.

In our school, after a few months of participating in the Reading Clubhouse, classroom teachers and parents would notice the obvious improvement in reading, behavior, or both. These children, of all nationalities and genders, were being taught through their interests and not through one teacher lecturing in front of the class. The students learned to work independently at their own ability level. They could monitor their own work to be done on corresponding checklists when supervised and guided. These students were showing ownership of their own learning.

Unfortunately for the classroom teacher, much of what she had to teach was mandated from the curriculum that was chosen for a particular grade level. Worst of all, much of what teachers had to teach was bound within the limits of the short school year.

When using this seven-step program, one will hopefully realize that passions or interests can change in children, but the basic learning tools will be well established in reading, writing, spelling, science, and math by third grade. Again, we must repeat that studies have shown that this grade level is critical for future success in education. A poor reader by the end of third grade will most likely struggle throughout school and possibly drop out by the time of high school.

Therefore, why do we need to rush our children? They will learn in their own time, dictated by their developmental age, not their year in school. We all need more patience, especially when it comes to our boys and how they learn.

THE TAKEOVER OF TECHNOLOGY

Almost nothing about the lives of boys these days concerns parents and teachers quite as much as our sons' seemingly boundless appetite for video games. Many parents of an underachieving boy are sure there is a link between their son's obsession with *Madden* and the Cs and Ds on his report card.[13]

Video games do have obvious effects on the boys who play them. During the school year, teachers, peers, and students themselves reported that behaviors changed. Some students were playing nonviolent games, such as *Sims* or *Madden*, and others violent games. The boys who played violent games for thirteen hours per week became more aggressive on the playground and in the classroom than those who played nonviolent video games. The aggression was related to how long they played the violent games.

Computer games, with their fast-paced graphics, system of challenges, and glorification of extreme violence, are hurting our sons in ways we really do not totally understand. These games can be found everywhere. Over one-third of all households have some kind of game console, and boys love them. Many boys report that they prefer video game play to television, movies, reading, and playing sports.[14]

Boys are now playing video games at younger and younger ages, and if they have a big brother, it is impossible to keep them away from the games. Parents are wondering what the games might be doing to their sons. Some psychologists who work with school-age boys think that video games are so harmful that they should be severely limited and that certain games should be banned. Games such as *Grand Theft Auto* and others are stealing the innocence of our young children, some say. Think of the pressure it puts on parents and their decisions about video game use.[15]

Gaming can make boys sit motionless for hours, with the hand controls gripped, oblivious to the world around them. What happened to riding our bikes, skateboards, or playing kick the can? Guess they are not as exciting. And with some, gaming becomes a habit, an addiction. We can learn much from studying the body during game time.

When a boy plays an exciting or violent video game, his heart rate increases, his breathing quickens, and his blood pressure goes up. In some cases, when games show surprising or disturbing scenarios, players' brains release the hormone cortisol, making it more likely that the players will remember what they have seen or heard.[16]

Unfortunately, gaming becomes a habit that some kids cannot kick. Are you saying, "Maybe playing nonviolent games is a form of brain exercise"? This may not be the kind of exercise you want your children to constantly engage in, and think of the time that is wasted. Technology has great uses but more in the arena of learning than in video games.

Teachers say that some boys who play video games often become progressively harder to teach. The attention spans of boys who play seem to grow shorter and weaker. Some of the questioned boys remarked that games grab their attention and demand fun types of concentration. In trying to win, the game becomes all-absorbing. When comparing that excitement to traditional schooling, with children having to move from subject to subject, boys are most comfortable zeroed in on a task. We already know that boys have trouble with verbal skills and verbal instructions.

It would make sense that boys need a limited time with any form of gaming or technology devices. There always has to be a balance of everything in life: too much of anything is not good. A child needs to know the difference between fascination and obsession. There must be shared time with sleeping, homework, interacting with friends, and active play. With young children, the technology can be used for rewards so that it will not be demanded later. Bad habits, as we know, are harder to break.

You will discover how wonderful computers can be when not overused and when they relate to any kind of learning and for schoolwork. When people say, "Just Google it," this reminds us of looking things up in the dictionary or *World Book* eons ago. With Google, the information is usually updated and more interactive with additional links.

In chapter 2, we discuss the daily use of the computer, recommended after the lesson is done and used more for reinforcement of skills taught. There are wonderful learning games, readings of interest, and vocabulary exercises, all accessible for free and for every age and subject. Still, this valuable use of the computer will be limited to no more than half an hour at a time. It can also be used as an incentive for good behavior or effort shown to enable the child to play the game longer. This is an excellent tool when controlled by the parent.

The information in this book can be applied to homeschooling as well. This book is written for parents, teachers, children, coaches, caregivers, and administrators who are serious about trying something new, leading to exciting results.

Many believe that over the past forty years of teaching, our antiquated school systems have changed very little. Education can spend all the money in the world but will still get the same lackluster results if we do not change how we are teaching. The hearts of parents, teachers, coaches, and all educators go out to all the young boys who struggle one way or another in schools today.

Others suggest that with computers and any technology, children will be able to catch up to where they should be in reading. Why do children need to learn math since they can find the answer on a cell phone or computer anyway?

New technology, used properly in schools, helps with the solution, but it still is not the whole answer by any means. A computer does not give you sincere compliments, encourage you to keep improving, or pat you on the back for effort. That same computer cannot help you with your home or school social issues. It cannot teach you to have empathy or even sympathy for those who need it. Computers should be reinforcement tools to help with skills being taught; they have to be used the way they were meant to be—as a resource for needed information.

Our children are glued to their cell phones, computers, or televisions instead of being involved with conversation or with their families. We are looking like a society of robots, when crossing the street, eating with others, or on vacations. The addiction of these devices should concern all of us. How will children ever learn to converse properly with adults, apply for a job, or learn to hear others' point of view?

THE REVAMPING OF OUR SCHOOLS WILL TAKE TIME

Scientific evidence and educational research will provide proof of what is discussed in this book. Much more of this important documented research is addressed in other chapters.

Sadly, the following definition sums up what has been happening over and over in school districts for decades up until now:

> The definition of insanity: Doing the same things over and over and expecting a different result.

The vision of revamping prekindergarten through third grade does not imply that young children should learn reading, writing, spelling, and doing harder math earlier and earlier in school. In addition, when talking about high school dropouts, children who are not ready to graduate and many who are unable to function in jobs become a moot point.

The remedy has to be from the bottom up and not a simple Band-Aid approach. For those who are able to attend college, only 50 percent of them graduate. The ones who do graduate often have to spend their lives paying back huge student loans. It is ludicrous that the richest country in the world does not help fund all students who can demonstrate their ability and who have the grades necessary to attend higher institutions of learning. After all, it is the future of our country that is important, too.

OUR GREAT EXPECTATIONS AND HOPES FOR CHILDREN

Already in kindergarten or even earlier, the child's attitudes toward school and learning and his abilities and self-worth are being shaped. This is our "window of opportunity" to help our young children succeed in a complex society. We must take advantage of this open window before it becomes too late to help.

Today, it would seem that what we all know in theory is not what we are doing in the classrooms. Again, we have seen a few encouraging exceptions to the rule.

SEVEN RECOMMENDATIONS FOR
SUCCESS TEACHING CHILDREN

Over many years of teaching and discovering through personal mistakes, there are seven recommendations that would change education as we know it today. However, this has to become a team effort, including parents, teachers, students, and hopefully administrators, to make education an improved model we all would support.

These seven recommendations are not the seven steps addressed in this book. However, all of these should work closely with the seven steps as an integral part of a child's successful learning:

1. *There must be more parental involvement.*
   This parental involvement has to be encouraged at home as well as in school. We all know that the parent is the first and, hopefully, the best teacher a child will ever have. (chapter 3)
2. *The curriculum must be developmentally appropriate.*
   This curriculum should be provided for children ages five to eight, with special attention to the way in which boys learn. We can no longer create programs geared to a child's age, as his developmental age may

be younger or older than his chronological age. The program must also be an integrated and exciting hands-on curriculum. (chapter 2)

3. *The curriculum has to meet the special needs of culturally and linguistically diverse students as well as the needs of exceptional children. (chapter 4)*

The world is becoming smaller and smaller with more diverse children moving here and attending our schools. One size cannot and should not try to fill all their needs.

4. *The programs should include outdoor exploration activities.*

Fewer teachers would be at the front of the class lecturing. More time would be provided for teacher observation of students while the children are engaged in learning. These observations could be placed in the child's portfolio. (chapter 6)

5. *Parents and teachers should have appropriate training.*

Naturally, for the most efficient methods of observing, teaching, and coaching young children, parents and teachers need training and in-services to help them.

6. *Recess time needs to be made available, not taken away.*

All children can thrive in the educational process with brain and body breaks between lessons. Teachers need recess, too.

7. *Assessment methods of children should be accomplished by observation and with student work folders or portfolios.*

The information in the portfolio would be a continuum from pre-kindergarten through third grade, easily understood by all, and passed from teacher to teacher and school to school. Naturally, parents could request to see them. The whole purpose of a portfolio is to give enough valuable information to help the child succeed in his journey of learning wherever he may be. A portfolio is a wonderful tool at conference time. (this chapter)

The two remaining chapters that are not referred to above are chapters 5 and 7. Chapter 5 presents a combination of teaching techniques to make writing fun while the child learns the difficult skills of writing, editing, and revising. Chapter 7 addresses bullying and how to solve this big problem facing children, teachers, parents, and coaches today. Therefore, both chapters are integrated into the above recommendations.

In a perfect world, these suggestions would already be currently in place at every school. Thus, if we truly want our children and students to become happily engaged with learning, then we must listen to what science and research tell us over and over. One would think that all these realities are falling on deaf ears.

If we could instill drive in children by discovering and supporting passions they have and teach them that no dream is too big, just think of what we could accomplish at home and around the world. The following quote by Ralph Marston certainly sums it up for children and adults as well in their quest to thrive:

Use Your Expectations

Expect to make a difference today. Then do it! Expect to use what you have, from where you are, to create new and meaningful value. Expect to use your time and skills to add real goodness to life. Expect to be kind, considerate, interested and helpful. Expect to be patient, understanding, generous and truthful. Expect bright new opportunities to come your way, and you'll see them when they do. Expect to find wonder and beauty, and they'll delight you everywhere you go. Expect to make this the most fulfilling day yet, and then act to make it so. Expect more of yourself than ever before, and see how much you grow. Use your expectations to create a shining path in front of you. *Then walk that path with persistence and passion and make your dreams come true.*[17]

On the whole, these may seem like high expectations, but why not simply try to retain a few at a time until they become naturally engrained into our daily actions?

Finally, we, as parents and teachers, need to build creative activities around the children's interests with a sense of challenge that is developmentally appropriate for the age of each child. This may sound redundant, but we cannot state enough that if the activity is too challenging, the child will lose interest and feel unsuccessful. Conversely, if the activity is too easy, the child will become bored. In both cases, the learning might be lost. No one wants a child to struggle through life or school. Children need our help and guidance while they are young and as they grow. We need to nurture their imaginations so that they can thrive during their critical years of learning. The two following quotes stress this importance:

Imagination is the eye of the soul.

—Joseph Joubert

Our imagination is the only limit to what we can have in life.

—Charles Kettering

We hope you are now convinced that, together with your child, you will find some interests or passions and begin to ignite your Adventure in Learning by using this book. So let's talk about how we can teach to that passion or interest next in chapter 2.

NOTES

1. Ralph Marston, "Be Amazing!," *The Daily Motivator*, February 24, 2014 (www.greatday.com).

2. Tom Mortenson, "What's Still Wrong with the Guys?," retrieved June 2, 2014, from wwwpostsecondary.org/last12/152guys.pdf.

3. Lesley Stahl, "The Gender Gap: Boys Lagging," retrieved June 14, 2014, from www.cbsnews.com/stories/2002/10/31/60minutes/main527678.shtml.

4. Madeline Levine, *The Myth of Laziness* (New York: Simon & Schuster, 2003).

5. *Scholastic Magazine, Read every day campaign; Lead a better life.* "The Reading Bill of Rights," retrieved June 15, 2014, from www.scholastic.com/ReadEveryDay.

6. Mihaly Csikszentmihalyi, *Flow: The Psychology of Optimal Experience* (New York: HarperPerennial, 1991).

7. Adam Gopnik, "Go with the Flow!," retrieved July 15, 2014, from www.the happinessexperiment.co.uk.

8. Csikszentmihalyi, *Flow.*

9. Ralph Marston, "Without Compromise," *The Daily Motivator*, June 23, 2012 (www.greatday.com).

10. "No Child Left Behind," retrieved March 14, 2012, from www.scoe.org/pub/htdocs/nclb.html.

11. Peg Tyre, *The Trouble with Boys: A Surprising Report Card on Our Sons, Their Problems at School, and What Parents and Educators Must Do* (New York: Crown Publishers, 2008).

12. Terry Husband, "Introduction," in *Read and Succeed: Practices to Support Reading Skills in African American Boys* (Lanham, MD: Rowman & Littlefield Education, 2014), xiii.

13. Tyre, *The Trouble with Boys.*

14. Tyre, *The Trouble with Boys.*

15. Tyre, *The Trouble with Boys.*

16. Tyre, *The Trouble with Boys.*

17. Ralph Marston, "Use Your Expectations," *The Daily Motivator*, October 8, 2014 (www.greatday.com).

2

Learning How to Teach to That Passion

Consider, Decide, and Do

Consider, decide, and do. Think about what's most important to you, and then put those thoughts into action. Take notice of the doubts and fears, learn what they have to teach, and then let them go. Make the commitment to move forward no matter what, and honor that commitment each day. Achievement is challenging but not particularly complicated. It's a matter of consistently putting your values, goals, desires and dreams into action. It's up to you to make your life the way you want it to be. Every day is filled with opportunities for you to make meaningful progress. Don't settle for being overcome with regret, wondering what might have been. Use this day, this month, this year to create the best of what you know can be. *Consider what truly matters, decide with passion and commitment to go for it, and do what you must do to make it happen. Today is your time to live with purpose, so go ahead and make it count.*[1]

BEGIN BY USING THE 7 ES OF EXCELLENT EDUCATION

Hopefully, by now you are thinking to yourself that it is possible to make a difference in the educational experiences your child will travel through from prekindergarten through twelfth grade and beyond. Just remember that this is a journey you both can share and look forward to when traveled correctly together.

This book shows you all the adventure and rewards available when your child begins to see learning as fun and with purpose and passion. Your student will experience exciting lessons that are hands on, engaging, developmentally appropriate, and changing daily. By working with your child at home and incorporating skills from school, you are also a tremendous help to the teacher.

Your child's current teacher will certainly appreciate your support, and keeping in close communication and contact will make the learning process less boring and frustrating to your child. This process will become more natural and happily anticipated, meeting the unique needs of your child.

Never forget the seven Es of your involvement in educational success: excitement, enthusiasm, entertaining lessons, engaging lessons, exploration, evaluating progress, and, most important, your encouragement along the way. All seven Es are important components and cannot be left out of your instruction. Be prepared for high energy and innocent wonder or curiosity with young children. With help from today's technology and so many online resources, you will never feel helpless. You will quickly see how many resources you already have around your home, so spending money is not necessary. Try to always be enthusiastic and express genuine interest in all you do with your child. Be inquisitive about what others are doing.

This attitude adjustment may be just what you need to jump-start the life of his dreams or passion. Most teachers love to share their materials—when the borrower takes care of them and then they are returned. Libraries in the community as well as at school abound with many types of exciting books, books on tape, learning CDs, and other media you can check out for free.

So you can choose to homeschool as a complement to traditional schooling. Even your own backyard and neighborhood have endless possibilities for hands-on learning. Many of us create stress in our lives by making the mistake of underestimating ourselves. Failing to have confidence in our abilities, wisdom, and intuition to try something new causes us to lean on others to guide and direct us. The decision is yours.

You will find simple, helpful lessons especially fit for boys, who are by nature curious and energetic. *The seven-step lessons begin with Magical Math Monday and end with Sunday Is Funday. The seven steps are done on seven days of the week and combine math, language, reading, literature, writing, and science into exciting, high-energy learning.* This learning is not accomplished by sitting at a desk, confined until the much-anticipated word "recess"—that is, if your child is lucky enough to even still have recess.

By working with your own child or students, you will observe their strengths, best learning styles, and even their weaknesses to remedy. In other words, you can not only make your lessons developmentally appropriate but also coordinate what you do with your child's teacher at school.

> The key to success is action; you may not know exactly what you're doing but with every action you are learning.

—R. E. Shockley

The dichotomy between the school environments that boys experience outside of school has become dramatically different for this generation of boys. While outside of school, students are multitasking and interacting with a variety of technology; inside of school, they are expected to sit still and maintain focus for long periods of time.

Although we see that boys thrive with greater access to technology, it is evident that they continue to need human interaction and contact as well. Most boys and girls do much better when they feel connected to the school environment. Unfortunately, we are seeing that boys are feeling less and less connected to school experiences. When they grow older, some boys find that connection by joining a gang instead. There is a crisis that is now facing boys in our schools. It is the result of the interaction between who boys are and the environment in which they find themselves.

When parents get involved in children's education in the early years and show their sons that school should be kept at a priority, attitudes can be positive for them. We also know they do better in school with a parent's support.

We know that not all parents feel comfortable volunteering in the classroom, but most teachers will beg for any help or support given at the elementary level. This book delves into participation and communication with the teacher in chapter 3.

STYLES OF LEARNING, OR "MODALITIES"

You have read many times about how children have different learning styles, or modalities. A huge first step is understanding which style your child learns best with.

Experts at university extensions say that parents can do a great deal at home to enhance learning. *First, it is important for parents and teachers to understand each child's learning style—the way he processes information.* Most children show a preference for one of the following three basic learning styles, or modalities:

1. *Visual learners* absorb information by watching. They call up images from the past when trying to remember. They picture the way items look in their heads. Forty percent of students fall into this category.
2. *Auditory learners* tend to spell phonetically. They can sometimes have trouble reading because they don't visualize well. These students learn by listening and remembering facts when they are presented in the form of a poem, song, or melody.

3. *Kinesthetic learners* are taught best through movement and manipulation or touch. They like to find out how items work and are often successful in the practical arts, such as carpentry or design. These students make up 50 percent of secondary students.

You might be wondering how you can determine your child's learning style. Here's a way that might help. Ask the child what he thinks of when he hears the word "cat." Some people see a picture of the animal, others hear a meow, and others feel the soft fur of the animal. Those who see a picture of a cat in their brain or see the letters "C A T" are probably visual learners. Those who hear the meow are probably auditory learners. Those who feel the soft fur are probably kinesthetic learners.

If your student or son is not performing well in school, you may want to explore the way information is being presented in class and approach the subject with your child at home using a different learning style. It is also a good idea to discuss this with your child's teacher. Much can be learned through observation of children and how they respond to different types or styles of teaching.[2]

When referring to the way very young children learn, we talk about the "five special senses," or learning by smelling, touching, tasting, seeing, and hearing. In these earliest of years, the child is still gathering information, and this collecting is accomplished as a physical or sensory action.

Therefore, it stands to reason that the more a child can experience a learning activity through his five senses, the greater the likelihood of that information being retained for future use. These children are too young to reason abstractly but need concrete experiences in learning. We know that children need many pieces of clear information in order to build a reference system to pull from. With more time, he should be able to process all these pieces, as in a completed puzzle. Hopefully, the child will be able to reach conclusions by figuring out relationships that finally make sense to him.

According to Donna Wood McCarty, an educational psychologist at Clayton State University, "Boys probably learn better in more actively learning situations and where they're able to move around, do something, or where there's some sort of visual-spatial component." Experts say that a parent can do at least two things: first, appeal to their school to energize the classroom, and, second, appeal to the boy's competitive spirit. However, parents need to know several other things, whether or not their child is having trouble in school, but certainly more so for the parents with children who are struggling at school or home. With brain research so prevalent now and available to parents, it should be mandatory that teachers, parents, and administrators have in-services available to those interested in using the best teaching strategies available and necessary for boys.

Here are seven appropriate approaches to use in helping your child succeed in school:

1. Make plenty of time to listen to your child's fears or concerns and try to understand them.
2. Emphasize the importance of study skills and hard work and follow through at home and in school. Help your child with his homework often.
3. Set appropriate boundaries for behavior that is consistently enforced. Children may voice that they don't want "rules," but in reality they feel more loved when rules are enforced.
4. Arrange tutoring or study group support for your son at school or through after-school people he may go to stay with if you are still at work.
5. Provide a supportive home and school environment in which education is clearly seen as valued.
6. Become more involved in school activities by attending sporting events, concerts, science fairs, plays, and so on, to show how you support his school.
7. Meet as a team with the student and a school counselor to share expectations for your son's future and to figure out how to support his learning environment.[3]

> There's just one small letter between can't and can, toss the t and go live your brightest destiny.
>
> —Rock Christopher

THE GOOD, THE BAD, AND THE UGLY OF COMPUTER USE

We have seen that technology needs to be used in conjunction with hands-on activities, outdoor exploration, exercises for our brains, and simple, old-fashioned, homemade games for exciting learning. We all know it is simple to sit a child in front of a computer for hours. When we think about it, getting him to stop is the hard part. Most children learn computers at a young age and can find their way around various programs without any help from us. Unfortunately, most of them know more than we do when it comes to operating these "new additions to our families."

Computers and all technology are only as good as the way they are used. They must be used to reinforce the skills and the curriculum that you dictate as a teacher. If not monitored correctly, the use of technology can become a waste of time or, even worse, dangerous.

By implementing the seven steps, you can assure yourself and your children that one size does not fit all for a curriculum necessary to your child's education. By following these seven steps and the seven recommendations in chapter 1, your child will be receiving one-on-one help without the negative peer influence and pressure sometimes found at school.

This book can be anything you want and need it to be, flexible enough to fit your family's unique lifestyle and situation. If a father or a spouse is available—even a brother, uncle, or grandfather—make sure to talk to him about becoming involved. Male role models can help boys tremendously, and you can bet that many did not think of traditional school as their favorite part of growing up (except for maybe recess, lunch, physical education, and summer vacation).

THE SEVEN STEPS OF AN ADVENTURE IN
LEARNING BY USING THE CORE STANDARDS

Our seven steps are done specifically for each day of the week, Monday through Sunday. At the end of each day of their Adventure in Learning, children get a designated amount of time to reinforce the daily step on the computer. Additionally, for every step, there are both indoor and outdoor activities to keep the learning active. Any child, depending on age and level of learning, can use these steps. If the child is beyond third grade, each lesson can be adapted for easier or harder lessons.

What Are the Core Standards?

Before getting into using the seven steps, it is important for you to research what the core standards are for your state. Go to www.corestandards.org to learn more about what they are, why they were established, and general information to answer your questions. Since these standards are mandated for each state, your child's teacher must incorporate them into his or her teaching. *If you can find a way to teach these core standards through your child's or student's interests or passions, you have found the "magic combo."*

Therefore, before setting up your daily use of the seven steps, print out the core standards for both your child's current grade level and your child's developmental level. For instance, if your child seems to be at the grade level below his class in reading, writing, or math, it is important to first review those core standards before challenging him with what is now expected in his current classroom. A meaningful foundation of skills must be built.

Or, on the other hand, if your child is one grade level above his class in reading, writing, or math, it is just as important to review current grade-level standards before progressing to the next grade level. Make sure you watch the three-minute video explaining the goal of the future for all K–12 children.

This core standards site is the official home of the Common Core State Standards. It is hosted and maintained by the Council of Chief State School Officers and the National Governors Association Center for Best Practices. It provides parents, educators, policymakers, journalists, and others easy access to the standards as well as supporting information and resources. Following is the introduction to the website referred to previously:

> Today's students are preparing to enter a world in which colleges and businesses are demanding more than ever before. To ensure all students are ready for success after high school, the Common Core State Standards establish clear, consistent guidelines for what every student should know and be able to do in math and English language arts from kindergarten through 12th grade.
>
> The standards were drafted by experts and teachers from across the country and are designed to ensure students are prepared for today's entry-level careers, freshman-level college courses, and workforce training programs. The Common Core focuses on developing the critical-thinking, problem-solving, and analytical skills students will need to be successful.[4]

Forty-three states, the District of Columbia, four territories, and the Department of Defense Education Activity have voluntarily adopted and are moving forward with the standards. The new standards also provide a way for teachers to measure student progress throughout the school year and ensure that students are on the pathway to success in their academic careers.[5]

Are you now interested in learning more about the Common Core Standards and the skills that students need to succeed? Parents, teachers, and caregivers need to be familiar with them. This new challenge to students, parents, teachers, and administrators may seem a little foreign and, to many, overwhelming. However, remember what Winston Churchill once said: "Courage is the first of human qualities because it is the quality which guarantees all the others."

Anything new is always daunting to those having to teach it and those having to learn the different skill sets. Time and repetition of particular lessons will make them more familiar, and soon the core standards will become part of everyone's vocabulary.

Things You Can Research to Better Understand the Common Core Standards

Find out what your state is doing to implement the standards, support teachers, and more on the "Standards in Your State" page at www.corestandards.com:

- Learn more about how the Common Core was developed on the "About the Standards" page. See what's different about the Common Core compared to previous state standards at the "Key Shifts in Mathematics" and "Key Shifts in English Language Arts" pages.
- Get the facts about the Common Core on the "Myths vs. Facts" page.
- Get more answers on the "Frequently Asked Questions" page.[6]

Now that you have access to this important website, you can save it to your "Favorites" or to a separate file for easy reference. Your child's teacher would love your help.

Now let's look at the exciting, engaging days of the week: active activities your child can look forward to. Let's begin in kindergarten to give you a better idea of what is expected.

YOUR KINDERGARTNER AND WRITING
UNDER THE COMMON CORE STANDARDS

Writing now advances from tracing the ABCs in kindergarten, then to writing them and to higher-level thinking skills, such as forming, organizing, and expressing complete thoughts.

What Does Great Kindergarten Writing Look Like Now?

Aside from decorative swirls, a few letters, and perhaps even their own names, most kindergartners start school not knowing how to write. You may have heard that kindergarten is significantly more academic under the new Common Core State Standards, and that is true: kindergarten writing standards include scary terms, such as "research" and "publish."

Kindergarten is still the year in which children first learn about writing, including listening, speaking, and thinking skills, along with physical writing, starting with the ABCs.

Writing Their Own ABCs

Teachers often start the year by introducing the letters of the alphabet, which we all agree are the building blocks of writing. Kindergartners learn how to form the shapes of letters, what sounds they're associated with, and how to combine those letters to create words. *While the Common Core Standards are more difficult, they are manageable if taught correctly.* This year, your kindergartner should learn to print most of the upper- and lowercase letters. Most children can do this with practice.

What Is Inventive Spelling?

Much of understanding the ABCs is figuring out how letter sounds combine to make words. In many schools, kindergartners are encouraged to spell words the way they sound to the child; this spelling is known as "invented" spelling. A child might spell the word "happy" by writing "hape." Children are often more comfortable using consonants and sounds at the beginning of words because they are easier to hear than vowels or sounds at the ends of words. Using invented spelling, children are demonstrating what they know. If we or they can read what they wrote, they are communicating.

Research shows that letting children use invented spelling allows them to focus on the purpose of writing: communication. Typically, with daily writing practice, kids learn the rules of spelling and later change over to conventional spelling, so do not fret.

By the end of the year, kindergartners should be able to do the following:

- Connect a letter or letters with most consonant and short-vowel sounds.
- Phonetically or inventively write simple high-frequency words they often see or hear in books.
- Write many consonant-vowel-consonant words, as in "cat."
- Write their own names correctly (not all uppercase).

Kindergartners Who Can't Read or Write Yet Can Listen, Speak, and Draw

Teachers and parents will read books aloud and need to ask questions along the way about the book itself. Ask the child, "What is the title?," "Who is the author?," "What does an illustrator do?," and "What do you think this book will be about?" All of these questions make the child think more about the book and all that reading tells us. It is important to ask what happens in a story and what your child notices about events and characters' actions. What happens first, next, and last is called the sequence of the story. This activity teaches the child to listen more carefully. This activity of asking needs to be done in all grades.

There are countless comprehension questions you might ask as well: "Who are the main characters in this story?," "Where was the dog hiding?," "Why do you think the dog is hungry?," and "Can you draw a picture to show something interesting that you learned?" You can also ask questions about the illustrations, or "What was the best part?"

Review with the child words such as "to," "from," "in," "out," "on," "off," "for," "of," "by," and "with" to express his thoughts. He should also learn to answer questions using complete sentences, not just one-word responses. Kindergartners also need to understand and use "question words," including "who," "what," "where," "when," "why," and "how," when they speak or tell you their writing so that they're familiar with these words when they begin writing on their own. They will also need to learn that these words signal the use of a question mark and that others will end in a period.

What Is Meant by "Research" in Kindergarten?

Most likely, your child's first experience with research projects will be listening to a few books by the same author or on the same topic. Students will be asked to recall information, such as the author's name and what they learned from the reading.

Then, with help and prompting from the teacher, they may draw pictures to accompany sentences told to them. They attempt to write one to three sentences about what they learned from these books. In kindergarten, this is called basic research. The skill of gathering information from different sources and using it in drawing, dictating, and writing to answer a question will enable your child to begin the three types of writing that kindergartners learn and for more advanced writing next year.

Kindergarten Has Three Types of Writing Now

Under the Common Core Standards, kindergartners should practice and learn three kinds of writing: opinion, informative, and narrative. These may sound like high school or even college directives. How on earth can you teach these seemingly advanced types of writing to a five- or six-year-old? Let's try to clarify by a few examples of how a kindergartner will perform these three—but with help.

All three will likely start with kids listening to books read aloud and responding to what they've learned. In an opinion piece, your child tells the reader his opinion or preference about a topic, such as a book, an animal, or an activity.

In an informative piece, your child names what he is writing about and gives some information or details about it. For instance, he might write, "I love space ships because they go fast and can circle planets in space." The third kind required is writing a narrative. This skill sounds difficult, but it is the same as writing a story. Your kindergartner will describe an event, putting the events in the order they happen and reacting to what happened. We call that sequencing in a story: "Then the third little pig stayed safe in his house of bricks."

By the end of the year, your child may be able to write a couple of sentences for each type of writing, but it's important to remember that under the standards, drawing and asking them to write sentences told to them to reflect their opinion and what they have learned and to tell a story count as writing, too. Therefore, the writing can be told verbally or even illustrated. The latter is the fun part and occurs naturally to them.

A big part of teaching kids to write well is helping them understand that writing is a process of several steps that take time. No one has to rush or have their writing done in a few minutes or even one day. Before your child picks up a pencil, prewriting begins with reading and thinking.

This may require rereading a book, discussing what your child has read, or simply brainstorming ideas for a picture or story. Then the teacher will likely go over your child's first-draft drawing, dictation, or writing with your child. More of the process of writing is explained in chapter 5.

The teacher or other students might ask your child questions about the work and suggest details that could be added or better ways to organize information. We always like to have one-on-one help when a child is past his first writing attempt to avoid any frustration. Next, your child may be asked to do a revision. After one or more revisions, the teacher will help your child with the final edit. This final step will focus on spelling, capitalizing proper nouns and the first word of a sentence, and adding a period at the end.

These steps of preparing to write, doing a first draft, revising that draft, and editing the final piece will help kindergartners learn that gathering and recalling information, organizing their thoughts, strengthening and clarifying their ideas, and improving grammar and presentation are all important parts of writing.

Finally, the Common Core Standards are big on "publishing" students' work. While this may mean putting it on the bulletin board or in the hallway for others to see, it is exciting for the child. We often would have the child take his Wizardly Writing to have the principal see it when she was not busy. This would really motivate the children to do their very best work.

These new core standards even ask for the uses of "digital tools to produce and publish writing," so don't be surprised when you get invited to read your child's blog that was posted.

What? We Need to Know Grammar in Kindergarten Now?

All year long, whether a child is following along as adults read to them or starting to write, kindergartners begin learning the basics of sentence structure, such as capitalizing the letter "I," as in "When I go out to play I run." They also know to always begin a sentence with a capital letter. They learn to end their sentences with a period and to end their questions with a question mark. They will also learn to identify which is a period and which is a question mark by naming them.

Because kindergartners' motor skills are still developing, the teacher will introduce handwriting with a range of approaches, such as finger painting, forming letters with clay, using salt boxes, and other tactile techniques, such as writing in the air with a finger or tracing letters. This kinesthetic approach is important for young children.

Kindergartners should learn how to hold a pencil correctly and practice forming letters by writing their names, which gives them practice writing letters, shaping and spacing letters correctly, and writing from left to right. Much of this can be practiced in the home; needless to say, this much-appreciated reinforcement helps your child and teacher a great deal.

THE SEVEN-DAYS-OF-THE-WEEK OVERVIEW: FUN STEPS FOR BOYS TO LEARN BY DAILY STRUCTURE

1. Magical Math Monday

Children will experience hands-on objects or manipulatives and simple games. A great deal of math can be pulled from basic cooking recipes used in the home and at school, and teachers and parents can use these with children whenever possible. This chapter even supplies a recipe for making ice cream. This recipe and others are suggested to practice the necessary skills and are age appropriate for your child or student. Hands-on activities keep all children actively engaged, enabling them to see number relationships much easier than simply by sitting with books, paper, and pencils completing assignments. Many of the skills relate to the state's core competencies. There are even some magic tricks that a parent, teacher, or child can do. Let your child anticipate this by telling him ahead of time to build interest.

2. Telling Tall Tales Tuesday, or Storytelling

Tuesday is a day of conversation, encouraging verbal skills by telling stories about exciting interests or passions the child has. Many suggestions will be given for materials needed and easy-to-make games, and time is given for creative illustrations. Children love this day. Parents and teachers can be involved here as well. Storytelling is captivating to most children.

3. Wizardly Writing Wednesday

Wednesday shows the parent, teacher, and student how much fun writing can be. Since actual writing is dreaded by most children, you will breathe easier when this day comes. This step will give numerous ways to "trick" children into enjoying writing—before they even realize what they have done. By introducing different ways of beginning to write or even forming letters, the fear of writing is eliminated before it can set in. Again, it is important to teach individually with each child or student so that some are not bored while others are still trying to learn the basics.

Using clay, salt or sugar boxes, individual whiteboards, and magical writing with disappearing ink makes writing too much fun to dislike. We often found good effort in writing displayed by the student when spraying a little shaving cream onto a desk, tray, or any flat surface. Little does the Wizard of Writing realize that he is doing you the favor of cleaning as well. The fresh smell is just as welcomed. Chapter 5 discusses the long process of writing, taking both Wednesday and Thursday to complete for children who are ready for this task.

4. Thinking Thoughts Thursday

Thursday is a continuation of the writing process started on Wednesday, as good writing cannot be done in one day. Once the child is happy with his writing, it is time to creatively revise and edit some parts before the illustration is done. The child may want to do this drawing first but will soon become accustomed to having to wait to illustrate until after the writing is completed. Their illustration is the icing on the cake to further explain the Wizard's wonderful writing. Here is where your child can shine in creativity, whether or not he is gifted in drawing, painting, or using colorful washable markers. As stated before, chapter 5 deals with the process of writing.

5. Free Fun Reading Friday

Friday is designed to use the material chosen by the child. He is able to select areas of interest or his passion. This activity can be performed in many ways, depending on the child's learning level. Some will be read to and follow along, seeing or pointing to the words spoken. Audio books are wonderful for this first step. Children can read it with the tape or CD after becoming familiar with the story and vocabulary. Since evidence has shown over and over that very young children learn far more through play than they do in a strict academic environment, more time is spent here on this important finding. According to Allison Gopnik, a researcher at the

University of California, Berkeley, and author of *The Philosophical Baby: What Children's Minds Tell Us about Truth, Love, and the Meaning of Life*, pretend play teaches children how to understand themselves and their world, leads to better adjustment in school, and helps turn them into what she calls "flexible and sophisticated thinkers."[7]

Most teachers know that the most important thing parents can do is to provide a rich language environment at home. Parents need to balance the instructive talk we do with our kids all day. Rather, try to use more description, referred to as "elaborative language" by some. This type of language makes connections to the brain and causes the neurons to work harder.

What do we mean, then, by using more elaborative language? You could be walking with a child not yet in school and see a "Lost Dog" sign posted. The parent could walk right past it; better is to elaborate on the learning from reading the sign. You should say something like, "How sad, someone lost their spotted dog! Look, the sign says his name is 'Spot.' What can you think of that rhymes with 'Spot'? Maybe we can look around the neighborhood for Spot. Let's make sure to look at the street signs so we don't get lost!"

All children need to make connections with what they see and read to become successful in all reading and learning. The child can be read to or read with, or you can have him read to you at home. It does not matter how the reading is done, but make sure that this elaborative language is used in talking about each page. Ask your child questions to see if he understands the book. This process will build comprehension and associations much more readily for your child or student.

Some children will read with their teacher or parent for more success. Still others can read to their parent or teacher and even share with peers who have better reading skills. However, one rule must be observed: the child gets to select the first book, and the teacher or parent chooses the second or third if time permits. However, that second choice must still be of some interest to the child. Again, remember that reading identifies interests and nurtures them. We identify, reinforce, and expand our children's interests through the selection of the books we read together.

Parents can help their children learn to read for the sheer pleasure of reading. Once good reading habits are established, the child will be receptive to reading more complex books and those with different viewpoints. Most important is that being informed of our children's academic strengths and weaknesses through our reading time helps us understand what is really going on in their lives.

Good books can change the life of a child forever. The book can encourage character development through exposure to good characters from great books. Similarly, reading can help develop a child's values and morality through exposure to good and bad characters and situations and their outcomes. Best of all, encouraging our children and students to select excellent reading materials strengthens their sense of self-worth, good judgment, and independence for the years ahead of them.

Shared reading is a valuable activity you will truly love, as will your child, while developing a lifetime of loving memories of reading together. The time that you and your child share together now will be remembered for the rest of your lives. In addition, reading with your child is a loving act. You grow as an individual by giving your time to your students or children. Finally, when we read to our students or children, we become their intellectual role models. This encourages our children to become role models for their own children. Reading is number one for success.

6. Super Science Saturday

Saturday is a real favorite, especially for boys. This day is spent mostly outdoors if weather permits. Some of the engaging activities are done through experiments tried indoors and some through exploration done outdoors. Even Dad can have fun with this one. The men can escape into the "man cave" of learning science. Some of the exciting activities include making a working volcano, building a bird feeder and birdbath, experimenting with making colors, and making types of clay and even your own ice cream.

7. "Sunday Is Funday"

This is your child's "day of rest." Thankfully, it will be your day to rest, too, and time to evaluate how the week went. Or maybe it will be time to tweak the things that did not go so well. Remember that each week gets easier and easier once you are organized. Organization is a skill that really pays off in the scheme of things. The instruction will become easier and easier as time goes by.

After a few weeks, all will run smoothly, like a well-oiled machine. Be patient. We have given just a hint of what these Magical Days of the Week will cover. The Adventure in Learning of math, language, reading, writing, and even science are the subject areas selected as most important. Consistency is the key to success. Let your student or child know that you are also starting something new, so all of you must be patient, remembering always that only practice makes perfect.

You might find that your child has trouble focusing on what he is not as interested in learning about. We as adults do the same, so why should this surprise us? The only problem is that learning at school is mandatory to success. That is why it is imperative to find those passions or interests early on so that focus is not a constant issue.

We all have watched a movie, read a book, or tried listening to a speech that we had no interest in. Now you can better understand how youngsters feel and why they often "tune out." But until you can find his passion or interest, here are some suggestions for better focus. We could all use some of these tips.

SEVEN HELPFUL HINTS TO SUPPORT YOUR CHILD'S FOCUS

Online schools are a wonderful resource for parents and teachers alike and provide many helpful tips. Does your child have trouble sticking with one task for long or finishing his homework? Here are some ways to help your child stay focused:

1. *Get the sleepy brain and body awake first.*

   Moving the body gets the brain going. Try having your child walk or bike to school, play outside after school, do chores around the house, or play on a sports team. Even doing jumping jacks in the house can help. Make sure your child has had a chance to run, walk, or jump around *before* sitting down to homework. You will see it works.

2. *Turn off screens and cell phones or any other distractions.*

   Before your kid tackles homework or does anything that takes concentration, turn off the television. Or, if others are watching it, make sure your child is far enough away that he can't be distracted by it. Also, shut down or move him away from the computer, and if your child has a cell phone, make sure that's off as well.

3. *Make a to-do list together for checking off.*

   Having a lot of chores and homework assignments can be overwhelming for kids. Help your child focus on getting things done by making a list together of everything he needs to do for the day or week. Then let him cross off each task as he finishes it so that he feels he is accomplishing more, and the list will become less overwhelming.

4. *Use simple, kind signals to help keep child on task.*

   You and your child can come up with a few basic signals. For example, when you point to his work or when you raise your hand, that means he needs to stop what he's doing and get back to work. For some kids, it helps to just lay a hand on their shoulder to bring them back. Try to avoid conversations when your child is working. To cut out distracting talk, you will assist with his focus.

5. *Take breathers to help with focus and attitude.*

During homework time, make sure your child takes a few breaks. After working for ten or twenty minutes (depending on his age), have him get up and move around, get a drink, and then go back to work. But don't let him get involved in something else during the break—for instance, no books, television shows, or games. Simply make that time a relaxing few minutes.[8]

6. *Remember to always compliment good focus.*

Whenever you notice your child trying to concentrate or focus on the task at hand, give immediate praise for him to continue working. You could even keep a tally of all those times for a reward at the end of the day after letting him know you will be watching for this behavior. Giving simple rewards is fine.

7. *Make learning fun with silly phrases of encouragement.*

We used to tell our students, "Hocus-pocus you *can* focus!" Always remember that children are still growing and changing, but for now try to make all learning as enjoyable as possible. Your enthusiasm and encouragement will keep them more engaged and excited. Notice we got to use five of the seven Es of excellent education: enjoyable, enthusiasm, encouragement, engaged, and excited.

Once you determine that special interest, none of these seven suggestions will be as needed for learning new things. More important, all learning days have to be individualized for the child you are working with, being age or developmentally appropriate. The interactive activities performed both indoors and outdoors will then be followed up by useful technology—but always done last. Consider it a reward for trying hard each day.

In the beginning, you may discover children begging to do the computer first. However, you must convey to them, "If you eat your dinner, then you can have dessert." Fortunately, with time, the child will love dinner, too— who knows, maybe even more than dessert. You may be thinking to yourself, "Wishful thinking," but wait and see.

HOW EACH OF THE SEVEN STEPS
LOOKS DURING THE WEEK

Let's go through each day with some ideas to jump-start your son or student. Keep in mind that each day will run more smoothly after you get your materials set up and organized. Additionally, try to learn different ways to access all the resources out there to help you. Once you begin, you will be amazed how many there are.

1. Magical Math Monday

Depending on your child's grade in school and developmental level, all lessons should be easy enough to master yet challenging enough not to become boring. The lessons have to include movement in the activity. For instance, boys absolutely love to go "fishing" with a simple magnet attached to a string and short pole. He can make his own colorful fish, cut them out, and have you label them with numbers, number words, or even math equations, such as 2 + 2 = (putting the answer 4 on the back of the fish). Find a large bowl or bucket to put the fish into and let the child fish.

This is a catch-and-release program the first time around. If two or more fish stick to the magnet, release all but one. The second time, the fish is caught with the right answer given, and the fish is added to the child's pile or decorated plate for dinner. This game can be played for a long time, and the fish can be changed to different task cards each time to further challenge the child.

Reinforcement of math can be done by writing on paper, forming numbers or equations in salt boxes, making clay numbers, or writing numerals on whiteboards. Make sure to use manipulatives for counting, doing math addition and subtraction, or tackling different word problems.

Children need a visual and something to move around to see number relationships. Change it up with Cheerios, fish crackers, miniature marshmallows, dominoes, shells, rocks, or whatever you can find. Let the child pick what he likes to use; if it is edible and he gets the answer right, let him eat some. Motivational manipulatives are the best type for young children. Anything we can do to add to the fun of learning is allowed.

Another magical way to have fun with math is by using the magnets in a different way. The magnets can be used to move a given number of straight pins or paper clips across the paper. Slide the magnet under the paper so the child does not see what you are doing. First tell the child or students that you have a magic trick to show them.

Everyone is intrigued by magic. Have the child count as the objects are moved from one side to the other side of the stiff paper or cardboard. Make certain the child does not watch under the paper but rather watches what is happening in the movement of the objects on top. You can use this magic to add or subtract amounts and have the child write down the equation you show to them, such as 5 − 3 = 2). He will need help at first, as will you, to perfect this magic. When the child finally discovers the trick, let him have a try tricking someone else who has not seen it performed.

*Cooking with Children Creates Valuable Knowledge
for More Than Math Skills*

Preparing desserts can be exciting for children. Because it does not require the use of an oven or stove, making ice cream is a good activity to begin with. Children can practice some of the basics of cooking as they learn about measuring ingredients and keeping track of time. Always use the freshest ingredients. How would your child like to learn how to make his own ice cream by learning first how to measure and then understanding the importance of temperature changes in liquids?

Depending on your choice, you can create new flavors, colors, and textures by mixing candy, nuts, food coloring, or crushed cookies into the ice cream after it has frozen. Encourage children to come up with suggestions for flavoring and serving their creations. This hands-on activity, using all the five senses of touch, taste, smell, sight, and hearing, is naturally a real crowd-pleaser.

Making Magical Monday Math ice cream might be used as a motivational tool to get your children or students to learn some particular math skills first. Whether it is addition, subtraction, multiplication, division, fractions, or money value, the skill will be learned quicker knowing they get to make ice cream as a reward. Little will they know that making ice cream seems like simply a treat, but in reality it is science.

To make ice cream, you mix milk or cream with sugar or honey. Some people like to put in some eggs before flavoring. Three of the most popular flavors are chocolate, vanilla, and strawberry, but there are lots of other flavors. You can even add some fresh fruit for flavoring. Once everything is mixed together, you put the mixture in the freezer, after discussing the temperature of 32 degrees Fahrenheit necessary for a liquid to freeze.

If you are working with a class, this would be the time to ask, "What is your favorite flavor?" The adult makes a bar graph with three columns, one column for each flavor. Next, using sticky notes, fill in a child's name so he can place his drawing of a cone with colored ice cream under his favorite type. Find out which flavor is the favorite, which is the least favorite, and which is in the middle. Also, do some adding or subtracting to determine your answers on paper. This is using math in a fun and creative way. We even could say you are using "sneaky math" for learning.

Materials Needed to Make Magical Math Monday Ice Cream

You will need to organize your mixing area first. Find one large bowl, a measuring cup, measuring spoons, a whisk, a freezer, a scoop, serving bowls, and napkins.

You can make the final product exactly the way you want by adding other ingredients and when serving your ice cream become creative. Use ice-cream parfait glasses, ice-cream sundaes with banana halves and toppings, or even a scraped-out cantaloupe or orange as a bowl to surprise your guests.

Ingredients

1 teaspoon gelatin
2 cups milk
½ cup honey
1 teaspoon vanilla
½ cup nuts
¼ cup warm water
1 cup evaporated milk

Directions

1. Put warm water in bowl, add gelatin, and blend it well.
2. Add 1 cup of the milk and honey and mix.
3. Add vanilla, the rest of the milk (1 cup), and evaporated milk and mix.
4. Put bowl and contents in the freezer compartment of your refrigerator.
5. Leave bowl in the freezer for 2 hours or set timer. Test to see if hard.
6. Beat the mixture with the whisk to make it soft and frothy.
7. Mix in the nuts, stirring lightly; you may use fruit if you prefer.

Finally, put the completed mixture back into the freezer and leave it there another 2 hours. Once it has hardened, take the ice cream out and serve it to your classmates or friends and family. Of course, you can always add other things, such as sprinkles, bananas, whipped cream, and strawberries.

Any type of cooking with children can teach many skills. The kitchen at home or the cooking station in the classroom can be a fascinating place. They see grown-ups working productively in there, see the steam rise from the pots and pans on the stove, and smell what is on the menu at home. Even the older kids might be intrigued by how baked goods and meals are magically changed into something that tastes great.

Younger children might be happy to watch what you are doing and help out with the smaller tasks, such as stirring something or setting the table, to develop the responsibility of helping. Older children can be taught how to crack eggs or measure the ingredients for math practice. Even teens might be attracted if you tell them they can choose the dish and help you prepare it with them. Make sure they know the rules about everyone having to help in cleaning up the mess.

There are many benefits to using this cooking time together, while the children simply enjoy the activity. Preschoolers will see how the dishes they eat are put together and get valuable hands-on experience. We know this is the best way for boys to learn, and they also feel pride in helping out. School-age children can learn some cooking basics and use more math skills as they help follow recipes and combine all the ingredients. You also can talk about healthy nutrition and why you chose certain ingredients. This is important to healthy eating now and in later years.

The chance to improve their cooking might be appreciated by teens. Who does not need to learn how to cook in the future? Teens might like to try different cultural foods they are interested in when studying faraway countries. Different cuisines, such as Asian, Mexican, Indian, Thai, and Chinese, are exciting to try and then cook later. Additionally, you could research that country, visit an Asian market to cook authentically, or see a learning video about the cultural differences there.

Parents and teachers can really enjoy this "togetherness of cooking" with children. The fun of everyone planning what they are going to cook, writing down the recipes, gathering the ingredients, taking turns, and finally getting to taste it together is a celebration of sorts. There is no end to all that can be learned by doing this engaging activity.

Seven Steps to "Happier Helpers" in Cooking

1. *Choose the right time for cooking or baking.*

   If you are going to have students or children helping to cook, you do not want to be on a tight time schedule. Instead of involving them in a time restriction with cooking, wait until there is a weekend or a block of time.

2. *Do not cook when tired or distracted.*

   With younger students or children, choose a time when they will be rested and not easily frustrated. You always want to be having fun while staying safe when you are cooking together. It is crucial to have another adult or parent helper help you keep an eye on everyone and what they are doing, especially if heat is involved.

3. *Choose the right tasks for the child's ability level.*

   Plan ahead a little when deciding what you will prepare. For the younger children, consider starting with simple dishes that have fewer than five ingredients. For example, children who can read can call out the ingredients needed. Another child can find those items of the recipe and put them on a table. A tossed salad or easy muffin recipe can be good to start with. You could also set up a pizza assembly, using English muffins and various toppings, sauces, and cheeses. Older children can take cooking to the next level with harder recipes.

4. Do some prep work in advance to save time and frustration.

For example, rinsing off items first will make the process move swiftly, but make sure they know the importance of what you did first. Get the paper towels, utensils, chopping board, knives, bowls, and recipe book or card out before having any child help.

5. Always stress safety in cooking and using sharp utensils.

Supervision of children is imperative when using a hot plate or stove. Preschoolers must learn not to touch beaters whirring, use sharp knives, or touch hot pots. Talk about which tasks are for adults and which are better for children. Make frequent reminders about what is fine to touch and the ones that could hurt them. It is very important to establish cooking rules, such as washing hands carefully and not licking the utensils until given permission. We found it helpful to make a visual chart to post near the cooking area and to review those rules often before beginning any cooking or baking activities.

6. Relax and have fun—messes can be cleaned up.

We know that children are not exactly neat in the kitchen or at school during cooking, just like many adults. Try to make your cooking time enjoyable by allowing for some big messes and show more patience for that activity. Remember when you were first learning and how hard it was to be careful. Most children make a mess when they eat, so expect it. Part of the learning is seeing the mess and learning how to clean it up.

7. Prevent cooking disasters and recipes tasting "icky."

To prevent cooking disasters, be certain your child is not measuring ingredients over the main bowl, causing a big "Yikes!" Make sure he knows the difference between salt and sugar in a recipe, even if they do look alike. Measure carefully and take more time to read and reread the recipe for clarity. Who cares if it does not turn out perfectly? Keep the smile and positive attitude. If the egg gets more smashed than cracked, show him how to do it right. Remind yourself and your helpers that cooking is a process and cannot be always perfect. Cooking takes many years of practice, and for some it is still a disaster. And thinking of how reading, writing, language, math, and science are all a part of this activity makes the process of cooking even more valuable. Finally, and most important, compliment your cooking helpers on a job well done. Bon appetite!

That was quite a diversion, but what a joyful, exciting, and engaging activity for all children. Now we can move past Monday and think about how Tuesday will go.

2. Tall Tales Tuesday, or Storytelling

The adult should first model telling a tale. It can be about a story or poem that everyone would know, such as "The Three Bears" or "Humpty Dumpty," except you add to the story to make it your own. You could even write down color words, spelling words, or any words that the child needs to learn. Part of the tall tale has to use a given number of those words for a simple prize or star on a chart. Any competition makes it more fun, and you can check off the word after the child uses it up.

The rule for boys is, the sillier, the better. Give them ideas from pictures saved in the "magic hat" that they choose from or let them decide about what story they want to expand. If they love dinosaurs or have any other passion or interest, encourage stories about those topics. This is a way to learn more vocabulary words and correct grammar at the same time. If the tall tale gets to be good and long, tell them you will record what they say or even type it later from the recording. Any incentive of encouragement is a must.

Finally, have the child illustrate his tall tale in any medium you both choose. Colored markers, chalk, pencils, pens, or crayons all are easily stored for future projects in empty cans or boxes. Thrift stores, such as Goodwill, are fabulous places to find containers to help keep all your material organized for the following day. You may even find new or gently used crayons, rulers, pencils, pens, magnets, or any other item you are in search of.

There is no rule about having to use new and expensive materials. If something gets lost or broken, you can always go back to a secondhand store or yard sale and search again, creating another fun activity to help develop language development while learning new vocabulary. The one rule you need to encourage daily is to make sure everyone helps clean up each day. This will build better teamwork and cooperation; both traits are harder and harder to find in some homes and schools today.

Let you child or class know that after the art of storytelling or telling tall tales is mastered, the best will be videotaped for all to see. Watch how many children try harder by using that motivation.

3. Wizardly Writing Wednesday

We have already discussed the difficulty involved in the skills needed for writing and that writing is even harder for boys. Here is your opportunity to change things. Do not even say that you are going to have them write at the beginning. Find a book or story that interests your child and talk about it together. Have the child pick out words he thinks are important to the story while you write them down on a paper. Ask him to spell them to you to help out. Then read them back together or even spell them.

He will be the Wizard of Words to help you make up sentences using as many of the words as he can on your list. You write them down as he says them. Make a goal of five to ten sentences. Always start small, as later you can increase the number written. When the Wizard of Words counts the required amount of sentences, you can read them together. After a few weeks of sentence stories, change to making a short story.

Depending on the ability and age of the child, the teacher or parent is the one to decide what that child might be capable of doing. When spelling words are required to be learned for the week, work those words into the story as well. Always remember that it is better to start with an easy task, as you can make it more difficult later. Frustration is to be avoided at all costs.

Just as you used the motivation of videotaping for storytelling, let the child know that when his final masterpiece is good enough, he can read it to the principal or be on the Author's Chair to read to the class. When children realize there is such a goal as even having their writing published for the library, the task takes on a whole new meaning.

4. Thinking Thoughts Thursday

This day is used to perfect your Wizard's writing or story that was worked on the day before. Depending on what needs to be done, Thinking Thoughts Thursday is used primarily to edit and revise his original story—to complete the masterpiece started by your young Wizard. Have your child or student read his story or writing over and over to see where there might be words he thinks are spelled wrong. The first day is always "inventive spelling," so the child can be freer with his ideas and length of story. As long as he knows what he wrote, the improvement of spelling can be addressed on Thursday. You will find many helpful tips in chapter 5 about writing that will make these two days much easier.

5. Fun Reading Friday

We have already discussed the early rush for young children to read and how many boys are simply not developmentally ready. *Education professor Susan B. Neuman agrees that supporting your young child's reading does not require special preparation or expensive programs.*

Neuman points out, "Parents can support early literacy just by taking advantage of all the regular routines of their day, like going to the bank, going to the grocery store, going to fill up your gas tank, or even following a recipe to cook something together. All of these activities get children used to seeing print in functional settings and help with reading."[9]

In regard to the television effect, the role of media and language/literacy development has been an early and ongoing topic of Neuman's research. During the 1980s, she conducted several studies that explored the impact of television on listening, reading achievement, and attitudes as well as specific reading skills, such as inferencing, comprehension, and vocabulary acquisition through exposure to captioned text.

In the midst of hot debates on the impact of television viewing on reading, Neuman challenged the traditional assumptions regarding the negative relationship between television and literacy development. In two editions of her book *Literacy in the Television Age: The Myth of the TV Effect*, Neuman systematically reviewed the developing corpus of research on the relationship between television media and literacy.

Neuman concluded that the relationship was complex and that, like other resources, television was "intrinsically" neither good nor bad. She characterized television viewing as a situated social practice embedded within family life and, as such, needed to be carefully examined within the context of a child's environment. Moreover, the role of adult mediators in that environment was a critical determinant of television media's positive or negative impact. Neuman urged those who would "banish" new technologies and media to shift focus toward harnessing the power of this media for positive educational purposes.

On Fun Reading Friday, why not go to the local public library? There are many choices of books, a variety of media to use, and even days that special people read to children for Story Hour. Libraries need to be thought of as not only a place for adults to do research but also a fun place to visit and check out books, learning DVDs, and books on tape and view newspapers and magazines. These varied items might excite your son to want to read more and discover how to find materials about his interest or passion.

Once the material is checked out, take it home to enjoy. Fridays will become a special day for learning about interesting things, not just a boring day of reading. The choosing of the material can be above or below the child's ability, as you can help with the reading if it is too difficult. If the material is too easy, use it to make the exciting challenge of your son reading to a timer or stopwatch. Each time he reads, record or graph the amount of time taken. Soon, this activity will make reading feel like enjoyment and develop confidence as the recorded time gets shorter and shorter.

Speed-reading is exciting, but the importance of careful reading has to be stressed. Read with a pencil to mark how far your child can go in a minute. Make sure to put a light mark (if it is your own book) on words he missed or skipped. Pronunciation is just as important. If he is reading a library book, write problem words on a list for him to study. It is better to point out only a few things to correct at one time so he will not become overwhelmed or frustrated with his reading progress.

Finally, use a tape recorder as an incentive to try after a few weeks of practice. Maybe Dad can do one reading and make a few intentional mistakes so that your child will see that everyone does not read perfectly. See if a big brother or big sister might want to do the same. The more involved you are with reading will set a better example for the one just beginning to learn to read with more ease and understanding. Make it a game for all.

6. Super Science Saturday

Whether the child is homeschooled or goes to a public or private school, you will see how exciting the weekend can become. Science lessons and experiments go hand in hand with how boys learn naturally. These lessons are motivating, engaging, hands on, and many times done outdoors. Try to get Dad or an uncle to become involved with choosing safe yet thrilling lessons and/or experiments. Watch their eyes light up when you tell them about the following:

How to Build a Model Volcano

We all have seen the exciting spewing volcano in science projects, at science fairs, or on television. This fun activity is wonderful for boys and can include many math skills in measuring the recipe for the liquid lava rolling out of the mountain.

Begin the lesson by letting your children or students know a little bit more about volcanoes before making their own volcano. This will motivate them to read, listen, and learn more about volcanoes before the experiment is done. For instance, tell them that volcanoes exist in many parts of the world but that most are inactive. Also, it is important that they see an active volcano having large, white clouds of steam and ash rising into the sky. Red-hot liquid rock, called lava, flows out, too.

Perhaps look up some of the most recent volcanoes that became active by going to the library, viewing a video, or researching further on Google. The children need to have background information and have a visual of what volcanoes look like before building their own. Let them know that after they have learned more, they can build a model volcano with vinegar and baking soda. Magical make-believe lava will pour out of its top even though there is no fire. Your children can build a realistic volcanic cone out of clay.

Here are the materials you will need to assemble first: a large glass jar, a measuring cup, a measuring spoon, baking soda, vinegar, water, detergent, food coloring, modeling clay, a flat wooden board, and twigs.

Make sure you do not take over the project, as learning comes when the children do most of the work. That is why we call it "hands on"—but their hands, not yours. You want this project (and all projects) to be a team effort but directed or coached mainly by the parent or teacher. There may be a bigger mess at the end, but they can help clean it up.

First build a model volcano out of clay. Decide where you might want the fun mess to be; outside is usually the best choice. If you do not want to use clay, you can simply pile up mud or dirt around the large jar to make it look like a real volcano. Leave the top of the jar clear for them to add the ingredients. Add the twigs at the bottom of the mud or clay and even some model dinosaurs for special effects.

When your model is dry and ready, put three or four small teaspoonfuls of baking soda in the jar. Mix together one-half cup of water, one-fourth cup of detergent, one-fourth cup of vinegar, and some red food coloring. Pour this mixture into the jar. Get ready for some real excitement now, as the smoke and lava you have made will start pouring out the way they come from a real volcano. Get the camera or video ready.

Use your perfect opportunity to talk about fractions with the measuring cup and measuring spoons. Meaningful math can be reinforced on Magical Math Monday at the same time. Experiment with how many fourths it takes to make a half cup and a full cup using water. If the child can write down the equations of one-fourth + one fourth = one-half and two-fourths or one-half + one-half = one whole, the learning of fractions will come easily. Also switch to pizza parts or pairs of items.

Make an Underwater Volcano

As a secondary exciting experiment, try this. Explain how volcanoes sometimes erupt in the ocean. Here is how to make an easy underwater volcano. To do this, you will need a large glass jar, a small bottle, string, and red food coloring. Fill the large jar with cold water. Next, fill the small bottle with hot water and tie a string around the upper edge of the bottle. Now add a few drops of red food coloring into the small bottle. Finally, hold one end of the string; lower the small bottle carefully into the glass jar and watch as the "lava" rises from the small bottle. You have just made a mini-underwater volcano.

If your children are older or gifted, it is an extension of this volcano building to let them know that mixing baking soda and vinegar produces the gas carbon dioxide. This reaction causes many tiny bubbles; it is the same kind of reaction that creates the air pockets found in certain breads made without yeast. Adding the detergent increases the bubbles but make sure to check the label; some detergents produce toxic gases when mixed with other substances.

Try This Website for More Science Excitement

For more information that will dazzle your child in science, go to www.sci-encekids.co/nz for excellent science resources in the form of lessons, experiments, games, and funny science facts, such as the following:

- Rabbits and parrots can see behind themselves without even moving their heads.
- Butterflies taste food by standing on top of it. Their taste receptors are in their feet, unlike humans, who have most on their tongue.
- Most of the dust in your home is actually dead skin. Yuck!
- Although the stegosaurus dinosaur was over nine meters long, its brain was only the size of a walnut.
- Humans get a little taller in space because there is no gravity pulling down on them.
- Because of the unusual shape of their legs, kangaroos and emus struggle to walk backward.
- A hippopotamus may seem huge, but it can still run faster than a human.
- Even if an analog clock is broken, at least it shows the correct time twice a day.
- Sneezing with your eyes open is impossible.
- The trickiest tongue twister in the English language is apparently "Sixth sick sheik's sixth sheep's sick." Give it a try and see for yourself.

7. Sunday Is Funday!

So here it is, Sunday, the day of rest. You all will need this day, trust us. This is just what Sunday Is Funday implies. Your child has studied diligently all week to work up to the reward of a free day off. Let him decide how to spend his time. You might be shocked and surprised to find out that he wants to learn more about his passion or interest. The new and exciting learning journey has really begun to make a difference in your child's life.

   As additional resources, there are many wonderful online schools that go hand in hand with the seven steps. Take the time to check all of them out for possible support in your educational journey.

QUALITY ONLINE SCHOOLS CAN
COMPLEMENT THE SEVEN STEPS OF THE WEEK

Over the past decade, homeschooling has become more popular than ever. We see more and more online options that coordinate curricula specific to state standards. Some of these programs have fees associated with them, and others are free. For parents choosing to homeschool, the quality of available online materials has improved tremendously. This online instruction can be used entirely at home or in combination with public or private schools.

Schools, homeschoolers, and anyone interested in teaching and learning can access the learning power of many growing collections of standards-based resources. You get to choose the kind of support and training you want, and the online schools supply what you need; many are standards aligned and free. From fast-action interactive online tours to a continuous schedule of online webinars with instructors, you can learn all about what these sites offer and how to use these valuable resources to meet your teaching and curriculum goals.

Some online schools even have professional development available to K–12 educators and to the faculty and staff of colleges of education, parents, after-school providers, and others interested in helping children learn beyond the classroom. Now you can also connect with a community of colleagues. Others are home to a huge online community of educators, administrators, parents, and education enthusiasts. A person can explore the collective wisdom of your peers and make your voice heard by others. Additionally, you can organize and save your resources so that they are always accessible.

Why not participate in discussions and create interest groups to expand your own network of contacts? For teachers, this program is invaluable when it comes to lesson plans. In the classroom, the library, computer lab, or your own home, there are now websites for enriching and expanding learning experiences. With resources in every core subject area for both the earliest learners and their soon-to-graduate peers, free online resources give educators great ideas, great materials, and an ever-expanding collection of high-octane instructional opportunities and professional development.

What Is ReadWriteThink.org All About?

Whether from home or at school, you will be able to access what you and your children need—and fast. You will see what is new and what is thematically relevant, and you will be able to search quickly for the material you need by state standard, content, grade level, type of resource, or content partner. As a teacher and literacy specialist for so many years, ReadWriteThink.org (www.readwritethink.org) is one of my favorites.

ReadWriteThink.org is a website with partners of two key associations: the International Reading Association (IRA) and the National Council of Teachers of English (NCTE). IRA is an international membership organization dedicated to improving the quality of reading instruction, disseminating information about reading, and encouraging the lifetime reading habit. IRA offers members new approaches to teaching literacy, easy ways to stay up to date on the latest research, and opportunities to connect with local literacy leaders.

Lisa Fink, project manager for ReadWriteThink, says this about the two outstanding organizations:

> The International Reading Association is an international membership organization dedicated to advancing the quality of reading instruction and reading research worldwide. The Association provides outstanding professional development and supports excellent teaching, critical research, and promotion of the lifetime reading habit. The organization has more than 1000 state, local and student affiliate groups throughout the United States, and 82 country affiliates throughout the world.
>
> The National Council of Teachers of English is a membership organization, serving 35,000 members and subscribers who are dedicated to improving the teaching and learning of English and the language arts at all levels of education. Since 1911, NCTE has provided a forum for the profession, an array of opportunities for teachers to continue their professional growth throughout their careers, and a framework for cooperation to deal with issues that affect literacy education. The organization sponsors 100 regional, state, provincial, local, and student affiliate groups throughout the United States and Canada.[10]

Both of these amazing associations are constantly striving to support our children and teachers.

ReadWriteThink lesson plans are organized perfectly for you. You can explore classroom resources, professional development, videos, and parent/teacher resources and after-school activities for K–12 students.

You will know exactly what the objectives are and what materials you will need. You will have access to student activities, additional resources, such as websites, and other materials at your fingertips. Be sure to check out what's new since there is always something intriguing for teaching and learning. In addition, there are fun, creative activity sheets that can be printed out for free.

We all know how much children love interactive games. There are games and activities that will give your children hands-on, meaningful, and fun learning opportunities. ReadWriteThink has made it easy for anyone to find just the strategy that will engage individual students, small groups, or an entire class.

If your child is interested in people from long ago or in history, you can access interesting facts about events that occurred and quick links to lesson plans and other material on similar subjects. The material is stimulating and full of stories.

Since we all know that specific state standards are now in place, first find the core standards for your particular state. With this super site, the subject area and grade level are available, then, magically, ReadWriteThink delivers a list of the resources available to address each of your specific state standards. There are hundreds of lesson plans. These standards-based lesson plans are written and reviewed by educators using current research and the best instructional practices.

One can download this app to use anywhere, so no Internet connection is required. The numerous engaging lessons show you the learning objectives, such as collaboration, comprehension, critical thinking, or the writing process. There are many themes to pick from, depending on your child's interests or passions. How convenient is that?

With the world changing so rapidly, you can search for just the right interactive activity to differentiate instruction while reinforcing core skills. Children who are ready to move ahead independently can do so. It is now possible to prepare children for the twenty-first century and tomorrow. This site can inspire creativity, critical thinking, and communication.

When you give students the opportunity to use ReadWriteThink resources in your home, classroom, computer lab, or library, it is possible to assign lessons as at-home activities. You will be able to integrate technology strategically and help children build important twenty-first-century skills today, enabling them to meet the needs of a constantly changing world. This is great use of our increasingly prevalent technology.

Wouldn't you like to capture your child or student's imagination? For summer and after-school programs, ReadWriteThink opens a world of cool learning experiences. You can find activities and interactive games that will help children practice and master essential skills and concepts. Best of all, you can find resources to help children excel in the subjects they find fascinating. This ties their passion or interest to the skills needed to constantly move forward in their educational journey.

This website is not only for children but for parents as well. It supplies a growing collection of materials that support family literacy. At the same time, it can help adult learners continue to build essential literacy skills. Educators who teach adult literacy will also find resources to enrich their instructional plans. With so many languages in our country now, this aspect is invaluable.

Parents, teachers, and after-school providers can find activities that match the standards that children or students are working on during the school day. How specific is that? How perfect to be able to incorporate core standards in activities done?

Thanks to the support of so many educators' significant commitment to improving education for all, the resources on ReadWriteThink are always available free of charge with no membership or access fees. Imagine having all this information available to our children at no cost.

This website is constantly changing and improving. It has delivered tens of thousands of lesson plans. The new website takes the best of what has made the site so popular and successful and adds powerful new twenty-first-century features, including the following: more topical content, searchable by subject, standards, grade level, and resource type; top and timely stories covering K–12 education on the home page; more robust and comprehensive search; and new ways to connect via social network links. In addition to these, there are more interactive and multimedia resources for students, teachers, and parents. Explore the new tools to help you organize lesson plans and save resources for the future.

From a fast-action interactive online tour to a continuous schedule of specific online materials, you can learn all about what this site offers and how to use these valuable resources to meet your teaching and curriculum goals. This exciting website is home to a huge online community of educators, administrators, parents, and education enthusiasts. A person can explore the collective wisdom of peers and make your voice heard by others.

You could certainly say that this is one amazing website and perhaps exactly what you have been looking for. Hopefully, administrators will also take a look at this website, which has been developed carefully for parents, students, and educators.

In summary, with ReadWriteThink now providing a unique, innovative, technology-based approach to literacy and student achievement, our methods of teaching and learning have expanded our horizons of what is possible. By combining best-in-class learning content, complementary professional development, and a growing online community for users, this website is helping students advance on their own with technology beyond the classroom.

Technology is now a huge part of our changing world; some is good, some not so good, for so many reasons. Out in public, it appears that everyone is "hooked in to" some type of technology. Certainly, it is not the answer to all of our school system woes. Many parents and teachers have a negative feeling about how it is "taking over our kids" and "taking the place of teachers." In some ways, this may be true. However, if it is used as a tool to reinforce what is learned and not as a substitute for human interaction and communication, today's technology can be helpful.

Virtual Learning through Online Schools Must Be Helpful to You

Whether you choose online schools to complement homeschooling or public schooling, the one you select must be right for you as well as your child. Additionally, if you engage in one that takes over educating your child rather than a local school, make sure you do your due diligence in finding out more about each. You might research your community to see which type is available, if fees are attached, and the school's reputation. Make sure they are funded properly so that they do not "up and leave" in a year or two. Make certain to attend any orientation before making this important decision.

To clarify further, some programs are done at home and not in conjunction with a public or private school. The parent's role changes to that of a "coach" rather than a teacher. According to some online schools, you are connecting your child to a love of learning. Naturally, the seven steps are still helpful to use with their lessons. Who said, "Variety is the spice of life"? This saying is even more true with children.

Other online schools can be an addition to what your child gets at school. You could say you are simply supplementing their education with different types of visual skill reinforcement necessary for your child's developmental level. These online schools should believe that a great school is not about classrooms and homework but rather about the relationship between teachers and students, between parents and teachers, and between students and their family members and peers.

The program is done only at home; teachers and students interact one-on-one, while virtual classrooms promote real achievement and exploration of a world of new activities for children. Some parents prefer to be their own child's teacher, and others like to share the responsibility with a teacher at a physical school. Still other parents might not feel confident enough to be "the teacher," or their busy schedule does not allow planning lessons for the day. Therefore, the latter group of parents will love learning how to use virtual learning that is engaging, enriching, and effective in most cases. You can learn how they combine the one-on-one instruction from superb teachers with, hopefully, an award-winning curriculum and a powerful digital learning platform. Make sure their program is regarded as a high-quality type. It is imperative for parents to now do "their homework."

What Are Some Benefits of Online Schooling?

Many students involved with online schools begin to see the important connections—with lessons, with teachers, with peers, and with their own abilities. Forming these connections helps the student succeed academically, emotionally, and socially.

If this type of schooling is available in your state, you can access everything your child or student needs for a well-rounded education. Some boast "exceptional teachers" who must be the foundation of these online experiences in order to be recommended. The teachers should be talented, passionate, certified, and specially trained to excel in online teaching. People who are happy with this online schooling seem to be drawn because they see that the school cares about kids and believe that personalized, one-on-one instruction really works.

These online schools have courses developed by experts. Most ensure that the curriculum meets national and state standards, including the quality guidelines of the International Association for K–12 Online Learning, which integrates the very best texts, materials, and educational resources from leading print and online publishers.

Most important, their curriculum team builds lessons that truly engage all of our children. Therefore, before setting up your daily use of the seven steps, print out your state's core standards for both your child's current grade level and developmental level for learning. By using a one-on-one approach, teachers get to know the learning styles, skills, and interests of each student so they can give every student the best opportunity to excel. It also allows students to accelerate learning in areas of strength or to get extra attention in areas of weakness.

They have opportunities to share ideas, compare experiences, and have fun learning together. Some types of virtual schools include opportunities to attend in-person field trips that bring classroom lessons to life. With clubs, activities, and other gatherings, the children can participate in more social options.

Finally, check to see if the online school you choose is accredited by AdvancED, the national accreditation commission:

> AdvancED is the largest community of education professionals in the world. We are a non-profit, non-partisan organization that conducts rigorous, on-site external reviews of PreK–12 schools and school systems to ensure that all learners realize their full potential. While our expertise is grounded in more than a hundred years of work in school accreditation, AdvancED is far from a typical accrediting agency. Our goal isn't to certify that schools are good enough. Rather, our commitment is to help schools improve.
>
> Combining the knowledge and expertise of a research institute, the skills of a management consulting firm and the passion of a grassroots movement for educational change, we serve as a trusted partner to 32,000 schools and school systems—employing more than four million educators and enrolling more than 20 million students—across the United States and 70 other nations. AdvancED was created through a 2006 merger of the PreK–12 divisions of the North Central Association (NCA) and the Southern Association of Colleges and Schools (SACS)—and expanded through the 2011 acquisition of the Northwest Accreditation Commission (NAC).[11]

Any online schools that you consider must be either accredited or in the process of being accredited by a local accrediting body or by one of the six regional organizations recognized by the Council for Higher Education Accreditation and by the U.S. Department of Education. The new schools typically begin the accreditation process after operating for a full year.

In conclusion, you are now hopefully aware of the crisis facing our boys. Each chapter will give you tools and strategies that parents, teachers, and the boys themselves can use. They are unique and more hands on to fit boys better in their learning styles. So now we will leave you with another fabulous passage by Ralph Marston related to the importance of passion:

Ignite Your Passion

Ability is about more than skill. Ability is about more than knowledge.

Though skill and knowledge and experience are important, there's something even more powerful that drives ability. It is passion.

If you do not have a strong desire, fueled by passion, it doesn't really matter how much skill you have.

If you lack passion, it doesn't matter how much experience or knowledge you have.

When you are truly passionate, that brings your skills and knowledge to life. When you are truly passionate, even if you lack sufficient skills you will find a way to acquire them.

Passion compels and enables you to connect with whatever is necessary to express and fulfill that passion.

Passion pushes you into action, and supplies the energy for perseverance.

What are the things that ignite your passion? It's well worth your time and effort to know.[12]

The following statement is from a dedicated teacher who taught all grade levels in numerous elementary schools in several states and is even now substituting after partial retirement. Lana Penrose, an elementary school teacher in Las Vegas, Nevada, could see the snowball effect of not meeting the needs of many boys at the age of five who are just beginning their educational journey:

After being a primary teacher for over 30 years, finally someone has addressed this valuable and extremely important subject . . . and she is a former colleague of mine! In my opinion, little boys at the kindergarten age are not ready for the confinement of the school structure of today. Too much is expected of a 5 year old now; while little boys are still wanting and needing to play and explore the meaning of things in their environment.

So many would do better with recess, which is now being eliminated. It is almost impossible for these young children to settle down to a structured academic learning environment, required of so many today. Therefore more motivation is needed to stimulate and balance their learning modalities. Hopefully, by eliminating some of their frustrations, by finding their interests first (too much time spent on one subject, or not enough time on another; one they are more interested in), is a logical place to start change. This change will make their learning come to them more readily. Their discovery of interest areas, combined with more multi-sensory activities, will increase and help the learning and enjoyment of education to take place!

In chapter 3, we will help you get more involved in your child's school, meeting his teacher, and learning about education in general, so let's get started. The importance of volunteering for Mom or Dad cannot be stated enough. We hear often about the positive relationship between better grades, more success, and capturing happiness when it comes to the parent's involvement by volunteering at their child's school.

NOTES

1. Ralph Marston, "Consider, Decide, and Do," *The Daily Motivator*, November 1, 2014 (www.greatday.com).

2. Robert Seith, "Connect with Kids," retrieved March 25, 2014, from www.connectwithkids.com.

3. Larry Eldridge Jr., "Connect with Kids," retrieved March 25, 2014, from www.connectwithkids.com.

4. "Core Standards," retrieved June 2014 from www.corestandards.org.

5. Department of Defense Education Activity (www.corestandards.org).

6. "Core Standards."

7. Allison Gopnik, *The Philosophical Baby: What Children's Minds Tell Us about Truth, Love, and the Meaning of Life* (New York: Farrar, Straus & Giroux, 2009).

8. Joan Kelly, "Moms across America" (www.momsacrossamerica.com).

9. Susan B. Neuman, *Literature in the Television Age: The Myth of the TV Effect* (Westport, CT: Greenwood Publishing Group, 1991).

10. National Council of Teachers of English, "Parent and After School Resources," updated July 2014, retrieved from www.readwritethink.org.

11. AdvancED (www.advance-ed.org).

12. Ralph Marston, *"Ignite Your Passion!"* October 28, 2010.

3

Meeting with the Teacher at the Beginning of the Year

The starting point of all achievement is desire. Weak desire brings weak results.

—Napoleon Hill

Napoleon Hill, an American author leading the new movement for new thoughts, understood how important desire is. *But desire has to be accompanied by enthusiastic and engaging effort to become real achievement that affects others.* When approaching any task of consequence, the more involved with that task, the better. In a way, it becomes a real team effort, working toward the same goal of a child's success in his educational journey. You, the child's teacher, the principal, and the child are all on the same team for attaining achievement.

Powers in Numbers

Tiny drops of rainwater are soft as they fall on your face. They yield to the slightest breeze. Yet if you gather enough of those raindrops together, and get all that water flowing in the same direction, it can destroy anything in its path.

Brief, tiny moments come and go all day long. Each of them seems quite trivial and powerless. Yet when you point enough of them in the same direction, by focusing your efforts on a clear and specific goal over a period of time, those moments can add up to a powerful, unstoppable force.

Are you tapping in to the awesome power which you receive one moment at a time? It is constantly available to you, yet you must use it as it comes. It does not linger around and wait for you.

Each moment comes, and then it is gone. It is up to you to use it, to forge it together with the other moments in your life so that you can build, create, accomplish and achieve.

Waste your moments, and they'll seem numbingly trivial. Harness them together and there's no limit to what you can achieve.[1]

HOMESCHOOLING, PUBLIC SCHOOLING, OR A COMBINATION OF BOTH: WHICH IS THE BEST?

As stated before, the parent is the child's first teacher and hopefully the best
one that child will ever have. Some children will be homeschooled, and
therefore most of the full responsibility of teaching the child will fall on the
shoulders of the parent. For some parents both of whom work, this is too
daunting to even consider as an option. With so many schools not fulfilling a
parent's expectations for their children, the dilemma of "what to do?" can be
very confusing and frustrating.

All parents want their children to be happy and to love learning. They
dream of their children leading happy, productive, fulfilled lives. Many feel
their own value system is not being truly reinforced in the public schools
and don't want their children exposed to bullying. Private schools may have
smaller class sizes and a different curriculum, but the cost of such schools is
out of reach for many.

There are things to be said for homeschooling when it comes to letting
children move at their own pace of learning. Brighter children are not held
back by the class or teacher. Additionally, students who are struggling can be
given lessons in the home and online at a lower grade level until they catch
up. Neither will have to endure so much frustration. Both ways can reach a
good solution to the correct pacing of learning, which is so critical in the early
years for academic success.

Children develop differently—and most boys more slowly than girls,
especially when it comes to verbal skills and reading. These brain developmental differences were discussed in the introduction and also in chapter 1.
As educators and parents, our teaching style must fit the child, as pointed out
in chapter 2.

Over the past decade, homeschooling has become very popular, with more
and more online options that coordinate curricula specific to the state's standards. However, if you are fortunate enough to have a school you love and
respect, with excellent teachers your child likes, public school may be the
perfect fit for you and your family. Let's say you have observed the teacher
working hard to find every student's strengths, teach to those strengths, and
challenge your child to learn creatively with lessons that further develop his
interests. Now you can relax, hopefully. Not so fast, as you must do your part
to support this excellent teacher!

IMPORTANCE OF INDIVIDUALIZED
INSTRUCTION AND OBSERVATION

With all these specific characteristics in place, the perfect combination of home and school instruction works great. For parents who need to be involved, this type of instruction is wonderful for all. At least your options are always open to change.

Furthermore, the teacher must be one who has individualized the instructional approach, not the one-lesson-fits-all approach. That teacher also has to make sure that he or she uses the technique of observation to determine each student's strengths and weaknesses as well as best learning style. Next, the teacher must create a curriculum to match those individual specific needs. By keeping detailed notes, checklists, and a portfolio for the year, much can be accomplished, providing invaluable information for years to come. This portfolio of progress is an excellent tool for teachers, parents, and students.

So now the curriculum is individualized for each student, while learning becomes age appropriate. Children will have a better chance to love school and feel they understand their goals and how to reach them. They are not overwhelmed with school and with homework they might not understand. School becomes more rewarding for all.

PARENT AND TEACHER COMMUNICATION
LEADS TO STUDENT SUCCESS

Teacher communication with parent and child needs to be done weekly or at least monthly. Consequently, the student's small successes experienced daily will lead to better self-esteem, more self-confidence, and less frustration for all involved. Hopefully, your "class clown" will find learning tricks to entertain himself instead of trying to entertain and distract others.

Let's assume, then, that you and your child decide to attend a school, public or private, and hopefully you plan to support the teacher in this difficult endeavor of individualized instruction. We would all desire that class sizes be no more than twenty, but who knows if this classroom perfection will ever happen? This is what it should be, but we do not often find classes of this size. In addition, a trained paraprofessional or volunteer can help with student documentation tremendously and help make each child feel there is another "coach" to go to.

Research over and over has shown that when parents are involved in their children's education, the children do better in school and, just as important, that the schools also improve. The parents and teachers need to build a consistent partnership. By working together for the child, the environment of learning is much more meaningful. Your child feels supported, starts the process of valuing education, and can thrive.

PARTNERSHIPS WITH PARENTS

As Jeffry A. Timmons warns, *"Always do what you say you are going to do. It is the glue and fiber that binds successful relationships!"*

Anne Henderson stresses the importance of this "partnership with parents." Henderson is a senior consultant with the Annenberg Institute for School Reform. Her specialty is the relationship between families and schools and its impact on students' success in school and through life. Since 1981, she has steadily tracked research and effective practice on how engaging families can improve student achievement, especially in diverse and low-income communities.

Over the past twenty-five years, Henderson has written, by herself and with others, a small library of reader-friendly articles, reports, handouts, and books. She has also written the Evidence series, which reviews research on the effects of parent and community engagement on student achievement. The latest edition, *A New Wave of Evidence: The Impact of School, Family and Community Connections on Student Achievement*, written with Karen L. Mapp, was published by the Southwest Educational Development Laboratory in 2002 (www.sedl.org/connections). The most notable ideas she points out from her research are the following:

- The benefits are not confined to early childhood or elementary education; strong effects result from involving parents continuously throughout high school.
- Parent involvement is most effective when it is comprehensive, long lasting, and well planned.
- The family, not the school, provides the primary educational environment.
- Involving parents in their children's formal education improved student achievement.
- We cannot view the school and the home as isolated from one another; we must see how they interconnect with each other and with the world.
- Involving parents in their own children's education at home is not enough. To ensure the quality of schools as institutions serving the community, parents must be involved at all levels in the school.

- Children from low-income and minority families have the most to gain when schools involve parents.[2]

After reading the last point, this parent/teacher/school partnership has even more importance or relevance today. *If we could bridge that language and socioeconomic gap, which hugely increases yearly, many more children might find enjoyment and success at school.* Naturally, again, struggling boys would benefit the most from the parent support. However, we need to realize that all children benefit.

WHY SHOULD PARENTS VOLUNTEER TO HELP IN SCHOOL?

Fortunately, parental participation has always been an important part of preschool programs as well as kindergarten, but this partnership cannot end there. Children love to have their parents at school, and this involvement helps parents see what is happening in the classroom. This visiting and participating is a key to see how your child interacts with others and his teacher. By the way, visiting dads can make the day more delightful. For children, having a father read them a story is incredibly important.

A young child's social development has a profound effect on academic progress. Children who have trouble getting along with their classmates can end up behind academically and have a higher incidence of dropping out in the later years. In the early grades, children should be encouraged to work in groups to develop conversations, comparisons, brainstorming of ideas, and cooperation with others.

Even the lost art of compromise can be established in the early years through small-group work. At this age, children are learning to judge themselves in relation to others. Many do not know how to distinguish between effort and ability. If they try their best at something and fail, they may wrongly conclude that they will never be able to do a particular task successfully.

Young children must find success at something to want to come back the following days. The action of sharing and taking turns is a lifelong skill. When parents observe group interaction while participating in the class, they can better help their child at home with additional learning and problem solving, teach new skills, and use techniques that work well for their child.

The importance of parents as partners cannot and should not be underestimated. This concept recognizes that parents should be the most significant and influential persons in their children's lives. When children begin school, they bring along their attitudes, values, and behaviors of their families. This framework of family attributes, through which the children's school experiences are interpreted, is influential for that child.

We find that the greater the continuity between the values, attitudes, and behaviors of the home and those of school, the greater the effect on the child's total development. Naturally, positive interaction between parents and school staff can ensure the continuity of attitudes and values that promote our desire for student success. We cannot overestimate the fact that schools are always in need of parent helpers in the form of volunteers.

Parents' jobs or having younger children at home often make taking time for your child's school very difficult at best. However, helping out does more than provide aid to a busy teacher and give you a warm, fuzzy feeling. Studies have shown that parental and community involvement in school has an academic benefit for students. Consistently, it has been shown that students whose parents volunteer in the school environment earn higher grades and test scores. They have better social skills and tend to pursue higher education as well.

Often the children who see their parents working in the classroom with the teacher show more respect in the classroom; this validates the child's role as a student and reinforces the huge importance of school in general.

Parental involvement in the school does change according to the age and grade level of the student. The parent might help with craft projects, prepare materials for the class, listen to children read, or help them figure out math problems. Yet in the upper grades, the parents might help sell cupcakes at a bake sale or popcorn at a game or do other jobs related to coaching. Here is where a dad can easily get involved.

You will see throughout this book how the male role model is lacking in our schools. Boys need to see real men involved in various ways as the child grows. Of course, Cub Scouts, Boy Scouts, or any other group for boys always needs help and leaders.

In elementary school, parent volunteers can often help directly in the classroom. Children of elementary school age love to see Mom or Dad interacting in their own class. As a parent, this can be very rewarding and a valuable opportunity to put faces to the names of the children your child talks about at home. Additionally, it is beneficial to see how the classroom operates and how your child gets along with others. You can get a feel for your child's teacher and style of teaching. Getting to know the school staff and office workers can help a great deal if you ever have questions or concerns.

Unfortunately, middle school parents often stop volunteering. However, be aware of the opportunities that are still available even if the tasks might be different from those in elementary grades. Many classrooms are closed to parent helpers, but there is a big need for assisting in the areas of fund-raising and in parent-teacher organizations. By this age, "tweens" are not that thrilled to see their parents in their classes anyway. Any small involvement does show your child that school is important. Best of all, by being in the school, you can always hear what events are coming up and at the same time pick up information to help guide your child throughout the school year.

When your child reaches high school, parents are relegated to a more supportive role. Volunteering at school events, helping the coaches, or working on fund-raisers demonstrates that you care about your child's education and life. Volunteering also models community involvement. Parents who lead by example tend to have children who grow up to be involved in their own communities. If your child sees you helping at school, involved with the Parent-Teacher Association (PTA), going on field trips, or possibly participating in coaching, they will probably do the same as a parent. That is a very hopeful goal.

SEVEN HELPFUL HINTS TO VALUABLE VOLUNTEERING

Sign up early if possible. Most schools have a background check and paperwork that must be completed before parents are even allowed to interact with students. Here are seven more hints:

1. *Never just drop in the classroom.* You must contact the teacher first and find the time he or she needs you the most. A phone call can establish this, or you can discuss your desire to help during the "back-to-school" activities provided.
2. *The teacher is the boss.* If your child or another student asks to go to the bathroom, refer him or her to the teacher. This is important for safety; the teacher needs to be aware of where students are at all times. Children can be sneaky. This fact is not exactly a surprise, right?
3. *Spend your time with students equally.* Try not to favor children you like the best or even your own child. All children need help and love the attention. Perhaps your extra attention will be the key to changing a child's behavior and even help develop positive feelings about himself and coming school.
4. *Minimize disruptions.* If your child wants to run up and hug you, yell when you come into the classroom, or climb into your lap, gently guide him back to his assigned task. Discuss at home your expectations, letting him know you will not be able to come back if the rules are not followed. This will get his attention.
5. *For older children, make sure to check in with your student to see the level of parental involvement with which they are comfortable.* Do not

let it hurt your feelings or think that they are ashamed of you. But teens regard school as their private place and might be happier if you keep behind the scenes.

6. *Dad would be more than welcome.* See if you can talk a dad, uncle, grandfather, or coach to come one day. Think of how special it would be for the students who do not have a dad.

7. *Finally, if you are unable to volunteer during school hours, check with teachers or office staff about tasks that can be done at home.* Teachers often need help with daily items that take time away from their planning of exciting lessons. Many classrooms and schools have websites or newsletters, needing volunteers to help coordinate.

Never discount your own talents as something that might be valuable as a source to the classroom or school. You might talk to the class about your job or hobby or do a demonstration for the class or at an assembly, or you can even read to them in order to explain what you are passionate about. Offer your talents. If you work in marketing, maybe you can help with flyers. If you are an artist, many teachers would fight over your artistic skills for help with never-ending bulletin board development. Just so you know, every skill is interesting to someone who knows nothing about it.

ATTEND PARENT-TEACHER CONFERENCES AND OPEN HOUSES

Nothing can replace face time with your child's teacher. You can ask questions about your child's behavior, his progress, his strengths, his weaknesses, and how you can better help him to thrive in his education. With more open communication, parents and teachers can better work together on how best to teach that child. Parents can and should help their children prepare for tests and review their homework. Students seem to be more responsible if they know that their work will be checked both at home and in school. Weekly spelling or math tests can become a breeze if the child is prepared.

If your child is being bullied, the best way to nip it in the bud is to discuss the problem with the teacher immediately. You can ask the teacher if he or she is seeing any of this inappropriate behavior in the classroom or on the playground. Often it can happen on the bus or on the way to and from school, so the teacher is not even aware it is going on. However, by making the teacher aware, he or she can better follow up by talking to other children or even the bus driver.

Open houses are a special time for children to show off what they are learning and making in school. The teacher and students take lots of time to dress up their classroom to make it inviting, friendly, and interesting. You will see displays of the children's hard work done over weeks of time. Sometimes it helps a parent to observe comparisons of other children's work to better see how your child is really doing.

Children love being able to walk around and show you what they do in their classroom and the projects they have been working on. Open house is a wonderful opportunity for everyone to enjoy the efforts of all and show praise for a job well done.

PTAS NEED YOU

All teachers strive to get as many parents as they can to join the PTA. They have classroom contests and prizes to promote joining this valuable association. The monies collected from each parent to join are minimal for all that the PTA board tries to accomplish that year. Meetings keep you in touch with what is going on behind the scenes of the school, and you can voice your opinion on school matters.

Remember that PTAs are not for females only; dads are needed as well to provide different points of view. In addition, the setting up of school carnivals, science fairs, bake sales, or school plays could always benefit by the extra muscle power and toolboxes often hidden in their man caves.

The PTA board members could not do all the things necessary for the children at your school without parents and the community working in conjunction with each other. Any amount of time you can dedicate to helping out the PTA determines what can be done in a school year and how wonderful it can be for your child to experience. The hardworking board members work tirelessly and seem to be recruited again and again, year after year, yet everyone should at least help in some way to support them. For more information, visit www.pta.org.

FUN FIELD TRIPS NEED CHAPERONES LIKE YOU!

Once you have participated in a field trip for your child's class, you might never forget it. That may be a good thing or a bad thing, depending on how the trip is organized and how many volunteers the teacher can bribe to come along. Unfortunately, there can never be enough supervision when it comes to the younger grades. Children can get overstimulated and want to go in their own directions at times. This is why more chaperones are a must.

Rules have to be discussed, gone over, and memorized weeks before the trip; still, with all the excitement and anticipation, you might think rules were never even mentioned to the group. To be fair, always give the teacher the benefit of the doubt. If children are to bring a lunch, a whole new nightmare begins. Lost lunches or forgotten ones can cause tears on arrival, and rationing becomes an art form. A hint to you: "Get ready!"

So whether it is visiting the pumpkin patch, the zoo, the fire station, the library, or the police station, be an "angel of the teacher" and volunteer early. You will make his or her life easier, and he or she will be able to sleep better at night. You might have fun, too. However, if you do not, pretend that you did!

In conclusion, twenty minutes of making copies for a teacher, helping prepare for art projects or science setups, or simply helping to update a bulletin board—all these tasks will be greatly appreciated but will be even more meaningful to your child. The smallest amount of help can make a tremendous difference, even if you think it is nothing.

We have had children team up with the PTA and volunteers to plant a community garden, which is something that needs constant weeding and upkeep for the garden to be a success. Even with all the time and work this project takes, much hands-on learning is done by the child. When harvest time comes, children love to have their parents come and share in the joy and pride of their hard work. Finally, if you really have no extra time to volunteer, at least try to donate materials needed by the teacher for upcoming projects or parties. He or she will certainly appreciate your effort to help in any way you can.

Now that we have discussed the immense importance of the parent and teacher partnership in the school, let's talk more about the beginning of a child's exciting journey of learning. Your child's first experience with school is just as important as—and might be even more important than—simple parental involvement. If the class is not hands on, engaging, exciting, developmentally appropriate, fun, and meaningful, you must take another look at the preschool and how it is being run. This first important environment of learning can make or break how a child feels about going to school and how he feels about himself when it comes to his ability.

A GREAT PRESCHOOL CAN BE POWERFUL—JUST ASK A TEACHER

Attending a preschool program might be the magical difference for your son to love school, or it may be the beginning of his disliking even going there to learn. This pre-K experience used to be rare, yet today over 5 million children attend these programs. Some states, such as Florida, Oklahoma, and Georgia, are passing important legislation to make preschool available to all.[3]

Due to many parents having to work now, preschool solves the issue of child care for most. A second factor is caused by the fear of crime being so prevalent.

Whether it is real or only imagined, knowing that your child is getting to play in a safe environment is comforting. Parents are now more concerned about any free play outside for their children. Years ago, it was different.

Riding your bike across town, playing hopscotch, jumping rope, playing kickball out front, or going over to people's homes you do not know that well can seem careless and even dangerous in today's society. Probably, this lack of exercise adds to the problem of obesity in some children, having to stay indoors most of the time. The lack of socialization with other children can be detrimental as well. Preschools can help solve many of these concerns when the program fits the child.

Usually, the benefits of preschool are considered obvious. This early introduction to education can definitely help children make that important transition. The child is now moving from family life to a world where he is only one of many. For some children, this is a rude awakening, having to share objects, take turns, and wait for their talking time with others in a group situation. As with schools, there are the average, good, and excellent types of pre-K programs.

If the preschool has done its homework, it knows how very young children learn differently than older ones. The instructors and helpers try to make their programs exciting, challenging, and engaging with hands-on activities. They know that all young children need to move and explore rather than sit and listen for most of the day. Hopefully, these preschools provide skills to develop their children's independence.

Of utmost importance is the value of children, boys in particular, being immersed in a language-rich environment, which is critical to their becoming good future readers The development of verbal and language skills will help them later in writing as well. You will see in the following chapters how important this is.

Does your child's preschool have activities that spark his natural curiosity, get him excited about schooling, and form the cognitive-building structure to help him become a lifelong learner? Additionally, preschool should offer a program that is interactive and child centered with play-based activities rather than academic-based ones. This last type becomes a horrible experience for many children who are not developmentally ready for structured learning. They may soon feel inadequate in school.

Therefore, the preschool needs to be active, not academic, at this young age of learning. Some boys who have to perform structured skills have difficulty, leading to frustration, feeling uncomfortable, and not wanting to go back. These high academic expectations do not fit his natural development and can leave him feeling alienated or like a failure even at the age of four. What a horrid way to begin your precious child's experience with school. Instead of creating a love for learning, preschool may not only turn him off from school but also, worst of all, lower his self-esteem for future years.

This book spends a great amount of time on brain research comparing boys to girls because of its relevance to learning styles. It is important that your child's teacher has some current knowledge of these differences, and as a parent you should inquire if he or she does. Perhaps you can suggest to the principal that a specialist in children's brain development come to discuss this topic with all the teachers and parents one evening. You just might make a huge difference in many children's quality of learning.

IMPORTANT QUESTIONS TO ASK THE TEACHER

Get ready for more reasons to note brain differences found in other research. Hopefully, your child's teacher is aware of teaching to the boy's (and the girl's) brain in general. You might say the learning has to be boy friendly.

According to Michael Gurian in Minds of Boys, the solution for under-achieving boys is a program of boy-friendly learning-based strategies tailored to the hardwired differences in male neurobiology. "New nature-based gender science can arm teachers and parents with successful methodologies to teach boys."[4]

Furthermore, PET scans of the brain suggest how teachers can teach boys more successfully. Testosterone, Gurian says, formats the right side of a boy's brain for spatial and mechanical tasks. "The further you are on the male spectrum, the more you will be visuo-spatially inclined. And the more you will have to move your body. You will also be less verbal. The visuo-spatial centers take over the verbal-emotive centers." More simply stated, that is why boys tend to supply less detail in their writing than do girls.

Gurian says that male brains tend to compartmentalize learning. A female brain shows more activation patterns than do male brains. "Girl brains are on alert. They are better at multitasking. When boy brains rest, they cannot pay attention. In fact, a boy brain at rest shows almost no functioning beyond digestion and breathing. I'm sure you have seen this at home."

You might think, "Well, that is insulting to boys!" But think back on our previous discussion of brain research. Boys have many strengths that are different from those of girls. And, as said before, brain studies do indicate that boys would need to experience learning in a more active way that keeps them engaged in what they are trying to learn. Many doubt Gurian's findings, yet they do substantiate the fact that boys often have to move around during learning times.

The more scientists study the brain, the more the interaction between its structure and experience become known. Hormones, genes, and the environment are much more important. "While genetics and hormones affect activation patterns, which in turn influence the impact of experiences, experiences can influence the activity levels, of genes."[5] Peg Tyre feels that the boy's brain is also "plastic" and is shaped by experiences and attitudes in which he is immersed.

We can all spend hours debating who is right about research regarding the brains of girls and boys, but why not go with what we know and apply that to a boy's early learning? Naturally, we cannot totally classify students, as each one is unique, developing at different rates. Doing so would put males and females back into gender stereotypes—highly unfair to children everywhere.

Ask, "What Skills Must My Child Learn?"

If we could incorporate boy-friendly academic strategies into some of our existing schools, both boys and girls would both benefit greatly. In the report "Raising Boys' Achievement," Younger and Warrington describe the results of a four-year study of gender differences in education. Working with more than fifty primary, secondary, and special schools in England, the authors worked to identify strategies that appear to make a difference to boys' learning, motivation, and engagement with their schooling while consistently raising levels of achievement.

Their research concludes that gains can be made in the areas below. The use of speaking and listening as part of the writing process and areas of reading and writing with targeted strategies are important. They include the following:

- Bringing more creativity and variety to reading and writing
- Greater use of technology
- Greater use of active learning
- Utilizing the arts
- Incorporating an understanding among teachers and students that individuals have different learning styles (modalities), including a focus on multiple intelligences
- Creating lessons that incorporate more learning styles and a greater variety of intelligences
- Using mentors to mediate and negotiate for their students and at the same time challenging their students to do more and better

- Targeting boys who have the greatest capacity to influence others and seeking to give them greater positive reinforcement in school
- Providing leadership opportunities for all boys

They do say that some of the results are not conclusive but that there is enough evidence to support the use of these strategies for mixed-gender classrooms, targeting the achievement of boys. They made it clear that girls also benefit from many of these strategies.

It is important that parents and teachers meet and work together for the success of the child. Both could work as a team to determine the best program that is doable for both. A teacher would not appreciate being told how he or she should teach a child. Additionally, a parent should not be happy finding out that all children in the class have to run on the same excessive exercise wheel of education that gets nowhere fast.

One way will never satisfy everyone, and it might be time for both parent and teacher to work together for the benefit of all children. Teachers want to do their very best, and parents want teachers and their children to do their very best. The combined desire and effort will result in students getting the advantage of a much-needed individualized program.

When a parent meets early in the year with the child's teacher, a bigger picture of that child's strength and weakness can be determined. Suggestions from you regarding the best ways your child learns, including interests or passions, can help the teacher tremendously. Teachers need the support of the parent, as does the child. Hopefully, a bond will develop between the family and the school that will last for many years.

Getting involved as a volunteer is best of all, of course. Many parents would love to help in the classroom but cannot due to working schedules. Regardless, everyone can take an hour now and then to keep contact with the school. Whether by phone, e-mail, or in person, updates of the child's successes and even failures need to be communicated to the parent and teacher at least monthly. If there is an obvious problem, weekly is certainly better. Communication is the key to building the best relationship between the teacher and the parent.

Ask, "Does My Child Appear Bored in School?"

Boredom in a bright child during class is inexcusable. Some boys will say, "This is boring!" for an excuse when they do not want to do the work or do not know how to accomplish a task. A teacher will hear a child say, "I'm bored!"

We all have heard this phrase many times in school and over summer vacation. However, bright children who are truly bored and who already know the material being taught should be able to be challenged more in the classroom.

Another option is to have children switch classes during their subject time. We did this often at our school, and the child was able to feel successful at his own level of ability. This easy switching solution can often help the child catch up—and without stress. Conversely, a brighter child can move ahead at his own pace. A teacher might even discover children displaying better behavior and happier attitudes.

Many young boys could be held back from receiving an appropriate education by a lack of advanced classes. This could cause the risk of social and emotional difficulty by "being tethered to an unrewarding educational program."[6] Why wouldn't a child act out with nothing new to learn or be challenged by?

Both teacher and parent need to discuss what is being done to help very bright boys achieve to their ability. The report *A Nation Deceived: How Schools Hold Back America's Brightest Students* is especially important today. The report states six ways that schools might be preventing children from accelerating:[7]

- Limited familiarity with the research on acceleration
- Philosophy that children must be kept with their age-groups
- Belief that acceleration hurries children out of childhood
- Fear that acceleration hurts children socially
- Political concerns about equity
- Worry that other students will be offended if one child is accelerated

Current research is showing that these concerns are not totally valid and that the benefits of acceleration can outweigh any concerns. In this day of mediocrity in many schools, it makes sense that acceleration for specific children, boys or girls, could be a ticket to the future happiness and success of any child who demonstrates above-average ability and maturity. Again, one program cannot and should not trap all children into learning the same things at the same time. We might improve what is labeled "boy behavior" as well.

Ask, "How Can I Help My Boy Who Struggles?"

Conversely, a parent and teacher need to discuss what is being done in the early years for struggling boys to help them love school or at least like it.

Boys need to find a niche or interest area early on that helps them develop a positive self-image and gives them goals and direction. We need to expose him to many interests—but his own, not ours.

The interest or passion can be that special key that unlocks the child's frustration with school and homework. Why does it matter what he reads about if he is reading, writing, drawing, or making up his own math problems? Isn't he still learning? That struggling boy has to be accepted and taught at his level or ability to ever find success and happiness. We owe all children and students our best effort.

When meeting with the teacher, let him or her know some of the seven steps you are doing in the home; perhaps some could be reinforced during school as well. Who knows? Maybe you can convince the teacher to try a few of these steps for fun. If time, bring a list of the seven steps done during the week.

The teacher would probably love your child to share what he has learned about his area of interest. As mentioned before, becoming the "expert" for a child is the ultimate compliment. Everyone gets to learn new information, and the expert gains the most while also developing his confidence and self-esteem.

If you are a parent finding that your child already hates to go to school or is making excuses when it is time to get on the bus, something is wrong. Talking with the child's teacher at the beginning of the school year might reveal the real problem. Is the work too hard or too easy for him? Does he have any friends, or does he keep to himself? Is someone picking on him at school or on the bus? Many questions might be answered.

When asked, many more boys are less happy at school than girls. However, if boys' needs are not being met, it stands to reason that they might become frustrated or aggressive at home and at school. When children are not happy at school, it is usually because of a problem or a group of problems. It might be trouble with friends, low grades, or problems at home.

If the child has trouble telling you what is bothering him, he might find help by talking to a counselor, a teacher, or another adult at school. Without finding help, these children are less likely to solve the problems they might be having. A bully may be picking on them daily, grades may be getting worse, or a family issue or divorce might be distracting them from doing their best.

Discussing any problem early in the school year might alleviate the distraction in the beginning. Additional help is imperative at times. It may feel odd to open up to someone whom you or your child does not know, but the school's staffs are not really strangers; they are all there to help you. It is imperative to at least give them a chance.

It would be normal for your child to feel sad or even angry if he has a tough problem to solve. However, counselors are experts in helping students with various problems. They can establish a plan and invite others to help if the problem cannot be solved. Meet with them early on, and your child will thank you in the end.

In order for your child to not feel weird going out of the class to see a counselor, have the meetings before or after class. Privacy can make the difference of going or not going and makes it easier for you to seek help. The teacher could be asked to arrange the meetings. If a child can start talking about a problem and begin to discover solutions, he might just decide to like school after all.

No parent wants to hear, "I hate school, and I am not going back!" Thousands of children are saying that every day. How sad. Hopefully, school is a place where things of interest are being taught. The child is making many friends and getting an education to help lead to happiness and the kind of future he desires and deserves. He is being challenged to want to learn more and more each day.

When meeting with the teacher, let him or her know if your child worries about school. A stressed-out child might have recurring headaches or stomachaches. He may say he feels like throwing up. Lack of sleep is also a sign of stress. If the child is not getting enough sleep or healthy food, just like adults, he might be grouchy or tired during the day.

Being stressed out might make it hard to make even simple decisions, such as what to eat in the morning, what to wear, or where you put your homework. Staying home might be their immediate solution, but it makes going to school the next day even worse.

Certainly the teacher would be concerned and want to know why your child dreads school each day. Is it that a bully is bothering him, he does not have friends, another child keeps hanging around with your child, or maybe he just doesn't like the teacher? That last concern will be a harder discussion to have, to say the least.

Often it is a problem with the classroom and schoolwork. Maybe the work is too easy, and he gets bored. On the other hand, perhaps the work is too hard, making your child not feel as smart as the other children. Either problem must be addressed as soon as it becomes obvious. Waiting too long may compound the issue.

Reading may be extremely hard for your struggling student, especially if he has to read out loud to others in the class. When a child feels like he is getting further and further behind, he may think he will never be able to catch up. This insecurity can develop more and more if not resolved early. Self-esteem and self-confidence will be affected in the long run. Perhaps one-on-one reading or reading with someone else he likes in the classroom is best. A child coach can really help.

So if the child is dealing with worries, stress, or problems that make it hard to concentrate on schoolwork, it is time for the parent or teacher to take steps to make things better—before that scary snowball starts rolling out of control. We all hope that the child will talk to someone about his problems at home or at school. Moms, dads, relatives, teachers, or counselors want to help but often do not know how.

SOME OTHER SUGGESTIONS FOR STRUGGLERS

Some children are so disorganized and cannot start to keep up with the homework, much less find it. Teachers and parents need to suggest step-by-step solutions that are not overwhelming. If everything seems too hard, it might be time for a peer coach or tutor to become involved. The school can provide suggestions for both.

Cleaning out closets, drawers, and desks is not fun, but perhaps a small reward to bribe the child to do so will work wonders. All children like immediate gratification for their efforts. Eventually, organization might become a routine and not as frustrating to everyone. Some children even find their lost lunch money during the organizing, the best reward of all. If the child is old enough, he can write about his feelings of school in a journal.

If too young, the child could even draw a picture or tape-record how he feels. The hardest part is getting the frustrated child to open up. You can write two columns of what he likes or dislikes about school. Maybe there will be enough likes to solve his problem easily. We all know that number one will be recess or lunch. Hopefully, there might be a couple other items, too. Try not to let the problems go on too long since it is much easier to solve a problem when it first begins.

Another technique is to ask for the child to list or tell you all the students he dislikes at school on one sheet of paper. On another sheet of paper, make him think of some of the students he likes. Go over the list with him and ask what he likes or dislikes about each child.

Suggest that doing his homework might help with his not liking it when the teacher asks him for it. At the same time, it might make a child feel more confident in class. Also, find out when share-and-tell or show-and-tell is so he can talk about a favorite thing. He might feel shy, but teachers know magical ways to get students to share. Finally, at the teacher meeting or conference, make sure to ask the teacher to encourage your son to bring a special item to share. Many times sharing a pet opens great conversations. (Ask the teacher first.)

You might not be able to change everything your child does not like about school, but discussing all problems with the teacher at the beginning of school is very important. When a parent waits too long, the problems get larger and may increase in number. Some parents did not particularly like school, either; if you are one of them, tell your child about your experiences. This will validate his feelings, and he will probably listen more to your suggestions of ways to solve his issues.

A bully may not simply disappear, but telling about it is the first steps toward improving the situation. Reading books and the dreaded writing assignments may always be difficult, and that is fine. Simply concentrate on the things you can change, and you might be able to help your child love school—or at least like it.

When that last school bell rings in the afternoon, hopefully the children will want to continue their day of learning when they get home. They may want to learn more about their interests or passions at home with this book. They might even be eager to get on the bus the following day to school.

In addition, perhaps summers would not become the time to escape school and the many types of learning activities, You might even declare, "It's a miracle!"

SUMMARY OF THE PERFECT PARTNERSHIP WITH SCHOOL AND HOME

The most important way to begin supporting your child's education and school is by making time for the special events planned for you. Usually, the beginning of the year has several of these to attend, with varied resources available from home. School-organized events, such as orientation night for parents, meet-the-parents sessions, open house, and back-to-school barbecues, are organized for the parent and child. Information-rich resources include school websites, newsletters, school memos, and notices sent home by school and teacher.

Attendance at school events such as meet-the-parents sessions and orientation programs give you a better idea of the school's policies and programs and how they work for the benefit of your child. They also provide opportunities for you to engage school leaders and teachers in face-to-face dialogue that will pave the way for both the school and the parents to work out effective ways of supporting your child. Be certain to always remember to first carefully listen to what a teacher has to say, and then it will be your turn.

The following quote by Ralph Marston points out the consequences of good and poor listening; this passage should be read by parents, teachers, coaches, and administrators. More would be accomplished making the educational changes that are needed, but only if we all would listen a little more to the opinions of others. More would be learned about children, their strengths and weaknesses, and how we all can better meet their needs. By listening more while talking less, we could all learn to understand each other better:

Carefully Listen

Stop worrying so much about what you're trying to say, and listen for a while. Though it may seem strange, one very effective way to express yourself is by listening.

Listen, carefully, lovingly and attentively to the world around you. Listen to others and listen to life.

Let go of your assumptions about what you expect to hear. Listen not only with your ears, but also with your heart and spirit.

Pay attention to what life has to say to you. There is no end to the valuable lessons you can learn.

When you think you know it all, you deny yourself the opportunity to learn new things. When you interact with others only to impress them with how much you know, they'll soon understand that you know very little.

The more you listen, observe and learn, the more powerfully you'll be able to express yourself. Take heed of what life has to say, and what you learn will carry you far.[8]

Actions speak louder than words, but words are important, too. We should remind ourselves to become more aware of the things we say around our children and to others. We might even be able to answer the question, "Where did you hear that?"

When you offer your child alternative phrases to be used in similar situations, you might be shocked when your son says, "But I hear you say it all the time!" Little ears and big ears are always open and listening to the things being said. The things we say and do have a bigger impact than we probably imagine. Our children are always paying attention to us, even when we do not think they are or do not want them to.

The good news is that this concept works both ways. Author James Baldwin says, "Children have never been very good at listening to elders, but they have never failed to imitate them." Understand that your children often will not hear your requests to clean their room, but the first time you let certain words or phrases slip out, they will certainly catch that.

There is an old children's story called "The Three Sieves." Before we speak about or to another person, we should let our words pass through three "sieves," straining out what should not be spoken. The sieves are truth, kindness, and necessity—all great values to teach to children and many adults as well.

Before we speak, we would do well to ask, "Is it true?" If it is not true, then we must stop, as the information is not worth sharing. But what if it is true? Then we pass our words through the next sieves: kindness and necessity. It might have been true that the girl is overweight and wears odd clothing, but would it have been kind or necessary for you to point that out? Of course it isn't.

If bullies spared others from mean remarks, think of the cruelty we would avoid. Bullies have the tendency to criticize, tease, blame, or belittle others around them. Those mean words not only hurt those they are meant for but also can be picked up by others hearing them, then possibly doing the same to someone else at a later time. This negative action can cause a reaction that is not kind or helpful at school, on the bus, or in the neighborhood. We need to teach to our children to lead by example while explaining how it feels to be the butt of a joke.

Now let's discuss some practical tips for building a strong working relationship with your child's teachers. Before conference time, show the teacher that you are working with your child as well as the school to make the year one of the best yet. Try to initiate communication with your child's teachers and let your child's teachers know how you can be contacted. Conversely, find out from the teachers the best way to get in touch with them. Establish the most effective mode of communication that will work for both you and the teachers.

Early communication can solve many issues, whether they are about homework, getting along with others, bullying, or behaviors in class. A child's strengths need to be challenged; naturally, his areas of weakness should be worked on as soon as possible as well. Teachers will appreciate seeing that you are as concerned as they are and will be willing to share their ideas and expertise in whatever your child might need.

SEVEN HELPFUL HINTS FOR BETTER COMMUNICATION

1. *Advocate for your child and share information about your child's personality, interests, concerns, behavior, and attitude with the teachers.* Where needed, keep your child's teachers informed about changes at home that may have an impact on your child's behavior, attitude, and academic performance. This allows the teachers to see any changes in your child in perspective and to provide the necessary support where needed.

2. *When your child shares conflicts and concerns that he experiences in school or in class, be certain to hear both sides of the story.* Contact your child's teachers to understand the conflict and concerns better. Realize that even in situations where your child has been misunderstood, learning to stand up for himself and articulating what really happened in a calm manner is a valuable life lesson.

3. *When your child's teachers share concerns about your child's progress and development, be open to the feedback.* Work in partnership with the teachers to follow up on jointly decided intervention strategies that will help your child overcome obstacles. Check on your child's progress from time to time to ensure that your child is on track.

4. *When you need clarifications on class projects and class-related matters, contact the teachers to understand and to provide feedback, suggestions, and ideas where appropriate.* A two-way, constructive, and open sharing of thoughts and ideas allows both you and the teachers to understand the perspectives of each other.

5. *Volunteer your time and expertise for class-related projects or trips according to the time and effort you can afford.*

6. *Show support to your child's teachers and appreciate the effort the teachers are extending to your child, you, and your family.*

7. *Remember that it has to be a team effort, with the goal of doing what is best for your child.*[9]

As parents, your involvement in your child's schooling is crucial, and your communication with the school and teachers is invaluable in bringing about positive change. This desired positive change is not only for your child but also for the entire school community. You may not think so, but your child will actually look forward to seeing your smiling face walking through that classroom door. Come to think of it, the other children will embrace you almost as much, and perhaps the teacher will appreciate you even more.

WHAT TO LOOK FOR IN APPROPRIATE INSTRUCTION

1. Instruction should be informal, interactive, and individualized. Formal instruction is limited. It is fine to hear "productive conversations" in the classroom by groups of children.

2. Teachers act as facilitators of children's learning, almost like a coach. Parents are actively involved in the education of their children.

3. Children are free to choose activities often throughout the day.

4. Class size should be no more than 24 but is best at 20.

5. Teaching and learning are based generally on the belief that the child constructs knowledge by interaction with the social and physical environment.

6. Program content values social, emotional, physical, and cognitive development.

7. Assessment evaluation is informal, with the purpose of tailoring the program to individual students. All children have a portfolio that is easily understood by all. This portfolio should include many dated samples of the child's work and assessments in reading, writing, math, and science. The portfolio should have a current photo of the student and an interview with him about likes and dislikes.

MORE QUESTIONS TO ASK YOUR CHILD'S TEACHER

1. What about readiness and retention?

Now that you are comfortable with your child's teacher, it is always important to ask what his or her policy is when it comes to holding back a child. As you probably already know, the final decision is made by the parent, not the teacher or the administrators. As programs for young children have become increasingly academic and less appropriate developmentally, either retention or delayed entry to kindergarten has been used to exclude children from school rather to ensure success.

The decision that a child is not ready for kindergarten too often means that his parents were advised to wait another year before entering the child into school. Just remember that each child is entitled to a public education when he or she reaches the legal age for enrollment. Having said this, there is often reason enough to keep an immature or small boy out for one more year of mental and physical growth. That final choice of enrollment is up to the parent.

The concept of readiness is also being used inappropriately to justify retention. The kindergarten child labeled not ready for first-grade work is retained in kindergarten for another year. The impact of that retention on both the child's achievement and the child's adjustment is often negative. By the time they complete first grade, most children who have repeated kindergarten do not outperform comparison students. They do, however, have slightly more negative feelings about school. Apparently, there is no achievement benefit in retaining a child in kindergarten or first grade, and, regardless of how well the extra year is presented to the child, the child still pays an emotional cost.

It seems important that the concept of readiness be redefined. Maybe *the school program is not ready for your child.* One could say that when the curriculum and instruction are appropriate to the children, the issue of retention fades away. *To reiterate, maybe it is time to have the school fit the child, not the other way around.* When we see all of the emphasis on reading earlier than ever before, one would wonder how good this is for both child and the parent.

2. *So, why does the push for earlier reading need to be questioned?*

When it comes to the push for reading earlier and earlier, parental anxiety can reach high levels. A few of the findings parents face on the journey to kindergarten and reading might be hard to understand or even accept, such as the following:

- The quality of a child's language environment at age three is a strong predictor of tenth-grade reading achievement.
- A child's vocabulary at age four is predictive of third-grade reading comprehension.
- A child who does not read proficiently by third grade is four times more likely to leave school without a diploma than is a proficient reader. This is scariest of all, according to research by the Annie E. Casey Foundation.

We bet you are wondering what the Annie E. Casey Foundation does:

The Annie E. Casey Foundation is devoted to developing a brighter future for millions of children at risk of poor educational, economical, social and health outcomes. Our work focuses on families, building stronger communities and ensuring access to opportunities, because children need all 3 to succeed. We advance research and solutions to overcome the barriers to success, help communities to demonstrate what works and influence decision makers to invest in strategies based on solid evidence.

As a private philanthropy based in Baltimore and working across the country, we make grants that help federal agencies, states, counties, cities and neighborhoods create more innovative, cost effective responses to the issues that negatively affect children: poverty, unnecessary disconnection from families and communities, with limited access to opportunity.

Since 1948 these efforts have translated into more informed policies and practices and yielded positive results for larger numbers of kids and families.[10]

Presently, parental worries have driven a thriving market of early reading programs, books, and other products. Parents in Manhattan are paying huge sums of money for various preparatory programs to secure a spot in gifted and talented public kindergarten classes. For the more budget conscious, the *Your Baby Can Read!* DVDs and flash cards let parents do the training themselves. Unfortunately, the company that produced these has gone out of business.

In July 2012, after its tactics were challenged in a *Today Show* investigation, a complaint filed with the Federal Trade Commission resulted in numerous class-action suits. Researchers say that the problem is

that no one knows if pushing your young child to read makes any difference. "There's no evidence that teaching children to read early is a
good thing," says Dr. Susan B. Neuman, a professor of education at the
University of Michigan who specializes in early literacy development.
"There's no evidence that says it's a bad thing either, but there's just
no evidence at all, so parents might be wasting a good deal of their own
. . . and their children's time, when they could be doing other things
that really do promote early literacy." Unfortunately, with the national
focus on reading brought about by the No Child Left Behind Act and
the implementation of Common Core Standards in today's classrooms,
not to mention the fierce competition for enrollment at top schools and
universities, parents are feeling more pressure than ever.

Parents, teachers, and administrators drive to get their children reading as soon as possible to ensure their academic success. "We see an
awful lot of parents who are trying to teach their children how to read
very early on, in infancy as a matter of fact," Neuman says. "We think
that some of this early push might be more focused on the parents'
needs rather than the kids' needs."

Dr. Shannon Ayers, assistant research professor at Rutgers University's National Institute for Early Education Research, states, "I find
the phenomenon shocking, but I don't blame the parents. Every parent
wants what's best for his or her child. But they're hearing about this
so-called 'window of opportunity' before age five, and they get scared.
The bottom line is: yes, there are critical skills your young child needs
before they enter school, but these skills are ones that they can learn
through play and through their life experiences, not flash cards."

3. *What types of assessments are appropriate?*

This is a great question to ask the teacher at the beginning of the year.
The major concerns in the assessment of young children are whether the
assessment measures what is being taught, as well as whether the assessment procedures being used are right. The question is not whether
there should be an assessment. Each teacher must continually assess each
child's cognitive, social, emotional, and physical development in order
to plan and present appropriate learning activities for that unique child.

The most effective tool for making that ongoing assessment is teacher
observation in addition to that seen by the parent. Samples of the child's
work and involvement in instructional activities should be taken over
time and dated.

During any instruction, as with teaching units about a particular subject, such as butterflies, the teacher might save any of the written work,
illustrations, and stories told to the teacher. This dictation of the child's

ideas lets him know the importance of letters, sounds, words, and meaning when put into sentences. Later, he will be able to do it on his own after learning how to write.

This book explains more about student samples of work, checklists, and portfolios that are saved throughout the year. The portfolio is invaluable to the student, parent, and teacher, especially when the child is moved to another school or room. The samples of work and assessments provide much more information than a report card.

As the child gets older, word lists and spelling and math tests will be included. This portfolio is like a snapshot of the unique child you are working with. It shows much that is meaningful.

In chapter 4, you will see that other assessments could be videotapes, audiotapes of children and their stories, oral questions asked about an area of study, and games or puzzles to solve. The inclusion of photographs and illustrations makes this collection special and invaluable.

When children grow older, there will be all types of assessments given in addition to those done by observation. Those assessments need to be criterion-referenced tests that show what is being taught and used for the measurement of student learning and comprehension. The core standards of the state should be reflected in the test.

Finally, standardized testing (the same test given to all by grade level) is particularly inappropriate for young children because each child comes from a different set of family experiences. What is available to one child may not be available to another. Some families travel extensively, and some do not travel outside their communities. Other children attended preschool or day care, and others did not. Maturity levels of young children are also very different. Therefore, decisions about student assessment must be based on multiple sources of information and never on the basis of a single test.

Now that you and your spouse have met with your son's new teacher and asked everything you wanted to know (and more), you have shown this teacher your true interest in helping your child in any way possible. Remember that there are not many male teachers at the elementary level, and having Dad volunteer would be a very special addition to the classroom as well as to other children who may not have a father at home. And if that teacher is very lucky, you were already convinced to help in their classroom as often as possible—or even to be the PTA leader.

> The measure of success is not the number of people who serve you, but the number of people you serve.
>
> —John Maxwell

In closing this chapter, recently an e-mail circulated that brought tears to many people's eyes but at the same time brought reality into perspective: "How much do we notice as we go through a day?" asked Lisa Beamer on *Good Morning America*, Lisa is the wife of Todd Beamer, who said "Let's roll!" and then helped take down the plane over Pennsylvania that was headed for Washington, D.C., on 9/11. She added that it's the little things that she misses most about Todd, such as hearing the garage door open as he came home and her children running to meet him. Lisa recalled this story:

I had a very special teacher in high school many years ago whose husband died suddenly of a heart attack. About a week after his death, she shared some of her insight with a classroom of students. As the late afternoon sunlight came streaming in through the classroom windows and the class was nearly over, she moved a few things aside on the edge of her desk and sat down there. With a gentle look of reflection on her face, she paused and said, "Class is over, I would like to share with all of you, a thought that is unrelated to class, but which I feel is very important. Each of us is put here on earth to learn, share, love, appreciate and give of ourselves. None of us knows when this fantastic experience will end. It can be taken away at any moment. Perhaps this is God's way of telling us that we must make the most out of every single day."

Her eyes, beginning to water, she went on: "So I would like you all to make me a promise. From now on, on your way to school, or on your way home, find something beautiful to notice. It doesn't have to be something you see, it could be a scent, perhaps of freshly baked bread wafting out of someone's house, or it could be the sound of the breeze slightly rustling the leaves in the trees, or the way the morning light catches one autumn leaf as it falls gently to the ground. Please look for these things, and cherish them. For, although it may sound trite to some, these things are the 'stuff' of life. The little things we are put here on earth to enjoy. The things we often take for granted."

The class was completely quiet. We all picked up our books and filed out of the room silently. That afternoon, I noticed more things on my way home from school than I had that whole semester. Every once in a while, I think of that teacher and remember what a lasting impression she made on all of us, and I try to appreciate all of those things that sometimes we all overlook.

Take notice of something special you see on your lunch hour today. Go barefoot. Or walk on the beach at sunset. Stop off on the way home tonight to get a double dip ice cream cone. For as we get older, it is not the things we did that we often regret, but the things we didn't do.

Life is not measured by the number of breaths we take, but by the moments that take our breath away.

—Anonymous

Onward to chapter 4 the one that your child will probably love the most. There will be many exciting, fun, engaging things and activities he gets to do to show proof of active, hands-on projects done for learning. Now your child or student gets to become the expert or star of the video, tape recording, or photos taken during the showing off of his new learning. Everyone now seems to want their fifteen minutes of fame.

NOTES

1. Ralph Marston, "Power in Numbers," *The Daily Motivator*, March 8, 2001 (www.greatday.com).

2. Anne Henderson and Karen L. Mapp, *A New Wave of Evidence: The Impact of School, Family and Community Connections on Student Achievement* (Austin, TX: Southwest Educational Development Laboratory, 2002 (www.sedl.org/connections).

3. Peg Tyre, *The Trouble with Boys: A Surprising Report Card on Our Sons, Their Problems at School, and What Parents and Educators Must Do* (New York: Crown Publishing, 2008).

4. Michael Gurian, *Minds of Boys: Saving Our Sons from Falling Behind in School and Life* (San Francisco: Jossey-Bass, 2005).

5. Mike Younger and Molly Warrington, "Raising Boys' Achievement," Research Report No. 636 (London: Department of Education and Skills, 2005).

6. Terry W. Neu and Rich H. Weinfield, *Helping Boys Succeed in School: A Practical Guide for Parents and Teachers* (Waco, TX: Prufrock Press, 2007).

7. Nicholas Coangelo, Susan Assouline, and Miraca Gross, *A Nation Deceived: How Schools Hold Back America's Brightest Students* (Iowa City: University of Iowa, 2004).

8. Ralph Marston, "Carefully Listen!," *The Daily Motivator*, November 6, 2013 (www.greatday.com).

9. Derrick Meador, "Parental Involvement in Education: Tips to Increase Parental Involvement in Education," retrieved July 15, 2014, from wwwteaching.about.com.

10. Annie E. Casey Foundation (www.aecf.org).

4

Fun Reporting about What Was Learned

Videotaping and Tape Recording of Subjects, Puppetry with Stories, or Writings, Reading, Math, and Science . . . Makes Learning Very Special!

Put Passion

Put passion into what you do, whatever it is. Your passion confers great power, and engages your best abilities, and you can put it into anything.

There's no need to search for, or wait for, or wonder about what will give you passion. Go ahead and give your passion to the moment you're in.

What provides you with passion is your choice to live it. What gives you passion is your decision to allow it to flow into your thoughts, words and actions.

Live your life not as a bystander. Live in this world, on this day, at this place as an active participant.

Discover how empowering it feels to give authentic passion to the smallest of details. Experience for yourself how great it is to care without holding back.

Put passion in this day, in this task, and in this circumstance. Be rewarded with exceptional effectiveness and meaningful achievement.[1]

This book has emphasized the importance of boys learning in a way that is more passionate, engaging, creative, active, and hands on. Too many children are spending endless, unproductive hours in front of the television, watching videos, playing video games, or just playing on the computer. All of these things in moderation would be fine, especially if the subject matter were rich with appropriate content. Unfortunately, many boys are not restricted to the amount of time spent in these activities or the type of content they are viewing. So, before getting into the types of fun reporting about what was learned during our daily activities while doing the seven steps, a discussion of how children are spending more and more of their time is necessary.

THE OVERUSE OF COMPUTERS AND TELEVISION

Years ago, we all watched television for a couple hours a day, then ran out to play with our friends. Television was exciting but made up only a small portion of our day. Now things have definitely changed. We read the media reports that link our huge use of television to health problems and obesity. You might be wondering what it does to the brain as well.

Dimitri Christakis, a brain researcher at Children's Hospital and Regional Medical Center in Seattle, Washington, has pointed out that the brain needs touch, hearing, seeing, smelling, and tasting, a complex interaction of the five senses, already discussed in chapter 2. These five senses also need to interact with the external environment in order to grow brain tissue fully.

Apparently, our brains rely mainly on direct and various sensory experiences for this tissue growth. *Christakis goes on to point out that this growth is largest in the child's first three years, when a child's functions of abstraction in the top of the brain have not developed yet. Therefore, screen time should be especially observed in toddlers and infants.* He has also found that such tissue brain growth continues into our twenties.

Of even more concern is what Christakis and other researchers have discovered. The relationship between brain development and screen time shows that "passive, hypermechanical stimulation," or watching images moving on a flat screen, can have lifelong negative consequences on the developing brain.

Christakis and colleagues presented research that followed 2,600 children from birth to age seven. They discovered that "for every hour of television watched per day, the incidence of ADD and ADHD increased by 10 percent."[2] This is a worrisome finding, to say the least.

Each of us, as teachers, parents, administrators, and members of parent-led teams, needs to monitor and manage screen time more carefully if we want to help our boys succeed in school and life. Long ago, children learned by moving around in nature, touching things, feeling things, smelling them, and hearing them while experiencing the five senses by using both fine motor and gross motor abilities.

Our country's mechanization and industrialization, with all its advantages in the areas of comfort, medical health, and personal entertainment, have cut down on our children's opportunities for natural brain development. Some of our children may be suffering attention and other difficulties. Too many hours each day, their brains do not receive fine motor and gross motor development based in physical movement and whole-sensory experience.[3] Sadly, all this time spent in front of some type of screen leads me to seven reasons we all need to be more observant of our boys' time and how they spend it.

SEVEN REASONS TO MONITOR AND MANAGE YOUR CHILD'S SCREEN TIME

1. The average child now spends 900 hours per year in school but 1,023 hours per year watching television.
2. In the average home, the television is on six to seven hours per day.
3. The number of videos and DVDs that families rent every day is twice the number of books read.
4. By the age of sixteen, your son will have seen 200,000 acts of violence on television, 33,000 of them acts of murder.
5. One-fourth of children under two years old now have televisions in their bedrooms.
6. Two-thirds of preschool boys sit in front of screens for two or more hours per day.
7. This is more than three times the hours they spend looking at books or being read to.

LET'S ALL MOVE MORE OR GET PHYSICAL

As a teacher, this is a poor commentary on what our youth are seemingly obsessed with during their free time. This current problem affects both girls and boys, but it has a special impact on boys. As we have learned, boys need a large amount of physical movement in order to grow their brains. Screen time does not allow this to happen. You will read about many engaging activities in this book to develop fine and gross motor skills that can be done at all ages, ones that engage the brain while having fun doing the suggested activities that are best for boys.

All children, especially boys, are fascinated by kites, how they fly, and how they might make one for themselves. Why not combine math skills, reading skills, science, and physical activity to explain more about the structure and flying of kites?

Kites are very old in history. It is believed that kites were first developed for military purposes in ancient China. Kite-flying contests have a long history in some countries, too. There are many different kinds of kites found throughout the world. Some are built in the shape of birds; others are shaped like boxes. The most common are shaped like diamonds. While most kites are small, some are large enough to lift a person (don't worry; ours will be the smaller version).

Remember those good old days flying a cheap triangle kite on the beach, in an open field, or on the lawn? We even put tails made of ripped-up bedsheets on the kite for better stability.

How Do You Build a Kite?

A kite needs a light, strong framework made of sticks. The framework needs to be covered with a thin material, such as paper or cloth. We have seen many different types of kites: some with pictures of faces, birds, and other fancy designs. Many kites are built in different countries and of different styles and materials. It does not seem to matter how they look, as they are extremely popular all over the world with children and adults. So go fly a kite and get into shape by chasing it down.

Let's learn how to build two different types of kites. One is a floppy kite, and the other is a paper bag kite. To build a floppy kite, you will need a roll of kite string, thin sticks, clear tape, scissors, and a plastic bag. First, cut a square sheet out of a plastic bag and make a large round hole in the center. Make a cross with the sticks and tie them together with the kite string, like an X. Use clear tape to attach the plastic firmly to the frame of sticks. Finally, take four strings the same length. Tie one to each corner, then tie them all to a long kite string.

A paper bag kite is more creative and will take a little more time and patience. You will need a paper bag, a piece of cardboard, kite string, glue, a felt-tipped pen, and scissors. First, cut an oval out of the cardboard that will fit in the bottom of the paper bag. Tie three pieces of string to the oval ring, equally spaced. Cut a hole in the bottom of the paper bag. Glue the oval to the bag so that it strengthens the paper bag.

Make sure to dry the oval part of the bag completely before the following steps. Next, draw a face on the bag with colored markers, crayons, or paint. Cut the open part of the paper bag to make fringe at the bottom by cutting slits with your scissors. Now go outside and enjoy your new creative kite with someone else and get some exercise while having fun.

On both kites, you must make sure that the sticks and strings are firmly tied together and that the material used to cover the kite is strong and fastened securely before sending it into the wind. If you find that the kites need more balance in stronger winds, attach streamers or a tail to your kite so it can fly better. Find a friend, Dad, Mom, or a relative to take you out to an open field where your kite can really show off. Do not forget the camera since there will be memories to remember long after your kite-flying days are over. Even if you decide not to build your own kite, you may buy one to take outside and enjoy. The fresh air and activity will do everyone good—we promise.

WHAT IF THE WEATHER IS BAD OUTSIDE?

During the winter months and long, rainy seasons, kites are not really an option or much fun to even think about. However, there are many other creative hands-on activities that are great for the development of fine and gross motor skills, teaching children lots about science at the same time. One such activity is making your own terrarium. A terrarium is like an aquarium but for houseplants instead of fish. It can be any shape or size, from a small bottle to a large glass tank, as in an aquarium. Once it is made, your plant garden does not need much care. Mom and Dad will love it for that reason alone.

Plants are quite hardy if planted correctly and watched for the correct combination of water and sunlight. What they need is indirect sunshine, clean water from time to time, and someone talking to the plants to keep them alive and healthy (the talking part is optional). However, if you decide to add some small frogs, turtles, or snails to your terrarium, you will have to take special care of them. How much fun would it be to have your very own miniature nature park or zoo? Think of what your friends would say.

One of the nicest parts of taking time to make a terrarium is that it serves as an attractive piece of a child's artful creation and a source of pride to him. It teaches about what plants need and about responsibility; it is a great tool for the observation of science at its best. Materials needed are soil, small sticks or chopsticks, a paper funnel, a spool, a large jar or big tank, scissors, small plants, and a water sprayer.

Seven Fun Steps to Making Your Own Terrarium

1. Pour soil through a paper funnel into a large jar until it is about one-quarter full. Make sure to pack down the soil well.
2. Dig the plants out of the pots very gently. Trim the roots and leaves carefully to fit in the jar. Try to leave as much of the roots as possible.
3. Plant the largest plants first and then arrange the smaller ones around them in a neat pattern. Your chopsticks will help you do a better job.
4. Place the spool on the end of the stick and use it to pack down the soil firmly and carefully around the little fragile plants.
5. Spray your arrangement with water from the spray bottle, using the mist spray adjustment. If you are using a bottle used for something else, make certain it has been cleaned thoroughly.
6. Wipe all the dirt and water off the inside of the jar gently with a paper towel or napkin. Wait for the leaves to dry before closing the jar with a lid.
7. Once the jar is closed, there should be just enough moisture inside to form drops of water. If there is too much moisture, leave the jar open until all the extra water has evaporated.

Our second-grade glass had a lot of fun and discovery in making the class terrarium for all to watch for hours of enjoyment. We did learn many things that we will warn you about so that you do not make the same mistakes. As we know, that is how you learn—by making mistakes, you have to observe what is wrong and then do some brainstorming or problem solving.

To make sure you have a successful terrarium, remember that plants thrive inside as long as there is the right combination of moisture, light, and air. Plants that like humidity and low light are best. For instance, maidenhair fern, wax plant, prayer plant, or peperomia all would love to live in your terrarium. Most plants will stay healthy in a peat-based potting mixture laid on top of a drainage layer of charcoal and gravel. Obviously, if you notice your terrarium drying out, try to mist more often. If you and your child have lots of questions about possible plant choices, go to a local nursery and tell them what you are planning. They will be thrilled to help you out.

Creating a terrarium is an excellent way to read and learn more about plants, what they need to survive, where they should be placed for adequate light, and the proper care of them. Why not bring up what those weird droplets are on the glass and discuss the big word, condensation? Explain how sun, water, and clouds all work together in the cycle of evaporation and condensation to make rain for the earth.

If you have used a large tank, a turtle, salamander, or frog will love its new home if similar to its own environment. Remember to find out what such creatures need to live and thrive as well. This is a good excuse to make a visit to your school or local library. Just think about how your friends can come over to see your own miniature nature park. This activity can last for years, providing enjoyment of a real-living learning environment, with entertainment for the entire family, neighborhood, or classroom. This is certainly one way to bring the outside indoors. This is science at its best.

WHY NOT GROW AN INDOOR GARDEN?

If your child is the type who wants to do more watching and waiting to see what happens, then why not grow your own plants? If you plant hyacinth or daffodil bulbs, they will sprout and grow. These flowers grow well when placed in the windowsill but take some time. You can also grow vegetables indoors, such as soybeans, spice seeds, and parsley. Transplant them into pots and take care of them so that they can grow into healthy plants that can give you a sense of satisfaction as you observe their changes.

Let's talk about some different ways to grow your own plants. If you take some mustard, dill, caraway, or coriander seeds and soak them overnight in water and then put them on a damp sponge, a magical garden might surprise your student or child. Keep the sponge moist by keeping it in a shallow dish of water. Place the dish in a bright area but not in the direct sunlight. The seeds should sprout in two or three days, so this activity is fun to observe. If you want to transplant them to a pot, they will grow into much larger plants if you take care of them. Now you have made an indoor garden of your very own.

Another fun activity is to put an onion or an avocado in a glass of water with toothpicks so that the bottom of the plant is in the water. Avocado seeds take longer but become beautiful trees when transplanted into a container and maintained. With the onion, you will see green shoots appearing out the top, and as the shoots grow larger, the onion bulb will grow smaller. Try to have your child or students figure this phenomenon out. Later you can also plant this into a pot with soil.

Next, try to grow some soybeans by putting a third of a cup of soybeans in a glass with warm water. Soak the seeds overnight and in the morning drain the beans and rinse them off in warm water. Cover the glass with cheesecloth and place it in a warm, dark place. Make sure to rinse the seeds with warm water each morning and evening. In three days, your beans will have grown sprouts. To stop them from growing any more, place them in the refrigerator. Now sprinkle your own fresh sprouts on your healthy salad.

If your child is really adventurous and you can help him a little, build a plant tank by trying the following activity. This plant tank is especially good for a gifted or older child. Many questions can be asked while doing this task. First, put water containing plant food in a water tank. Keep the water clean and warm, using an aquarium filter and a heater with a thermostat. You might get them from a fish store.

Place a small cherry tomato plant in the tank and wrap the stem with paper. This will hold it up and prevent the loss of moisture. It may also be necessary to support the base and stalk of the plant with string and a frame to keep it from falling over. Finally, make certain to put it in direct sunlight.

The plant should begin flowering in a month. Pollinate the flowers by hand. To do this, take some pollen grains from the male stamens of the plant and very gently put them onto the plant's pistil (get a book about flowering plants to explain the parts of a plant). Keep the water at about 50 to 60 degrees Fahrenheit (10 to 15 degrees Celsius). Remember to add plant food weekly, and with luck and your green magical thumb, you may eventually grow some cherry tomatoes of your own to add to that growing salad of yours.

Planting and growing things is meaningful when children or students do it themselves. There is no end to the things they can try to grow, such as carrots, tomatoes, beans, eggplant, and other vegetables, all of which can be easily grown indoors. They will grow wherever there is plenty of sun, water, and fertilizer. Gardening is a good hobby to share with your classroom or child in the home. Think of all the science learning that can be done through daily observation and the math skills that can be practiced through measuring and graphing, not to mention all the verbalization that can be incorporated. All the while, your children and students are just thinking they are playing and having fun.

RELEVANCE OF SCREEN TIME TO BOYS AND THEIR BRAINS

Given what we know about boys' brains, it should not be surprising that mainly boys suffer from attention and hyperactivity disorders. Their brains do not grow and develop as easily or naturally as girls, when it comes to the type of learning required in school. Boys, therefore, are prone to attention problems linked to passive entertainment, screen time, and passive hypermechanical stimulation. Setting limits may seem impossible with teenagers, but certainly we can help our younger children cut back on screen time.

There are many things a parent can do easily to help curtail problems from media. For instance, do not let the child start an early attachment to the computer. A few minutes per day for a three-year-old is part of the excitement of growing up. But an hour or two on the computer at that age can have the same effect as television and videos; it can hurt the developing brain of the young boy.

Try to avoid the use of videos and DVDs as a babysitter for your son. We all know how nice it can be to have children quiet and sitting still, but make sure that what they are watching is of excellent quality. When using media as a babysitter, your son could end up with educational problems.

Maybe scheduling only television programs that are developmentally appropriate, with good content, will give better outcomes. Ideally, after watching a program, you should share a discussion with your child about what he learned and what he saw. Bring up any questions he might have. Make sure you never put a television in your child's room, regardless of his age. This may seem too restrictive, but how else can you know what is being watched?

Regarding video games . . . make certain your child understands the time limit you have set for your family, and then stick to it. You might even set an alarm for both of you. Try to preview the games he is playing, or you might be shocked at what he is watching. Tons of fun learning games are available on the Web simply by doing a little research.

When talking about going to the movies, first do your homework. Make sure you are not taking very young children to movies that contain any content you feel might be difficult for them to understand. Naturally, violence should be avoided at all costs, and remember that a toddler has a very short attention span. Studies have shown that their brains want to learn in bursts of movement, and developmental learning will stop occurring for much of the movie anyway.

Finally, when your child reaches an age when you believe using television, videos, or DVDs is appropriate, again make sure you have researched or previewed any videos shared with your son. Do this same research and preview when it comes to television shows.

Double-check with other parents and teachers to make certain the content is useful and meaningful to your child. They can be the naysayers so that, if worse comes to worst, you do not have to be "mean mom or dad."

The argument for the early use of computers is a strong one from many. They believe that if their children get exposed to everything when they are young, they will be more mature, more successful with school assignments, and sophisticated later on. By adolescence, they will know everything that is out there. We are not sure that is such a good thing. They may be more independent and mature as adults; these same children may do better if they attend college, but they might also be viewing some very inappropriate material.

Others totally understand the argument against too many hours in front of the television but still think that computers are the future. They want their young children to become adept at computers as early as possible. These people did not read what psychologist Jane Healy has shown in her seminal work on computer use, *Failure to Connect*.[4]

Healy found that even if a child starts using computers for the first time in adolescence, within months he gains computer skills equal to those of children who began as toddlers or young children. Therefore, being good with computers does not depend on starting as a young child. In 2004, the Alliance for Children completed a major worldwide study that showed the same results as Healy.

Naturally, it is the parent's final decision, but with the potential disadvantages to male brain development from the overuse of computers, television, movies, and other screen activities, hopefully you will put your parenting decision making on the side of caution.

Now that we have pointed out the warnings about too much screen time, this is a good opportunity to talk about the various creative and engaging ways your child or student can report to you, his school, or others about what was learned in the seven steps done throughout the week. Get ready for some real fun now using puppetry.

TYPES OF PUPPETS TO MAKE FOR MORE ENJOYABLE LEARNING

Now it is time to get into the fun of making different kinds of puppets and using them to show what was learned. Since Sunday is Funday and a free day, anything can be done that the child wants to do. Maybe he wants to watch you make a puppet, or, on the other hand, should he make the puppet himself? Perhaps you both can make one together. What a special way to spend some quality time together.

One method that is quick and simple is making a sock puppet; this is really fun. What's especially fun about sock puppets is that you can make each one unique and individualized so that each has special characters. And they don't have to be human; animals and aliens are great possibilities, too. If you choose one that is not too complicated, it is best if your child or student makes it or at least gets involved in making the puppet. He will have so much more fun using his own creation.

Start by assembling your special materials in a large shoe box with your name on it. You'll need at least one clean sock of your choice, a large needle, and some strong, thick thread. This is just the bare minimum. Of course, you can add any other decorating items you want to use, like glasses, jewelry, and special hair material, to embellish and decorate your sock puppet, making it more original. Your teacher will have some decorating materials on hand in class (assorted buttons and beads, wool, pipe cleaners, felt material, and so on) as well as all the rest of the items required to make your puppet, such as scissors and glue guns. Again, we must stress using all tools under supervision and following all safety rules. Have your child read the following directions with or to you.

Seven Steps to Making an Easy Sock Puppet with Variations

1. *First find a clean sock that covers your hand and wrist.*

   It can be any color you like, and it should be long enough for you to stick your arm in. Preferably, the sock should almost reach the elbow. Avoid socks that are too thin or that have holes. Any material will work just fine, but if you plan to bring out the scissors, you may want to use a material that won't automatically fray (like cotton).

   Of course, the type of character the sock puppet has is, in part, determined by the sock chosen. For example, spotted socks suggest creating leopards, cheetahs, Dalmatian dogs, and so on, while striped socks suggest creating zebras, tigers, and jailbirds. Plain socks could be a wide range of things, but the color can help, so a white sock could be a white mouse, while a gray sock could be an elephant. When choosing the sock, let the sock's feature be a part of what decides your puppet's final character nose or something you might not expect.

   This is your puppet, so your body parts are yours to create and position as you please. However, make sure you get adult supervision if unsure how to do this. Superglue can be trouble, as can needles, so don't be afraid to ask for help. Once the glue is dry, stick your hand in.

Form your hand into the shape of a mouth, with your thumb below your fingers. Use your free hand to force an indentation mirroring the inside of the mouth. Your arm should look like a snake.

Puppetry takes some time to feel comfortable with, but as the child or student watches others and then practices with his own puppet, the actions start to occur naturally. The best part is how a child changes his voice to fit the character he has decided to create. There is much creativity that can delight everyone involved.

2. *Next . . . what about the rest of the basics?*

For the tongue, you can use either a smaller oval in a different color to simulate a tongue or an actual tongue shape that hangs out. In fact, a felt tongue can be made and cut with a "V" at the end to look like an authentic snake or reptile monster.

3. *Then, glue by using a glue gun and hot melt glue or sew on the googly eye or eyes.*

(The number, size, and color are your choice.) You can attach the eyes either to the bottom of the sock, at the toe end, or pretty much wherever you'd like. Experiment with a few placements before you glue them on. The eyes might look good really close together, such as close to the slit in a snake's tongue. This is very realistic.

4. *You can also make a nose using felt.*

Cut a small triangle or circle to form a cute little nose. Either sew or glue it into place above the mouth. If you've added whiskers, keep these below the nose. Help your students or child with the small details that will make all the difference in how the puppet looks, whether he wants it to be realistic or silly-looking.

5. *Make your sock puppet have whiskers.*

Now cut whisker-length pieces of string or cord and sew into place at the top center of the mouth. Just make sure it doesn't look like a mustache—unless you'd like your puppet to have a mustache: and why not? This is your own cool creation. The same string can be used for hair, or look around the house for other materials to use. Consider a pile of string for hair; being messier makes for a more funny character. Try more pieces of felt for spikes or scales glued upright. Does it have ears? These could easily be cut out of felt and sewn on wherever you want them to be. Since this is your child's or student's own puppet, encourage him to make it original and exciting.

6. *To make arms, simply roll up a length of felt with a pipe cleaner inside.*

The pipe cleaner will make your puppet more believable. Glue the roll closed, with one end attached to the puppet. To make fingers, simply make two cuts into the end of the roll of felt. Two cuts will result in three fingers. The two cuts should force the end of the roll to splay out, resembling a hand. Round off the edges as you'd like, sculpting the puppet.

7. *Finally, add on the exciting extras.*

Your puppet could have everything down to eyelashes, hoop earrings, bow ties, hair ribbons—it's all up to you. You can even dress it up. If you like making clothes, give the sock puppet a few, too.

Supervise children if they are stitching a sock puppet on their own. Young children with little or no sewing experience will definitely need full attention and help from an older, more experienced person. Fingers stuck by a needle are not fun and can get messy!

Naturally, it is even easier to make finger puppets. Just use any of the leftover fingers from a glove puppet. You can add details with permanent markers, sew on eyes, or glue on the extras for special effect. There is no end to the types you can make, so get going. Even the shells off peanuts can make wonderful finger puppets with some ink. Why do puppets work so well? One of the reasons is because they are so multisensory. It doesn't matter if kids are small or if kids are very tall—you can reach them with puppets.

Puppets are easy to make, keep children eagerly involved, and are a tool that will make any type of learning more fun. In addition, many hands-on skills can be developed. Boys with fine motor skill problems need exactly this type of activity, and often!

There are many other types of puppets, including marionettes, paper bag puppets, and even puppets made from silverware. Sack puppets can be made and enjoyed by everyone, kindergarten through adult. You decide how much time and artistic effort you want to put into your sack puppet projects. They can be quickie puppet play stand-ins or works of art. It is up to you. We usually recommend that you cover the puppets with construction paper folded to conform to the folds of the sack.

Then with a little glue and a few "found objects" (such as material scraps, buttons, bristles, pipe cleaners, yarn, or any variety of items you can gather), you can give your puppets whatever features and costumes they desire. By typing in "How to make puppets" on Google, you can access endless resources and YouTube videos to make it all crystal clear. This is another good use of the computer for learning more engaging skills. Of course, you can save time and get them at garage sales, at toy stores, and online.

Just as important as the puppet is a place for the show or videotaping to occur. Why spend over $100 for an already made puppet theater when you can easily convert a large empty box from a television, oven, or refrigerator? Even an appliance store might have just the size you want. Creativity is the key in how you and your children or students decide to paint or decorate this future fabulous puppet theater.

Seven Steps of Working Your Puppet Like a Pro

Until the appropriate gestures and voices are added, a puppet is only a wiggling lump of cloth and not very interesting for anyone to watch. The way you hold and move your puppet is important. Here are seven suggestions to help you become ready for videotaping in your home or classroom:

1. *Puppet anatomy is important for movement.*

   Your arm has four puppet duties. They are the movement of your fingers, wrist, elbow. and shoulder. Your fingers form the puppet's upper jaw. If you pull them back, your puppet scrunches its face. If you open and close your fingers, your puppet talks slowly. If you combine the movements of your fingers and wrist, the puppet can cock its head, answer yes or no, or do neck exercises. Add your elbow and shoulder movements, and your puppet is ready to do almost anything. It can walk, run, fall, laugh, cry, do double takes, sleep, or sneeze.

2. *Lip sync takes practice.*

   Every time your mouth moves, your puppet's mouth should move, too. This may sound easy, but lip and hand coordination isn't as natural as one might think. That is a great brain skill for all children to master. To practice, have your puppet say the ABCs, recite "Humpty Dumpty," or sing your favorite song. By practicing in front of a mirror, you can always see what you are doing. Watch your puppet carefully. Are you convinced it is really talking? Does your puppet look a little fake to you, or does it really capture your attention?

3. *Puppet posture can give you away.*

   When you are using a stage, watch your puppet's height. If it is to look like it is walking, make sure its feet or the bottom of the puppet line up with the edge of the stage. When your arm or wrist is hanging out, some of the reality can be lost.

   On the other hand, a head puppet must not show more than its head and neck. Marionettes with strings should be saved for the adults or children who have devoted more than a few minutes to how they work. Untangling the nightmare of crossed strings can stop a puppet show in its tracks. Imagine how a real person or animal moves and try to copy that movement to make your puppet look more realistic to others watching.

4. *Natural position looks better.*

   Find your puppet's "natural position." In other words, how does the puppet need to stand so it is looking straight ahead? Most mouth puppets require a slight forward bend of the wrist. Ask your teacher, parent, or friend if your puppet seems natural to them. Try these exercises: Have your puppet look out the window, at the floor, and out the door. Have it read a book, do a double take, or do any movement you can think of.

5. *Don't ever sleep on the job.*

Keep your puppet awake at all times. If another puppet is talking, make sure your puppet responds with slight gestures. Just like a person, your puppet must look like it is listening and paying attention to the other puppet that is talking. This movement will make the audience truly believe the puppets are real. If you let your arm go limp, it will look as if your puppet has died onstage. On the other hand, don't go overboard and upstage by too much movement. This is a quick way to lose friends!

6. *Learn to bow politely.*

As the perfect puppeteer already knows, your audience will clap and cheer at the end of your fabulous performance. You do not want to look like a dud and just stand there while they are showing appreciation. Practice an elegant bow so that your audience can clap even more. When you are being videotaped, the bow is imperative.

7. *Always put all your puppetry materials neatly away.*

Remember that there is no magic fairy in your classroom or in your home. Everything has its own place, so it is your responsibility to take care of your own things; keep them in good condition for the next fabulous show. Your dog may want to play puppeteer if your puppet is left out, making a different creature out of your original puppet.

Using Puppets Is Great Fun to "Show Off" Learning

It seems that children have loved the use of puppetry since the beginning of time. Can't we all remember those great times ourselves, using a marionette with strings, a store-bought puppet, or even a simple homemade sock puppet embellished with buttons and yarn? In classrooms everywhere, young children can "hide" behind that puppet to eliminate shyness and have more fun developing unusual voices.

Boys who are uncomfortable reading aloud or telling a story can often be convinced to participate when puppets are involved. They soon realize that the audience is watching their puppet instead of them. This is extremely comforting and takes away the fear of being in front of others. By using this tool of puppetry, a child can totally relax.

As an example, the Hungry Monster Hand Puppet can gobble up many cookies, which are just paper cutouts that look like cookies. Each cookie has vocabulary words to read, spelling list words to spell, color or number words to read and spell, math problems to solve, or any other skill you might want your child to practice. The skills are endless along with wild imagination.

Make sure the rules are established first. No cookie may be kept unless the Hungry Monster Puppet knows the answer written on the back of the cookie. No matter how hungry the monster is, he cannot rip or bend his cookie that is drawn out of the cookie jar.

He also has to close his eyes when getting a cookie. If two or more play, the winner is the one ending up with the most cookies or correct answers.

Videotaping of Math, Writing, Reading, and Science Learned:
Using Puppets

The wonderful advantage of using videotape to show what was learned is that this process makes the child the "expert" or "star" when recording him. Videotaping, photos, or even tape recordings can be saved for many years and shared over and over. You could equate these to old home movies but with new and exciting learning being demonstrated.

Earlier in this chapter, we give suggestions for making your own puppets, different types your child might like, and easy ways to have him make them himself. When the child or student takes the time to make this creation of art, he will have more ownership and pride in showing off what he has learned with it.

MATH ON MONDAY

So now you know that Magical Math Monday is the real first day of our seven steps. Next, we will discuss fun reporting of what was learned in math first. You will note the fun usage of puppetry, too, in order to make the learning easier to demonstrate.

When videotaping math, simple games are best used. Most boys love fishing out of the "magic hat" or pond with a magic wand or magic fishing pole. As described in chapter 2, a magnet is tied to a string or yarn. The hat or pond is filled with fish, dinosaurs, or anything else that the child first makes and cuts out. The items must be large enough to write word problems or math facts on one side and the answer on the other. Make sure to use large paper clips for easier catch, and only one can be pulled out at a time. Using math symbols, number words, and numerals is a great practice as well.

As with the writing of a fun story or when reading with a partner or alone, all math problems need to be practiced before any videotaping is done. This gives your child or student additional practice and confidence before making the final product with a video.

When you use the incentive of videotaping, motivation for your son will elevate, and his enthusiasm for learning and doing more will skyrocket. Your child or student will learn more quickly, try harder, and become fully engaged in what he is doing when using puppets.

Seven Steps of Using Puppets to Teach Math Concepts and Problems

After some practice, videotape the learning from the lesson ideas or scenarios below while the child uses fun puppets and hopefully ones he has made:

1. *Have a puppet that loves to take things apart.* Mr. Tricky Puppet can use the old triangle-pieces-of-pie trick, or he can take one shoe from a pair by the door or in the closet. Give your child a felt board with cutout pieces of felt or give him a bunch of blocks. Have him take some away and change that into a number sentence or "equation" to prove that he really understands simple fractions. He or you can write fraction skits; in other words, show him what "1/2" is but in a fun way.

2. *Have a puppet that never gets the right answer.* Poor Mr. Wrong Puppet may try and try, but the more he thinks, the more muddled he gets. It is surprising how much kids love to show him his errors. But then Mr. Proud Puppet has to finally find the right answer and prove it to his audience with a kind correction to Mr. Wrong.

3. *Have a puppet that is always backward.* Sadly, Mr. Backward Puppet adds instead of subtracts; he multiplies instead of divides. He even counts from 1 to 10 backward. Have the kids point out his errors and correct them. Better yet, let Mr. Proud Puppet explain kindly what Mr. Backward Puppet is doing wrong. On paper, write the symbols for what he needs to do to be correct. Show the symbols for addition and subtraction, multiplication and division, fractions, and more than and less than. Much will depend on the ability level of the child or student.

4. *Have a puppet worried about the Meter Stick.* Mr. Confused Puppet is always left out because he doesn't understand the correct amount in a meter. Mr. Proud Puppet will explain what a decimeter is and demonstrate on the meter stick. Next he will show the difference between a yardstick and inches when compared to a meter stick.

5. *Drill work is much more fun if you have a puppet do it for you.* So, if you are like most teachers or parents, drill time is not the high point of your day. Make the learning more meaningful by putting a puppet on your hand. The student or child who can give the correct answer gets to be Mr. Proud Puppet. Chances are you all will have a fun and engaging time and the kids will learn much faster. Finally, let them know you might videotape the child who is next.

6. *Have a Mr. Crazy Puppet that goes crazy every time he hears a certain number.* Choose your work problems so that the number is in the cor-

rect answers; whoever gets the problem right first gets the puppet for the next problem.

7. *Have a puppet that always has a secret number, concept, or word.* Mr. Secret Puppet will give the kids only hints or clues. When one child figures it out, Mr. Secret Puppet will be approached by another child with a puppet, which will tell him a new secret. The puppets add interest, and paying attention is easier for all. Children can figure out the secret answer from the clues given after one is done as a model. Since they all want to be Mr. Secret Puppet, they try harder to solve the answer by listening more carefully.

TALL TALES, OR STORYTELLING, ON TUESDAY

The next day of the seven steps is Telling Tall Tales Tuesday and can make a teacher, parent, and child giggle. There are few rules, so the stories can be as silly and ridiculous as your child wants. Naturally, the subject matter must be appropriate.

Help the child decide what he would like to tell a story about and discuss how tall tales have been used as a form of storytelling throughout history. As a role model, tell them you will go first by asking, "Would you like me to tell you a story?" Do not get nervous; you may not realize it yet, but you have a wealth of stories to share. Do not think you have to invent them on the spot. As a teacher or parent, you could share personal stories from your childhood or from books you have read for starters. Children never tire of pet stories or from the mistakes you made.

Preschoolers and toddlers enjoy stories about characters from their favorite books. You can certainly take a story and change it to make it end differently, make the characters have names of people you know, or make it sequentially backward to get the child's attention. Children love to hear stories that describe them and the experiences they have had. Remember, as said before, the sillier, the better.

Older children can appreciate a funny twist to a story they know or take a favorite story and turn it upside down. You can change the setting, character, or plot. Again, for boys listening to a story that you tell or, better yet, one that they tell, just remember that the sillier or more outlandish, the better. As mentioned before, make your child or student the main character of a crazy adventure that fits his interests, whether it is trains or dinosaurs.

Most children really enjoy stories about you and your family, such as the time you got your first pet, lost your first tooth, or met your spouse. Perhaps as a parent, tell about the whole day and the events leading up to the child's birth. Some stories are true, but others can be tall tales. Thinking about

Mommy and Daddy can bring out stories for children. Maybe you want to pass down a story your grandparents told you or even a weird story from a neighbor about a ghost living in their attic always making noises. A favorite story might be one about when you got in trouble as a child. Children and students need to be able to relate to you and realize you were once young, too. Stories that tell about your shortcomings, mistakes, or failures helps them know we all are human.

So consider expanding the storytelling experience with your child at home or with students in the classroom. After sharing your stories, ask if someone has a story of his own. Tell him it can be real or make-believe, fact or fantasy. Sometimes it is fun for the audience to guess which type they think it is after the story is told. The only rule is for laughing to be appropriate to the story. Common courtesy is a constant rule.

Pick a reliable student to start with, and if you need to brainstorm vocabulary words of their interest, all the better. These key words can be written on the board for all to see. Spelling words of the week can be incorporated for double effect in learning them faster.

Once the child thinks he is ready to tell his story, encourage anything he comes up with. Brevity is not an issue at the beginning of this activity. Often it is fun to have the first child stop in the middle of his story and another take over, adding to the first story. We call this "pass it on" or "story building." Many more will volunteer if they know they are not the only one doing the storytelling and that there are no real expectations of how the story has to flow.

When people tell stories, they show how to put words together to make meaning. The class or child is practicing verbal skills and happily not having to write or spell. The children can draw images or illustrations as the story is told. This way, everyone stays on task and is engaged. Photos or magazine pictures for real stories can help everyone visual meaning much more clearly. Before any videotaping or tape recording is done, make sure the participant is comfortable and willing.

It is amazing how after one child does this easily, everyone's hand will go up in the classroom, wanting to be next for taping or recording. For those reluctant storytellers who remain, have the child or student make some face masks out of paper plates to match what his storytelling is about. By hiding behind the mask, a new character is born with self-confidence to perform for you or even the video camera.

Again, the use of puppetry can be used successfully in storytelling. The art of storytelling lends itself easily to the puppet's being the speaker. For instance, rather than having to think about being up front, the puppet's movement can be easily mastered as the child tells his story. The puppeteer can hide behind his puppet.

Teaching children how to make shadow puppets is a perfect tool for children who are overly shy or lack self-confidence. So here is another time to incorporate some science. Explain to them that whenever you are in the light, you cast a shadow; a shadow is usually the same shape as the object that casts it. Objects that are colored and allow light to pass through them cast shadows of the same color.

You can make shadow puppets of cats and dogs with your hands, stuffed animals, or cutout shadow puppets from paper. If you darken a room and cast shadows on a thin white cloth, sheet, or piece of paper from behind, you can make your own shadow puppet theater.

It is easy for children to make shadow puppets at home or in school. They will need some large pieces of cardboard or whiteboard, different colors of cellophane, some long sticks, scissors, tape, and glue. Next, draw a design on the cardboard. If you want more than one character for your storytelling or play, you might need to draw several. Be sure to leave places where you can cut out holes for the eyes or mouth. Use your colorful cellophane to tape over the eyes or mouth to add emphasis. Finally, secure the sticks firmly to the back of the shadow puppet with tape.

As all seasoned puppeteers know, you do not want your shadow to show up on the screen. Depending on how elaborate you want to make your theater, parents or teachers can help find other objects to have at the base of the sheet, piece of paper, or cloth. A child's world is full of things that can cast interesting shadows. Have your children take empty bottles of various shapes and cut silhouettes out of paper to place on the necks of the bottles. These can then be used to cast shadows against a wall or from behind a sheet. The transparent bottles and the opaque silhouettes will create different visual effects.

Encourage your child or students to identify common objects by the shadows they see cast. By building and performing in a shadow puppet theater, storytelling can be more inviting to others while providing the actor with confidence to be videotaped. In addition, children can learn something about the relationship between shadows and light sources.

WIZARDLY WRITING ON WEDNESDAY

All children love to be seen by others in a video, especially when it is about their areas of interest or discovered passion. For instance, if your son or student loves the study of the different dinosaurs, you can help him develop a story about a particular type. To make the Wizardly Writer's story more humorous and engaging, done on Wednesdays and Thursdays, let your Wizard name the dinosaur after himself, a movie character he loves, or perhaps a good friend. This gives the video more personality and gets the child more excited about the final product of writing and reading his story aloud.

Mom could even make one about Dad, or big brother, big sister, or anyone would work well being involved in the writing. Modeling is always helpful.

Your child may have to brainstorm some appropriate words for his story by making a list of possible vocabulary he will want to use. Make sure he incorporates his weekly spelling list with many descriptive and action words to make his writing more interesting.

EDITING AND REVISING WIZARDLY WRITING ON THURSDAY

Once his first draft is done, go through the process of editing and revising. In this book's seven steps, it is done on Wizardly Writing Wednesday and Thinking Thoughts Thursday. If he becomes tired and has a hard time finishing, keep reminding him that his best final product will be videotaped for his classmates, relatives, family, or anyone he wants to share it with. This adventure in videotaping is a great motivational tool for all students and can be edited over and over until the child is proud of his efforts.

FREE READING ON FRIDAY

Another way to use videotaping is in reading activities done on Free Reading Fridays. We discuss the area of reading more than some of the other days of the week since reading is the key to success in becoming a great student or learner.

This reading on Friday is naturally easier, as no writing is involved. Instruct your child to find a book he loves and practice reading it with you first many times. Use a pencil to read with and underline lightly any words he does not know how to pronounce. He should do the same for any words he does not know the meaning of. Even before he lets you videotape him, have your reader practice in front of a mirror and maybe another family member.

Stress the use of voice to make his story exciting by showing him the boring way and the exciting way a story can sound instead. The sillier you make it, the better he will like doing these practices prior to being videotaped. You can even read with him in the video if that makes him relax more. Another way is for the parent or teacher to read one page, and then the child reads the next. This will help him pay attention to where you are and when it is his turn to read. If you can talk his father, big brother, uncle, or friend into sharing the reading with him, this will help develop his self-confidence and lead to better self-esteem.

Some children are hams; others are shyer about being taped or recorded. Once you determine how your child reacts, it is easier to decide the best way for him to be involved. It is always fine to first model what you want him to do to make the activity run smoother.

You may have a reluctant reader, and for many children reading just does not come easily. Some have difficulty connecting letters and their corresponding sounds; others discover a special story that sparks their imagination and shows just how much fun reading can be. We all know that, for them, being comfortable with letters and their sounds and words is an important foundation for learning throughout life. Therefore, read to and with your child or students as often as possible.

Try some simple ways to help them become eager readers. Begin with some of your child's picks. A comic or joke books may not be your first choice to help with literacy, but the reality is that they are motivating to the child. You might be shocked and amazed how well they can read if it is something that they really want to read.

Sure, some of these texts are not very substantial, but they can help children understand some fundamentals of reading. How events take place in a story, or sequence, is learned along with how stories are laid out. They can even help build vocabulary and show that books can be visually appealing. Once the child is comfortable with the experience of reading, you can encourage other literature selections with a variety of more challenging content.

Electronic books, or e-books, can sometimes get reluctant readers to read. When your child or student gets interested in a book, regardless of the format, it will help him make connections between the story and the child's life. The child can relax more, follow along with the book, and hopefully read along on his own.

Teachers and parents often see their children wanting the same book over and over. This is a great way to learn text and eventually read it with ease and confidence through repetition. Each new reading of the book also may help them notice something they did not see the last time and understand the story better. This confidence will inspire children to try a new book the next time.

Reading aloud to children helps them build their vocabularies and introduces new concepts, ideas, and facts. By doing this, you are showing that you enjoy reading just for fun. Children also need to see men reading more for enjoyment. With repeated reading, the child will relate sounds with letters on the page. Who doesn't enjoy this together time? The fallacy of needing to stop this activity once a child becomes older is a missed opportunity. The comfort of a teacher's or a parent's voice and having their total attention is something all children love and need more than ever in today's rushed world.

Opportunities to read and write beyond the book pages are important for children. They need many chances to read every day and not just from books. You can write notes and leave them around for your children to find. Teachers can write notes and questions for the student to answer in their daily journals. Ask friends and relatives to send letters, cards, e-mails, or text messages. Magnetic letters and words on the refrigerator might encourage your child to create their own words, sentences, and stories.

Family car rides provide a perfect opportunity to point out common signs or to play word games to strengthen language skills. "I Spy" is a great game for this ("I spy something that starts with a 'b.' What is it?"), as are games that categorize things, such as "Animals" (everyone has to name an animal that begins with a certain letter).

If you are truly concerned about your child's or student's lack of progress when it comes to reading, get help from the specialists at school or in the community. One cannot wait until it is too late, when it will be harder for the child to catch up or even feel good about reading. There are many new techniques out there for children with dyslexia and other developmental issues.

For some children, reading is almost a natural reaction to print, and for other children, the struggle is so much greater. Some children fall somewhere in the middle (the majority), learning to read at a normal progression with appropriate support and stimulus.

To reiterate, in general, boys start reading later than girls do. Boys tend to be later in showing interest and later in getting started with the process of reading. However, they generally catch up right away once they start if no other problems are detected. Teachers and parents need to tailor reading time to a boy's gross motor energy. Keep it short, sweet, and relevant.

Most children will begin reading in first grade. But if by the beginning of second grade your child has not shown an interest in reading or a teacher has pointed out concerns about your child's reading progress, try to be proactive. Once you are aware of a problem, address it and increase the reading environment at school and home with continued support. You could even consult a reading specialist for added advice and help with activities to strengthen the skills that are not developing.

Make sure to read to your child as much as possible no matter how young he might be. We cannot stress the importance of this enough.

Seven Steps to Help Support Early Literacy at Home

1. *Show your child nonfiction books as well as storybooks.* Many boys are more interested in books that have information related to their passion.
2. *Visit the library every week and get to know the child's librarian, who can give you lists of good age-appropriate books.* The sight of new books each week can lead to excitement about learning and reading. All types of books are good, ranging from those that are repetitive to those with nursery rhymes. Inquire about a Story Hour when children can come to hear books read to them in the library.

3. *Be enthusiastic about Wizardly Writing.* Give your child a pencil and paper when you are playing restaurant so he can write down what you want to order. Inventive spelling is fine, as later you can work on the spelling correctly of words.

4. *Try to stick to real books, not electronic ones.* Dr. Shannon Ayers quotes research showing that with electronic storybooks, parents talked about the book only 59 percent of the time. The rest of the time was spent saying "push this button" and so on, whereas with a traditional book, 92 percent of the parent's time was spent talking about the story.

5. *Introduce your son to bigger ideas to think about.* Instead of the usual "How was your day?" conversation, talk to him about something you found interesting in a book. It makes your child feel more grown up and stretches his brain. This will help prepare him for a future world of reading with better comprehension as well.

6. *Do not ignore how books on tape can help a struggling reader.* These books are available in the library for checkout and can make a child love learning. Instead of struggling with words, meaning, and pronunciation, he can concentrate on meaning while the skills are being developed.

7. *Remember that it is okay to use puppets when reading books or stories.* You can hold the puppet at first to show how the mechanics of the mouth movements need to coordinate with the words read. Being realistic gives the book more meaning.

SCIENCE ON SATURDAY

Super Science Saturdays lend themselves easily to videotaping with many fun things to do, learn more about, and see outside. Most boys (as well as girls) are fascinated by birds and their busy behavior. We all love to watch birds out the window, playing and showering in the water dish and building nests in the spring with various items found, and enjoy seeing them come to a feeder the child has made for them.

What is a good way to invite birds into your yard you are probably now wondering? The best way is to build a birdbath or bird feeder in a quiet part of the yard where people do not go. Birds are fearful of humans and other animals, so prepare food that birds will like and be careful not to disturb them when you watch.

If you are observant and quiet, you might be lucky enough to see various varieties of birds. When time permits, it is fun to look them up in a bird book or on the computer for more information about their habitats and characteristics.

A great place to build a bird feeder is in the garden or in an empty spot near the house and a window. A balcony can be a good place if people do not use it often. Remember that birds of the same type look very much the same. If you want to tell them apart, you must pay close attention to their beaks and legs. That is where birds are most likely to be different. The materials you will need are a wooden box, a post, a short stick, some short nails, a hammer, some net, and some string.

Seven Easy Steps to Making a Bird Feeder (two types: box feeder and hanging net feeder)

1. Nail the wooden box to the top of the post. Use enough nails to make certain that the box is sturdy. A wobbly box might scare the birds away forever.
2. Place your bird feeder outside. Secure the post into the ground, against a tree, or next to the house where it can be observed and videotaped.
3. Scatter seeds and other food in the box, such as bread crumbs, sliced oranges, apples, berries, or seeds or buy wild birdseed at the store.
4. Fill the net with seeds and other food mentioned above. Use another post to put into the ground and another stick to secure with strong string to make the letter "T" shape as your post structure.
5. Tie the bag of bird treats or feed to the top of the "T" to hang down for the birds.
6. Let the birds get used to seeing your new contraptions for a week.
7. Get out the videotape or camera to record what you have made and what you observe as an "official bird-watcher." Binoculars are great for this.

Building a birdbath is exciting, and it is fun to observe birds bathing from a safe distance so as not to disturb them. Birds will shy away from people and decide to go to a puddle the next time they want to take a private bath.

This birdbath is easy for any child to do, and you need only a tin box, some strong glue, and a thick stick. Glue the empty tin box to the top of the stick or use a nail if the glue does not hold. Make sure the hole does not leak water. Fill with clean water and watch how much fun the birds will have taking a bath. Finally, videotape what happens.

Birdhouses are more difficult to make, but we are sure a dad can help figure out the best way to form the holes and frame for a bird wanting to nest. This may take longer to observe, as many birds feel safer up high in trees, but it is worth a try.

Before making any of these bird items, explain to your students or children that the use of pesticides and the cutting down of forests have seriously threatened many species of birds. Inviting birds to your yard is good not only for your child but also for the birds. You can try changing the type of seeds and other food in the feeder to discover what kinds attract different species. You can include math by graphing what you discover each day of the week, what birds like best to eat, or how many birds took a bath.

With a little practice and a good bird book, children can learn to identify different species of birds and keep a simple record of those they have seen. Be sure that your feeder and birdbath are high enough that the birds will not be in danger from stray cats or other predators. Also make certain that the water stays fresh and that the food does not rot. We do not want to make any of our wild feathered friends sick.

All of the above activities in this chapter lend themselves perfectly to photos, videotaping, and recording of observations made along the way of the child's fun discovery while learning new things. Even if you have to borrow or rent a video camera, regular camera, or tape recorder, the enjoyment can last for a lifetime. Who would not want to show "old-time videos" to their own children many years from now for laughs? Wouldn't we all love to have our own memories like these from the past?

Our goal in this book is to provide different strategies and ideas to keep the child stimulated and actively engaged with all types of learning and enjoyment. We need better ways to learn new things other than sitting in front of the computer or any screen for more than a few hours at a time.

Ralph Marston makes this book's thoughts crystal clear about the great need for creativity and how it can lead to more learning and adventure and become the avenue for following one's passion, purpose, and joy. He points out how very young children change from being confident, curious, and full of joy when learning to living with mediocrity as they grow older. We, as parents, teachers, and administrators, need to heed his warning when teaching our children of the future:

Creative Genius

There was a time when you knew you could do anything, and you did. There was a time when you were not afraid of your own possibilities, and you acted on them, and brought those possibilities to life.

There was a time when you created purely for the joy of it. There was a time when you learned just because you were curious. You still can do all those things and more. Your capabilities extend far beyond anything you've ever done with them.

Instead of living with mediocrity, or worse . . . you can live with passion, purpose, joy and fulfillment. Instead of giving in to the fear that you'll be looked at as weird for following your dreams, you can truly celebrate and live those dreams.

When it comes to living your own life and fulfilling your own purpose, you are the world's most creative genius. Imagine how great it can be to put that genius to work. Imagine, and then live all the good things you imagine. Imagine, and then put your imagination into fulfilling, joyous actions.[5]

Hopefully, this chapter has given you many new and exciting ideas to help become the launching pad for you, the child, and the teacher and to show you that learning does not have to be boring or repetitive. There are many creative ways to make learning more fun and meaningful for all involved. If your child is bored, then try another approach; moods and emotions can change daily, so do not give up. Try the same lesson on a different day and in a different way with even more determination and enthusiasm. Our last suggestion is to the parent, teacher, or caregiver: borrow if you must, or rent a camera—but do it!

Living in an adult world sometimes makes it hard to think and act like a child does. However, you will accomplish much more with children if you can get down to their level. Besides, we all need to find our own "inner child," don't we? We were all children once, but our busy world makes us forget about that carefree time long ago and far away. Our goal is to have all our children thrive in this exciting educational adventure, whether it is in the home, outdoors, or in the classroom with their peers.

NOTES

1. Ralph Marston, "Put Passion," *The Daily Motivator*, September 22, 2014 (www.greatday.com).

2. Dimitri A. Christakis, Frederick J. Zimmerman, David L. DiGiuseppe, and Carolyn A. McCarty, "Early Television Exposure and Subsequent Attentional Problems in Children," *Pediatrics* 113, no. 4 (April 1, 2014): 708–13.

3. Michael Gurian, *The Minds of Boys: Saving Our Sons from Falling behind in School and Life* (San Francisco: Jossey-Bass, 2005).

4. Jane Healy, *Failure to Connect: How Computers Affect Our Children's Minds and What We Can Do About It.* (New York: Simon & Schuster Inc., Oct. 1999).

5. Ralph Marston, "Creative Genius," *The Daily Motivator*, June 13, 2013 (www.greatday.com).

5

Writing a Simple Book for Peers, Parents, Teachers, Relatives, and Even Pets

Patience and perseverance have a magical effect before which difficulties disappear and obstacles vanish.

—John Quincy Adams

WHY IS HANDWRITING NECESSARY WITH TODAY'S TECHNOLOGY?

Of all the skill areas, the process of writing seems to be the one activity in school that creates the most problems for boys. Like reading, many parts must come together to make this such a significant area of frustration. Unfortunately, with the newer standards of the past two decades, writing has become a greater focus in school. Now writing is required on the mandated tests, even in math. Children are asked to explain in writing how they found their answers. Seems like that is testing them again in writing, not math. This is another reason for change.

Two major problems for boys when it comes to writing are not only writing skills but also their attitude toward the task. Many boys have the attitude that language arts is not something they are good at. You will also hear the excuse when they say, "Writing is an activity for girls, not boys." They wonder why they need to write at all.

The humorist Dave Barry commented on male attitudes toward writing in his 1995 book *Dave Barry's Complete Guide to Guys*. He commented that "very few guys write thank you notes or any other kind of note. Guys would probably commit a lot more kidnappings, if they weren't required to write ransom notes."[1]

Some believe that, with the arrival of the digital age, we are handwriting less and less and that everything is being done by computers. Now we write e-mails instead of letters, and essays are typed out and printed instead of handwritten; even doctors' prescriptions are typed and printed. For doctors this is an improvement! Will there be a day soon when we see handwriting disappear altogether?

How important is handwriting anyway? According to some, not important at all, but a 2012 study from Indiana University begs to differ. Researchers have found that when things are handwritten, we have a better connection with the words that we are writing. It also helps when we read words. This study found that handwriting fires pathways in the brain that lead to better reading as well as comprehension skills. The Common Core Standards focus on handwriting in kindergarten and first grade only and then move directly to learning how to type. What does this do to the reading skills of our children?

Karin James led the previously mentioned Indiana University study. Children were given a letter and then told to duplicate the letter three different ways. They could trace it, draw it freehand on a blank piece of paper, or type it out on a keyboard. Monitors were put on the children to measure brain activity while they were completing this exercise. The researchers found that the reading and writing center of the brain was very active when they chose to draw the letters themselves. When they traced the letter or typed it out, there was little activity in those areas of the brain.

James stated that the reason extra activity occurs is because there is a lot more thought that goes into drawing the letter. You have to look at the letter, think about its shape, and then make a plan as to how to draw it accordingly. With a keyboard, you need only look for a button and then hit it. With tracing, you need only follow a black line.

When we look more carefully at all of the skills involved in writing a story, it is easy to see why this may be the most complex school activity that boys have to perform. Remember that hard things are put in our way not to stop us but to call out our courage and strength. Here are the major hurdles in writing for boys to try to overcome:

- Thinking what to write about
- Putting words into meaningful sentences
- Making topic sentences
- Organizing sentences with details and thoughts into paragraphs
- Revising and editing the writing for a beginning, middle, and end
- Using grammar, punctuation, and spelling correctly
- Making handwriting legible (difficult for most boys)

Don't panic. These skills are developed over many years of school. Doing any of this is overwhelming to most children, especially as they begin to learn the basics of writing in kindergarten. For any difficult challenge, we all need to give ourselves an extra push to accomplish the task. This includes parents, teachers, and administrators, but most of all this is true for children learning a difficult skill. Just as Ralph Marston wisely points out, perhaps an extra push is necessary for success in writing or any area of difficulty:

Give Yourself a Little Push

Think of what you can do today to show yourself that your life really means something. Think of what you can do today to get yourself refreshingly outside your comfort zone.

Challenges and new situations will put you a little on edge and make you a bit uncomfortable. And as such, they will empower you greatly.

You can do much more than you now imagine you can do. Let yourself find out what that is.

There's more to life than speculating about what you might be able to do, and wondering whether or not you can. At some point you must find out for yourself.

Give yourself a little push into something that will challenge you in a meaningful way. Jump in and get busy transforming what you wish for and what you dream about into what is.

Discover how truly purposeful, creative, capable and effective you can be. Feel how much stronger and how much more alive you can become.[2]

The main thing we all must remember is for the "little push" to be small, attainable, and done with quality. A wonderful quote by Henry Ford, the great car innovator, also said, "Quality means doing it right when no one is looking." This seemingly lost trait of doing things carefully for your own satisfaction and not only when someone is watching you is important for a child to learn. Completing a task well done—not for awards or recognition—is certainly more worthy.

If we could all instill this rare quality of pride in our workforce today, think how much better our country could become. No matter what the job might be, whether the person is a great doctor or scientist, a hardworking janitor of a school, or a garbage man, one's dedication to completing that endeavor should be done with pride, dignity, quality, and effort every single day.

Perhaps some of the blame for careless work in some of this generation's workforce might be attributed to how much earlier we are now pushing our young boys to do schoolwork that is too difficult or often developmentally inappropriate for them. This rush may be setting up our society for a lack of pride or quality in jobs done, never the time given to do well before moving on to the next task.

When did our society forget to take the time needed for perfection of the products produced? Doesn't the rush lead to "haste makes waste," providing poorer products in our race of constant competition with other countries?

How many "recalls" do we constantly see on the news? Some of these have caused the deaths of many.

THE RUSH IS ON, UNFORTUNATELY

As mentioned over and over, elementary school has become a place of the "hurried child." Schools move children from the magical world of childhood toward a much more complex world. Reading and writing, concrete reasoning, abstract thought, and time management skills are expectations that are certainly too high for many children who are not developmentally ready.

Twenty or more years ago, kindergarten was the place for a child to learn more social and emotional development. Reading did not happen until first grade but only after taking more time to know their letters and over the year master the sounds of those letters. Little by little, as the children became ready, they were introduced to some words by sight and could read short sentences. They did not fear writing small words.

Writing happened only after a few sentences were understood and even then was done as a slower process. By second grade, the children had a better grasp of letters, sounds, and words and how they worked together to make sentences. That sounds logical, right? They learned that a sentence had to begin with a capital letter and end with a period or question mark. This puzzle of making stories or writing spelling sentences was just starting to make sense for some in second grade and others in third grade.

You can already guess how this acceleration of the curriculum affects young boys. Many parents, teachers, and caregivers see that the rushed approach has led to disaster. Even perfectly smart boys tend to start reading and writing a few months later than girls. Unfortunately, few allowances are made for differences in their learning timetable.

"What happens to the second-grade boy who spends writing period hiding under his desk?" Ro Costello, who had been a kindergarten teacher for twenty-five years but now she teaches special education and fifth grade in public schools, sees the effects firsthand: "Much of the work that teachers routinely assign children in early elementary school borders on developmentally inappropriate for many kids but is especially bad for young males. It is good to set a high bar, and all good teachers want to take kids as far as they can go. But you also have to remember that not every child is the same!"[3]

This sounds familiar, doesn't it? And Costello goes on to explain that she has seen the repeated heartbreaking pattern of boys who become frustrated with writing. By third grade, a second-grade boy's fear has turned to frustration. By fifth grade, he is the class clown. In middle school, he becomes aggressive and begins to be labeled a behavior problem or even a bully. By high school, he is in special education—if he is still in high school at all.

HOW TO BEGIN THE WRITING PROCESS IN MORE EXCITING WAYS

Even though we write every day, writing is one of the most complex tasks that humans learn to do. It involves both motor and critical thinking skills. Learning to write is a challenging process that takes years to complete. Writing has to happen in order, with each skill building on the last. Just like reading, children are aware of writing from infancy, especially if they are exposed to it regularly. When you read to a child and he sees you write, he starts to understand very young that written words have meaning.

Quickly you see children trying to create words on their own by scribbling, an activity most toddlers love to do. Many times they scribble on any and everything! They need some coordination to hold the crayon, keep the paper still, and apply enough pressure to make a mark. With lots of continued practice, they will start to realize not only that they can they make marks to create a pattern but also that, by doing that same movement, they can make the same pattern again. This is a good time to introduce the use of clay for more fun in forming letters, learning correct letterforms, and making their name and numbers.

Clay Can Make Learning Letters Fun and Hands On

Modeling clay is one of the most valuable educational materials children of all ages can play with. The use of clay also develops those necessary fine motor skills needed for writing! As they mature, they can attempt increasingly more difficult techniques, such as making statues of people or animals. Small children are content to work with clay using only their hands at first, but little by little the addition of various tools can be helpful.

Remember that oil-based clay stays soft, so you can use it over and over. Water-based clay hardens when it dries; when that happens, you can paint the clay. Bright plastic clays can be mixed to make many different colors, another opportunity to involve hands-on science. Children feel like it is magical the way two colors can make another. To explain better, start with red, blue, and yellow. These three are called the primary colors. When you mix them in different amounts, you can make all the colors in the rainbow. For instance, show the child how red + blue = purple. blue + yellow = green. and yellow + red = orange. Another time for math symbols?

Here are some universal recipes you can make with your children's help. Many lessons in math, reading, writing, and science can be worked into these recipes. Making all these different types of clay is not only hands on but also keeps your child or students engaged for hours to come. Make sure you allow all of them to help in the cleanup as well.

Molding Clay Recipes

Traditional Clay

Ingredients

   1½ cups baking soda
   ⅔ cup cornstarch
   2 cups warm water

Directions

Mix the ingredients together in a pan. Heat over low heat until thick. Stir constantly. Place mixture on a pastry board or breadboard to cool. As soon as it is cool enough to handle, knead well. At this time, you can add in tempera paint or food coloring if you choose. Roll out flat. Use cookie cutters or cut shapes freehand. Place unused dough in a plastic bag, as it dries fast. Paint your finished projects and brush with shellac or clear nail polish to preserve.

Quickie Molding Clay

Ingredients

   ¾ cup flour
   ½ cup salt
   1½ teaspoons alum powder
   1½ teaspoons oil
   ½ cup boiling water

Directions

Mix dry ingredients together and add water and oil. Mix well. You can add food coloring or tempera paint if you wish. Mold into anything you wish and leave to dry overnight. Store this material in a jar or plastic bag. It will keep for months, especially if kept in the refrigerator. If the clay becomes a little too sticky, just add a little more flour.

Sawdust Clay

Ingredients

2 cups fine sawdust
1 cup wallpaper paste
water (see below)

Directions

Mix sawdust and wallpaper paste together. Slowly add water. Blend enough water until you have a mixture the consistency of clay. Turn it out on a couple sheets of newspaper and knead until all the ingredients are very well blended. Use the same as any other molding clay. Let it dry for three days or bake in an oven at 200 degrees Fahrenheit for about 2 hours. Sand the forms to a smooth finish. Finally, paint by using shellac, spray finish, or varnish to top off your masterpiece.

Coffee Clay

Ingredients

2 cups flour
½ cup salt
⅛ cup instant coffee
¾ cup warm water

Directions

Dissolve coffee in warm water. In a separate bowl, mix the salt and flour together. Form an indentation in the dough ball and pour in about half of the coffee. Mix until creamy smooth. Add more coffee water as needed and work until it is a claylike consistency (not sticky). Design away. Bake finished goods in a 250-degree-Fahrenheit oven for an hour or until dry. Paint and finish with shellac, varnish, or plastic spray finish. Store the remaining dough in a covered jar or plastic bag.

Use these recipes responsibly. Many of them require using the stove. Some require using ingredients that might be dangerous if ingested in quantity. Parents, teachers, or caretakers must supervise children.

Children may start to practice writing by three or four years of age. Some of the scribbles become letters, like in their name, and are randomly put on different parts of the paper (and not on walls, hopefully). This is because children learn to write individual letters before they learn how to put them together to make a word. Here is another reason for children to work with clay often to help develop their recognition of letters and sounds later when they are developmentally ready. Boys especially need more hands-on work for the fine motor skills needed in writing, as previously mentioned. You are never too old to outgrow your need for clay. Even adults love using it.

TRY WRITING SECRET MESSAGES

In addition to clay, letting children discover the magic of writing with some fruit or vegetable juice or vinegar on paper is fun and definitely engaging. It leaves no stain when dry, but if the paper is then heated, a stain will show. Young children love feeling like they can make secret messages for others, and it helps further develop their fine motor skills at the same time. Only someone who knows the secret will be able to read their "invisible letter."

Materials

One lemon, one orange, one radish, and vinegar
Dish for the magical solution
White paper
Paintbrush

Directions

Put some lemon juice, orange juice, radish juice, or vinegar in your dish. Dip your clean paintbrush in the magical solution and write letters, words, numbers, or math.

After doing some skills, you can make pictures to enjoy. Why not try many fruit juices or vegetables to see which others might work? This could be another whole lesson for your child or students. When the juice dries, hold the paper near a hot lightbulb to bring out the secret message or picture to amaze your friends.

Before showing your students or children this magic technique, give them a brief background of how, before microfilm was invented, spies sometimes sent messages written in invisible ink. The secret message could be hidden between the lines of a letter or a book. Invisible ink is not nearly sophisticated enough for today's spies, but children can still have fun experimenting with it. To prevent accidents, be sure to instruct your child or students in the careful use of heat sources such as hot plates and lightbulbs.

Tell your children or students that you have a secret letter for them that is placed in a sealed envelope with their name on the outside. This sparks interest and can be a great introduction to writing secret messages at home or in the classroom. When the child opens the letter, there will be nothing there. Explain about how it was written with magical invisible ink and that the secret to being able to read what it says is by using heat.

Next, have them place the letter under the hot lightbulb to read what it says. The message could be a question, spelling words, new vocabulary words, or a math problem for them to answer. Some children love seeing a map to find the next letter for them, like being on a treasure hunt.

Another exciting form of using this invisible ink is in combination with pencil or crayon. Have the child make an animal's face (eyes, antennae, and whiskers), a part of a car (wheels and windows), or anything else that they partly draw before using the invisible ink. Others try to guess what it might be. To find out the secret answer, put the paper under the hot lightbulb. You could advance this game by doing spelling words and leaving out certain letters for the children to guess; do the same with the sequence of numbers, or math equations, leaving out a number for them to figure out. The parent or teacher can even get suggestions from the children.

Some of these activities take a little more time to set up, but think how much more fun they have, as the child is engaged in wanting to learn and participate. All of these techniques are definitely great motivational tools for encouraging better behavior, better listening skills, and whatever you feel is needed with certain children. They all want to have a turn to write in secret messages.

In addition to sending messages in invisible ink, children like to invent their own secret codes for writing those messages. Encourage children to create a new secret code that can be made up of everyday symbols, numbers, letters, or a more elaborate hieroglyphic formula. Look up the word "hieroglyphic" together so that they learn the meaning.

This activity can include beginning writing of letters, name writing, basic numbers 1 through 10, or simple addition and subtraction facts. The parent or teacher can also write a question with invisible ink and have the child write the answer on paper with a pencil or even invisible ink. You both can check to see if the child got it correct. This magical method of writing can be applied to reading, writing, math, and science. You will see that children never tire of seeing what they or others have written in a secret message.

LEARNING MORE ABOUT CONVENTIONS OF PRINT

Children then start to understand how words work and how groups of letters can make words. Between kindergarten and first grade, most children learn to put letters together into words to label pictures they draw. Later we discuss "invented spelling," but you can probably predict what it is. They start making words with no vowels, such as "prpl" for "purple." When kindergartners use inventive spelling, they are practicing writing words the way they sound; this process helps them as they learn to read.

With lots of practice and formal schooling, children learn about the "conventions of print," including writing from left to right, the difference between uppercase and lowercase letters, how to put spaces between words, and how to use correct spelling. When these students get older and develop better motor skills, their handwriting becomes smaller and smaller. Years ago, between second and third grades, children progressed into learning how to write in cursive by joining the letters together and how to use the conventions of print without even thinking about it much.

Many schools are now deciding that cursive wastes time and so are eliminating it. Sadly, many second graders could not wait to get into third grade just to learn how to do fancy writing called cursive. At any rate, students will have to take notes and tests sooner rather than later as well as complete homework. Those who struggle with the mechanics of handwriting will have a harder time, not to mention how it might affect their self-confidence and attitude toward school.

In order to read, a child must first understand that letters stand for sounds and that the sounds are put together to make words. When preschoolers start to copy the letters they see around them, they are demonstrating that they understand the connection between the sounds they hear and the words they see on the page. Experts think that developing writing skills reinforces reading skills and vice versa.

Fortunately, as children grow older and begin using a keyboard, the motor control and communication skills they have internalized through handwriting will help them become more successful writers, and the neatness does not count as much. For boys, it is much easier for them to transfer their thoughts into words using a keyboard.

WHY WRITING IN KINDERGARTEN?

Now we can move back to kindergarten writing, but this long detour explained why writing is not learned over one year or enjoyed very much by many children due to its complexity. Journal writing has become the norm required for most five-year-olds, even when many struggle to write their names correctly. From their first experience with school, children are asked to at least write the beginning sound they hear in the word they are trying to write. This is fine if the child can decipher sounds or knows any letters. The task would be like trying to do geometry while never having learned the basic skills needed for the concepts to make sense. It's easy to see why boys are made to feel incompetent early on.

You can reinforce this journal writing at home using a big notebook for your child to write down fun things he likes to eat, see, feel, hear, and smell. This will remind him about the five senses, and he can make one-word answers with illustrations.

For children to develop early literacy skills, the teacher needs to give them lots of practice. Fat crayons or chalk (even markers with large paper) make the writing easier and more fun. As they grow older, a special writing center disguised as an art activity with colored pencils and paint should be in the home and at school. At home, in order to be more active, have your child practice writing and drawing on the cement with chalk and even water with a paintbrush. Learning anything outside the house for boys is usually the best.

Young children are developing their fine motor skills by first developing their muscles, skills, and coordination needed to form letters. This water painting works well at school on a sunny day for struggling children, but everyone will want to do it. Salt, Jell-O, or sugar box lids are fun, as is clay for forming letters in the beginning. This kinesthetic approach can help boys in particular. If you have Etch-A-Sketch or erasable whiteboards to practice writing, you will make a hit with the future writers and future authors of the world, too.

Most teachers know that the best way to begin is to have the children tell the adult what to write down for them first. Next, the child reads it back to the teacher with help, seeing that letters and words do have meaning. Finally, the child can illustrate what his story is about, which will help him remember what he wrote. Then, when he takes it home to share, he feels proud and confident. The children usually love to use crayons, ink markers, or paint, and that creativity takes away the dread of writing for many. Teaching letters and sounds in kindergarten does not have to be so painful.

WHY NOT LEARN LETTERS AND SOUNDS THE FUN WAY?

This teacher discovered that boys learn letters and sounds much quicker if taught through silly and catchy poems, songs, or chants, such as the following we made up in our classroom. By introducing difficult words to students, they became curious as to their meaning. The class would draw on large cards to illustrate each silly letter/sound story. Helpers would hold them up over their heads when we came to their letter jingle.

For children (or even bilingual children) having difficulty with language development, this visualization helped to anchor meaning to letters, sounds, and words. The child's use of the English language happened much more rapidly and naturally. The retention of these short jingles was also more likely when memorized for fun.

This enjoyment of learning our silly A-to-Z tongue-twister jingles seemed to be true for our girls as well as the boys; we would even hear these chants below as they jumped rope outside. Many parents came to conferences referring to how their children loved learning them. Some parents jokingly said they were "sick" of hearing them daily at home. Others said they could not get them out of their heads. When learning expands to the parents from their child, the teacher knows he or she has succeeded.

Phrases to Learn for Fun

"Here We Go from A to Z"

*Abraham Ape Ate Apricots in April and August in Arkansas (long and short A)

Bobby Brown Bent Backwards Bumping his Big Boy's Blue Bike in Bakersfield

Carol Cat Carried Candy in Crazy Colored Ceramic Carts to California (hard and soft C)

Danny Dog Dunked Doughnuts in Delaware for his Dad's Dinner in December

*Emanuel Easter Bunny Eats Éclairs Eagerly Every day in Egypt on Easter (short E and long E)

Freddy Frog Feels Fine on Freaky Friday in Florida during February

Gary Gray Gives Giant Green Gifts to Girls, Giraffes and Goats in Georgia (hard and soft G)

Harold Horse Hid Happily in His High House on Haunted Halloween

*Ida Idolizes Icy Ice-cream on the Ice skating rink with Icicles in Indiana (short I and long I)

Jerry Jack-in-the-box Jumps Joyfully and Jokingly in January, June, and July

Katy Kangaroo Kicks Kites with Kathy Kitten in Kansas

Larry Lion Loves Lemons and Lemonade Lately on the Lake in Louisiana

Mary Mouse Moves Many Merry Mice to Maryland on Monday in March and May

Nancy Nightingale Nibbles Noodles Nervously Next to Nevada in November Now

*Over by the Ocean in Oregon we eat Outstanding Orange Oats in October (long O and short O)

Pamela Penguin Picks Perfect Purple Pansies and Plump Peaches in Pennsylvania

Queen Quartet saved Quarters Quickly and Quietly in Quebec

Roger Rabbit Runs by the Rushing, Rolling River over Rough Red Rocks

Sammy Silver Seal Sits Silently on a Slippery Sunny Saturday in September with his Silly, Slimy Soap in Salem

Tommy Turtle Talks To Terrific Tiny Timmy Tortoise Tomorrow on Tuesday in Tucson

*Use your Ukulele Usefully in Unison on the way to Utah, Ulysses (long U)

Vicki Victoria Visits Virginia on Valentines with her Very Vivacious Violet Velvet Vacuum

Wally Walrus Walks and Waddles on Wonderful Wednesday to Washington

X marks the spot for an X-ray; X is extremely hard to use for an excellent example (X and ex)

*Yellow Yams were Yummy Yesterday in Yakima when we were Yelling "Yahoo!" to You (short Y)

Zelda Zebra Zips her Zipper at the Zoo Zealously, singing "Zip-a-Dee-Doo-Dah"

"Whew, so much reading and now we are through!

We did the 26 letters with sounds, A to Z.

So, please tell me now, aren't you proud of me?"

The children learned many skills, such as which letters are consonants and which are vowels. (A, E, I, O, U, and sometimes Y are the vowels, and all the other letters are consonants.) They discovered that some vowels are called short, while others have the long sound that say their own name. The students heard that C and K could sometimes sound the same, as could G and J and C and S; therefore, some totally different letters might have the same sounds. The teacher explained that any word with the letter capitalized was to emphasize the letter and sound in the jingle.

The class looked up the meaning of new vocabulary words and found locations of cities, states, and countries on a map. Reading, spelling, and writing color words, days of the week, and months of the year was practiced. Holidays and even descriptive words, used in the upper grades of elementary school for better writing, were learned and became familiar to them.

The students really had to brainstorm to illustrate a visual picture of something that fit each letter's story jingle. But since they worked as a group, all children enjoyed participating in their collaborative team. The teacher did only four or five a week so that they would remember the jingles better, and a review was done the following day before introducing the next day's jingles. The class would move on, but only if they were ready. Remember, it is okay to take more time when children need to.

IS TRICKERY ALLOWED IN LEARNING?

The older children were informed that we were doing this project to help our school's kindergarten kids learn their letters and sounds. They really loved doing it; they felt smart and important in being able to share their knowledge with the kindergartners. Little did the upper-grade children know that this was an assignment to give them more practice with vowel sounds and new vocabulary words, their meanings, and how they are spelled.

Since the activity was active and interactive, done collaboratively, and engaging to all involved, much more was accomplished. The lessons were done in a fun way, and giggling was allowed. The process and final results appeared magical to all of us. Our new mantra became, "Trickery is not a bad thing when teaching and learning is achieved!"

After learning the entire jingle, we would invite other classes to see the pictures and hear the chant. Soon everyone knew the entire jingle by heart. They could easily find the "mystery word" requested by the teacher and circle it with pencil on a large printout or overhead projector.

The teacher would say, "Please find the word 'Egypt' and circle it," "Can anyone spell that word or country?," "Why do we need to use a capital E?," or "Does anyone know where Egypt is on the map or globe?" On another day, the group could even use their math skills or Google to see how many miles away Egypt was from our country. Think of all the skills a class could incorporate with just one word or silly jingle.

Helpers would circulate to make sure no one was lost. The so-called bad behavior was gone due to the changing, challenging, and interesting lessons with activities using the alphabet jingles. By involving the children in helping to make the jingles, they took ownership.

The teacher could go line by line and let the children raise their hands to choose the mystery word for the class to find. This would happen only if they knew what line we were on and were paying attention. All eyes were totally engaged and glued on their papers. Now they were practicing concentration as well as expanding their verbal skills. The competition between students to become the next teacher was always remarkably fun for adults to witness.

So, is it because teachers have so much power being up front, or do children just like to be chosen as the leader? None of us knew for sure. Human behavior can be studied in another book. In reality, the teacher did not care, as it was working so well for all types of students, whether they were advanced or strugglers. The children were happy to help each other in a cooperative and supportive environment. Each day, they came back excited and wondering what jingle was next.

For the youngest child, just printing a few jingles a day worked the best. The jingle printed with large letters enabled the young children to copy on top of the words or trace over them with pencil or magic marker. Their verbal skills improved, and they learned from each other and through interactions with the teacher.

Our goal was for them to circle the beginning sound we were working on while developing fine motor skills. Finally, they read the jingle to us, first as a group and then alone if they wanted to. No one was ever forced to read, taking the pressure off. Children relax more when they have no fear of the possibility of failing. Later they will try or even whisper read in your ear with encouragement.

If you want to take these jingles one step further, you could print the jingles out with long lines drawn below the word and let the student copy that jingle from directly above the line. For kinesthetic and visual learners, salt boxes work well for single words. Sometimes sugar- and Jell-O-filled box lids are fun but also give cause for licked and sticky fingers. This tasty activity is better used at home. Salt is not as tempting to the young for obvious reasons. Even hands-on spelling of the words works well with plastic or magnetic letters placed on the table or on the rug. Really struggling boys can form letters with clay, yarn, or strings.

Many boys might have trouble copying from the board from the start. Their eye–hand coordination may not be developed yet, so a child might have difficulty when looking up to the board and then back down to the paper in copying. Often they can lose their place. *Always avoid anything leading to frustration.* Think of using strategies of the easiest type and then progressively make them harder. More learning can be accomplished with children while developing better self-confidence.

Children love using individual chalkboards or whiteboards with markers as long as it does not turn into a doodling session. Rules have to be established first and consequences understood before passing out the boards. Students quickly learn that the privilege is lost if they do not follow your directions. No one wants to have to go back to plain paper and pencil if everyone else has an exciting writing board.

THE POWER OF POETRY

In first and second grade, it is better to begin writing by copying fun poems that students read together as a group and memorize beforehand. For instance, in science and reading, our class learned about caterpillars and metamorphosis. After watching the eggs hatch into wormlike caterpillars, we fed the caterpillars, measured them as they grew, and graphed how long the hatching took. The students observed the hatching of their own cocoons and then set the butterflies free. Some children knew they must be set free, but it was difficult for many to lose their new friends that they had observed for so many weeks.

The class and teacher made up the following poem and copied from the whiteboard in front of the classroom. After writing it on large, lined paper, they got to illustrate the poem story. The class painted egg carton caterpillars as well as beautiful tissue butterflies. The butterflies were made to hang from the ceiling for us to marvel at daily. Almost every subject area was covered—reading, writing, verbal skills, math, science, and even art—while having fun with live caterpillars and butterflies. The students sat for only short sessions when writing and made sure to do some jumping jacks in between.

Much of our study was done through observation and movement around the room or by going outside. As said before, the engagement of watching, moving, touching, and feeling all played an important part in what the children learned about the metamorphosis of the butterfly.

Our Cute Cuddly Caterpillar and Mariposa

Caterpillar, caterpillar, brown and furry, winter has come, so you'd better hurry!
Find a big leaf under which to creep; spin a cocoon in which to sleep.
Then when warm weather comes to stay, you'll be a butterfly, and fly away!
Someday soon, your eggs you'll lay, and more cute caterpillars will come to play.

This fun writing exercise as poetry taught the children about the metamorphosis of the butterfly through observation, reading, math graphing, sorting, and illustrations with art.

New vocabulary words were given, contractions were pointed out, the correct use of punctuation was demonstrated, and rhyming words were identified. As you can see, the teacher even put in some Spanish. Writing now did not seem as scary or impossible.

Do not ever forget that children can learn language (speaking, writing, or reading) only if it is presented in ways that make sense to them. Better yet is the learning experience when the activity is fun.

Children's first efforts at writing need not be letter perfect, as stated before. Spelling and grammar can be learned year by year. In the beginning stages of writing, the children should simply get used to the idea of daily writing of some type but in a fun, relaxed way. By playing instrumental CDs or classical music, the child learns that everyone needs to have some creative thinking music to help us write. (Many had never heard of classical music and decided it was "cool" for thinking.)

It's easy to think, "Okay, I taught or helped teach my child to read, whew—I'm glad that is over." But writing might be the hardest thing your child will do all day. By combining reading skills with fine motor skills and adding some spelling, your child is learning to better communicate via the written word—a skill that will be used and refined for the rest of your child's life. When a first grader writes, he must simultaneously recall ideas, vocabulary, and rules of spelling, punctuation, and grammar while writing them on a piece of paper.

GREAT EXPECTATIONS FOR WRITING IN FIRST THROUGH THIRD GRADES

Since all states are embarking on the core standards now, and curricula vary from state to state, it is important to find out the core standards in your own state. However, children working at the standard level at the beginning of first grade will do the following:

- Name and label objects
- Gather, collect, and share information
- Stay on topic (maintain focus)
- Can write in chronological order
- Incorporate storybook language (e.g., "They lived happily ever after") into their writing
- Think in a more extended fashion than they can write so that some thoughts must be extended orally

By the end of first grade, students working at the standard level will do the following:

- Communicate in writing
- Reread their writing to monitor meaning
- Begin to use feedback to change their writing either by adding more text or by making minor revisions
- Revise their writing by inserting text in the middle rather than just at the end
- Make deliberate choices about the language they use
- Use punctuation and capitalization more often than not[4]

At the end of first grade, your child was probably writing full sentences. In second grade, children will continue to further their writing skills by including more detailed aspects of grammar and style. They will be asked to read and write a variety of writing structures, such as letters, plays, and poems.

They will also be introduced to a new writing style: cursive in very few schools now. In second grade, children will begin to read and write a variety of things, and it is generally the first time children will be asked to write book reports, demonstrating reading comprehension with writing skills.

Here's what your child should be able to do before starting second-grade writing:

- Communicate in writing
- Reread their writing to monitor meaning
- Begin to use feedback to change their writing—either by adding more text or by making minor revisions
- Insert text in the middle of their writing rather than just at the end
- Make deliberate choices about the language they use
- Use punctuation and capitalization more often than not

By the end of second grade, students working at the standard level will do the following:

- Write about their own ideas
- Pick out nouns and verbs in sentences
- Explain the problem, solution, or main idea in fiction and nonfiction
- Revise their writing to make it clearer
- Read and understand stories, poems, plays, directories, newspapers, charts, and diagrams
- Write different types of sentences[5]

In third grade, writing becomes much more complicated. Not only will your child be writing book reports, but he will learn to do research papers. Just remember this suggestion concerning confidence from R. E. Shockley: *"Confidence is born in your mind and developed by your thoughts and actions. Therefore you are the author of your confidence."*

Third graders are asked to respond in writing in almost every subject, even math, so they need to know how to write their thoughts and ideas. Third graders will continue to focus on the parts of speech and how to use them to make their writing more interesting. In addition, now that your child can finally print well, it's time to learn and perfect his cursive writing. Again, many schools are now doing away with this form, however.

Want to know what's "normal"? As mentioned, the curriculum varies from state to state, but there are a surprising number of constants. Students who are working at the standard level at the beginning of third grade should be able to do the following:

- Write about their own ideas
- Pick out nouns and verbs in sentences
- Explain the problem, solution, and main idea in fiction and nonfiction
- Revise their writing to make it clearer
- Read and understand stories, poems, plays, directories, newspapers, charts, and diagrams
- Write different types of sentences

Students who are working at the standard level at the *end of third grade* should be able to do the following:

- Communicate in writing
- Use writing to inform others
- Use writing to persuade others
- Identify nouns, verbs, adjectives, and adverbs in a sentence
- Use adjectives to describe things and enhance their writing
- Correctly use conjunctions
- Correctly use common spelling rules
- Identify sentence types
- Write compound sentences[6]

SEVEN HELPFUL WAYS TO HELP BOYS IN WRITING

Many believe now that with computers and keyboards, there is really no need to learn how to write. But children still need to learn to write by hand. Handwriting is much more than simply putting letters on a page. It becomes a huge part of learning to read and even communicate. You will find that developing writing skills reinforces reading skills and that reading skills help with writing. They interact with each other. When children get older and do use the keyboard more and more, the motor control and communication skills they have received through handwriting can help them become better writers. How? They will now know better the way to transfer their thoughts into words when typing. If your child's handwriting continues to be messy and hard to read, even after several years of instruction, here are some hints:

Seven Helpful Hints for Writing More Neatly

1. Take it slowly.

Help your child understand many children struggle with writing because they try to do it too quickly. Encourage him to take more time to form the letters correctly. Remind him, "Practice makes perfect!"

2. *Reinforce letter formation.*

First find out from your child's teacher how the letters are to be correctly formed. Different styles are used in school. Next, encourage your child to practice writing using those patterns over and over. Start with free form, as with salt or sugar boxes, and then move on to lined paper.

3. *Make sure your child has the strength in his hand to write.*

Give your child some resistive-type materials to squeeze, such as Nerf balls or sponges, modeling clay, play dough, squirt toys, small balloons, or even cookie dough to mix. Can you guess what will happen here?

4. *Expose your child to many words.*

Read stories together daily or as often as you can. When in stores, point out words that are all around you that he might know or, when driving, talk about basic street signs he can spell. It will be easier to write and spell words learned first.

5. *Is the pencil properly positioned in his hand?*

Many have trouble grasping the pencil the right way. The pencil should rest near the base of the thumb, held in place with the thumb and index and middle fingers. Bad habits are much harder to break as children grow older. Pencil grips found in office supply stores might help as well.

6. *Erasers help—but not if used in excess.*

Some children want everything letter perfect and then use the eraser too often. However, big holes made in the paper are worse than the messy word. Let them know that erasers are there to help sometimes since everyone makes mistakes, even adults.

7. *Using the keyboard can help some boys.*

Of course, it is better for children to be able to learn how to write by hand so that they can take notes and tests later in school. But for a boy who is really struggling and refusing to write, begin letting him type letters and words. At least he will learn keyboarding skills, enjoy writing more, and associate spelling with words used. Point out to him that some letters, such as "g," "a," and "q," might not be the form that their teacher uses for handwriting.

Depending on the age and ability level of the child, take the time needed to back up to where he is comfortable. There is no problem with pulling out the clay and the use of magical disappearing ink again, especially if it gets him motivated to work harder.

SIGNS TO WATCH OUT FOR IN WRITING

What if your child shows extreme writing problems that you feel might indicate something is wrong? Sometimes writing problems can be a sign of other issues, such as a learning disability, dyslexia (reversal of letters), or a developmental delay. As mentioned over and over in this book, children develop at different rates, and like in adults, handwriting varies greatly among them. Some children will have trouble learning the direction the letters go and how they are to fit within and below the lines. Others struggle to use the cursive form of writing; they have more trouble with letter formation and neatness. Some just have better fine motor skills, and always will.

You should be on the lookout for various signs of problems in handwriting that can affect the child's ability to write. We are not trying to alarm our readers but feel it necessary to point out some things to watch for. If a child has memory problems, then these will prevent him from remembering spelling, grammar, or rules of punctuation. For instance, dysgraphia is a neurological disorder characterized by writing difficulties regardless of reading ability. The child might display odd-shaped letters or misspell words over and over.

Learning disorders may affect as many as one in five people in the United States and can not only inhibit a person's ability to learn and communicate effectively but also directly impact a person's self-esteem. Learning disorders include dyslexia, dysgraphia, dyscalculia, and dyspraxia. Descriptions of these learning disorders and possible signs and symptoms are provided here.

Dyslexia, one most of us have heard about, is a reading disorder characterized by difficulty recognizing letters, learning letter sounds, and identifying rhyming words. Young children with the disorder may also experience delayed language development and have trouble learning to spell and write as they reach school age. Here are some that are not so well known:

- *Dysgraphia* is a learning disability characterized by distorted and incorrect handwriting as well as issues with fine motor skills. Symptoms include problems learning to tie shoes, zip a jacket, and write legibly (i.e., can't form letters properly) and avoiding coloring or other motor activities that most kids enjoy. Some children with dysgraphia have strong verbal skills to compensate for their writing issues and are often good readers. Because little is known about the disorder, it can often be misdiagnosed as dyslexia or dyscalculia.
- *Dyscalculia* is a disorder characterized by problems with learning fundamentals that include one or more basic numeric skills. Often people with this condition can understand very complex mathematical concepts but have difficulty processing formulas or basic addition and subtraction. A person with the disorder may struggle with visual-spatial relationships or processing what he or she hears.
- *Dyspraxia*, also called *apraxia*, is a condition characterized by significant difficulty carrying out routine tasks involving balance, fine motor control, and kinesthetic coordination. Signs of the disorder in early childhood include not reaching developmental milestones on time as well as

clumsy and uncoordinated movements. *Verbal dyspraxia* describes a difficulty in the use of speech sounds that may be the result of a developmental delay in the speech production area of the brain. Verbal dyspraxia may appear as a stand-alone disorder or accompany dyspraxia.[7]

HOW BRAIN BALANCE CAN HELP

At Brain Balance, we believe every child can connect with success. If your child is having difficulty learning to read and write or appears to have marked issues with motor development, we invite you to consider the Brain Balance Program. Our program is a multi-modal approach that includes a comprehensive assessment and 36 sessions of customized sensory-motor work. In addition, your child receives behavioral, cognitive, and academic training, nutritional testing and planning, and an at-home program for continued success. Our approach is a thorough and holistic one that takes the whole child into consideration when designing his or her customized program. Since learning disorders are neurological in origin, strengthening brain communication and improving rhythm and timing can decrease negative symptoms and behaviors.[8]

If a child has attention-deficit/hyperactivity disorder, or ADHD, just sitting still long enough to try to write is almost impossible. Any child with special needs might have difficulty learning to write. If a child has trouble with visual or sequential ordering, then he will usually have trouble with spacing between words and putting his ideas in order. There are many signs that a child may need additional assistance with learning how to write. If the child has totally illegible handwriting and uses a very awkward grip on the pencil, these are indications that more help is needed.

Difficulty forming letters, many misspelled words, uneven spacing between letters, or difficulty with writing even though the child has good spoken language skills may concern a teacher or parent. In addition, speech problems can cause difficulty with word pronunciation, spelling of words, and sentence structure. You may choose to have your struggling child or student assessed by an occupational therapist who can help you decide if your child needs therapy and tutoring or simply an easier fix with more writing practice at home.

WRITING A SIMPLE BOOK: LEARNING TO WRITE BY WIZARDLY WRITING

When referring to a "book" written by a child, the teacher does not mean 206 pages with an introduction, bibliography, and index. A book can be any number of pages written, revised, edited, rewritten, and then stapled together. Naturally, the cover and back pages need to be decorated. Let the child make a title page and number each page at the bottom right-hand side of the paper (let's get in those math skills and sequencing at the same time). The child will love putting his name as the author. The date is helpful if you are saving the book for comparison as the child improves. This improvement will show him that any work of art takes time and practice to be great.

Sometimes it is best for a teacher or parent to first make a very simple book as a sample so that the child does not get too anxious at the thought of making one himself. Pick something interesting to your child and choose words from a list. He can help you brainstorm for words he wants you to use. Often it is wise to get the weekly spelling list from the teacher so that those words can be reinforced and incorporated into his book.

Beginning writers can use inventive spelling, such as "I Luv Butrfliz!" Who cares if the spelling isn't perfect? As long as the child can read what he wrote, the correct spelling will come with time. Pay closer attention to the school's spelling words, however. The teacher will love you forever for the additional help at home—before the spelling test is given.

The Wizard of Writing needs to always start with a capital letter and end with a period or question mark. Other punctuation marks can come little by little with more writing practice. Many children, especially boys, like what is called "Rebus" reading and writing: substituting a picture now and then for a word they do not know how to spell. This additional drawing makes writing and reading less tedious, and bigger ideas can be expressed by pictures drawn in between other words.

Previously, we explained that Wizardly Writing is done on Wednesdays. Then, on Thinking Thoughts Thursday, revising, editing, and the rewriting portions of the book, writing, or story takes place. Thursday is the day to pay more attention to neatness of letterforms. The child needs to learn the differences between revising and editing done on Thursdays. These two parts of any writing process are tricky for children (and sometimes adults) to understand.

Revising is making changes, such as adding or deleting words, reorganizing sentences or ideas, and often responding to comments from the teacher, parent, or peers. On the other hand, editing involves reviewing punctuation, capitalization, grammar, sentence structure, and correcting any mistakes. After a child starts to see that the two parts are different yet equally important, he learns that writing does not happen in one day. Time can be taken on a different day to go back, reread the writing, and, with help, make the necessary changes to make his writing a Wizardly Writing.

REVISING AND EDITING FOR A BOOK IN SEVEN STEPS

Begin by making sure the child knows that revising is not a matter of having done something wrong; it is his chance to make his Wizardly Writing even more magical. For children just learning to write, naturally the revising and editing process will take less time and will be much simpler:

1. *Read the writing out loud to the child exactly as it is written.*

   Ask the child if he could hear or see any words that might be missing. Does he see any ideas missing? After the child has addressed those two questions, read his writing again but see if he hears a beginning, a middle, and an end. If any of these three things are missing, help him make sure they are there with more additions.

2. *Ask the child if he sees any words that might be spelled wrong and tell him that is why it helps to use "inventive spelling" for better writing.*

   Go word by word and let him make a mark by any of the words he is not sure of. This way, you can show him the real spelling and at the same time let him know his inventive spelling made his story longer and even better. Also check for capitalization of people, pets, places, and the beginning of all sentences. Have the child change any words that he used more than once in his Wizardly Writing. If he is old enough to use a dictionary, thesaurus, or word list, show him different words to replace those duplicated words. These tools help with spelling and capitalization. Naturally, when typing, he can access the spell-checker to make sure of the word spelling. Don't we all just love this feature?

3. *For children with more writing experience, you should do all of the things listed in step 2 above and add a few more things.*

   After reading the piece aloud, ask him, "Did you describe what the characters look like? Did you describe what your characters feel? Did you use the right action words with your nouns?" Make any changes he notices with your help. Have the child reread the writing once again. When beginning the editing with a more experienced writer, start by taking a closer look at the paper. Now have the child reread the piece and think about the order of sentences and paragraphs. You might see if he can determine whether to change the order of one or two sentences to help make the writing more clear. Ask if there is a way to make his point just once. Make sure that each paragraph has one main idea.

4. *Now the Wizard of Writing is ready to edit the magical masterpiece for spelling and grammar.*

   Just like with the younger writer, you should check for misspelled words and capitalization. Have the writer also check for apostrophes in contractions, such as "won't," "can't," and "he'll." Look for any missing apostrophes in possessives, such as "cat's paw," "boy's bike," and "dog's bone."

5. *Reading through his work several times not only is reading practice but also increases the likelihood of finding more errors on his own.*

Do not try to change all the errors at once; in the first reading, work on spelling only, and in the next reading, focus on capitalization and so on. Your Wizard of Writing will feel more confident little by little and not as overwhelmed. Naturally, any author or Wizard must not try to edit or revise until after the first draft on Wednesday is done. You want his writing to flow and not be slowed by all the correcting along the way. That is why writing is a process and needs at least two days to complete the masterpiece well. If the child is having trouble coming up with just the right word, you can come back to it later or give him a rhyming hint, such as "The word you might like to use here rhymes with 'bikes.'" Again, with boys and writing, the last thing you want is frustration or refusal to continue. Step-by-step wins the race.

6. *Give your young Wizard of Writing some practice revising.*

You could have him write a letter to his best friend about what he did yesterday. Then have him write the same letter to Grandma or Grandpa. After rereading both, see if you together can find any differences. This letter writing is just a way for your child to double-check for errors by writing the same thing from memory twice. This is a great practice for him at sequencing as well.

7. *Finally, and most important, do not forget the "power of the pen" for future publishing.*

When both of you take the time to create a magical masterpiece that is also illustrated, the pride and self-esteem gained can be amazing. When the Wizard turns his masterpiece into a book for the class or library, uses it for a wall or bulletin board display, or even reads it to the entire class, these events can be special. Just sitting in the Author's Chair suddenly lets him see that writing can be fun and very rewarding! As mentioned previously, the promise of videotaping does wonders.

THE AUTHOR'S CHAIR FOR THE WIZARD OF WRITING

As a teacher or parent, always remember to try to develop appreciation for the way boys like to write. Boys usually write for each other, while girls write for the teacher in school. Let boys write about what they want, even if it is a little silly or gross to you. In order to get boys to enjoy writing, we have to become more tolerant of their subject matter and allow even a little violence (but only if there is a good guy who wins). We as teachers have a very hard time with this, and certainly the parents can be just as reluctant. The true goal should be to encourage boys to write more and more. Then they might not groan at the thought or suggestion of doing it. They may even one day become the next Stephen King—and why not?

Children soon learn that good writing is not done in one day. An author needs to be a Wizard and use his magic pencil over and over to make writing wonderful. Illustrations can be done in any medium, including pencil, crayons, markers, or even watercolors, after the writing. This final drawing is like the dessert part—after eating the broccoli or peas. When the author knows it is the best he can do and you agree, ask the classroom teacher if he can share it at school.

Before the big show, he can practice by reading his book many times to his parents, brothers, sisters, grandmas, grandpas, and especially pets. Remind him that "practice makes perfect." Animals are the best listeners of all and never interrupt or point out mistakes that they might notice in your book. In reality, we need to learn more courtesy from our pets. Do not forget reading to stuffed animals since we all know they will never complain or walk away from a boring story.

The first book will be the most difficult, as you will discover, but after doing one each week, the writing process will come more easily. Your Wizard of Writing will look forward to Wednesday and Thursday. He can save all his books to show visitors in his own library of written books. The creative books will become keepsakes for years to come and maybe to show their own children some day.

Tell your child or students, "If your writings are good enough, your teacher or librarian might put them in the Publisher's Place." This is a real incentive to work even harder at home.

We are all still asking: What is causing boys, in general, to keep falling further and further behind? This gender gap in education is due to the way boys are taught (or maybe not taught). Why are so many boys turning off in education by fourth grade or earlier? The research has been out there for decades about how boys learn differently than girls—all the more reason to teach our boys in a more conscientious way. If we do, perhaps one day they will say, "This Wizardly Writing is fun!"

WHAT IS THE SECRET TO ANY SUCCESS?

Finally, most of us want to know the secret to success at anything, whether it be in reading, writing, math, verbal skills, science, music, getting along with others, sports, or any other skill being developed. The necessary time put into doing something well is not as easy as it may sound. The child has to have determination, perseverance, and a desire to improve. The desire might be the obstacle when it comes to literacy skills as we see in most children, especially in boys. Naturally, boys will be more determined to perfect a certain skill, such as football, soccer, baseball, or any sport, *before* caring about literacy skills.

This last observation about success and how we might all achieve success in writing is another reason teachers and parents have to start earlier in presenting these literacy skills as important tools needed to pursue their interests and passions. By making the learning more boy friendly and meaningful to each unique student, we have a better chance at changing the trend of boys falling further and further behind in school. Read and reread carefully what Ralph Marston says the "secret to success" boils down to. All of us, as teachers of our future generations, could learn much from this evaluation of success and how one can obtain it:

Success Is Not a Secret

Success is not a secret. It is a choice, a choice that is made over and over again. The choice that brings success and achievement is more than a one-time event.

It is a choice that is integrated into every moment of life. It's one thing to decide upon a course of action and then leave it at that. Such a strategy will leave you with nothing but empty wishes and good intentions.

Real achievement comes from choosing to achieve, again and again, moment after moment, until the goal is attained.

Real achievement comes from choosing to achieve, and then continually reaffirming that choice with action.

Choosing success is really quite easy. To actually reach that success, just keep on choosing it.

Keep on choosing, and acting on that choice, for as long as necessary. And anything is within your reach.[9]

Anything in life is possible if you work hard enough. We always hear that said so often by adults, especially teachers and parents, even coaches. However, "working" is the operative word and is the hardest part to do for many boys. Again, "practice makes perfect," or at least practice can help improve any skill.

With that secret in mind, let's move on to one of the keys for any success, self-esteem and self-motivation, discussed in chapter 6.

NOTES

1. Dave Barry, *Dave Barry's Complete Guide to Guys* (New York: Random House, 1995).

2. Ralph Marston, "Give Yourself a Little Push," *The Daily Motivator*, September 4, 2014 (www.greatday.com).

3. Quoted in Peg Tyre, *The Trouble with Boys: A Surprising Report Card on our Sons, Their Problems at School, and What Parents and Educators Must Do* (New York: Crown Publishing, 2008).

4. From Amy James, *First Grade Success: Everything You Need to Know to Help Your Child Learn* (Hoboken, NJ: Wiley Jossey-Bass, 2005).

5. From James, *Second Grade Success: Everything You Need to Know to Help Your Child Learn* (Hoboken, NJ: Wiley Jossey-Bass, 2005).

6. From James, *Third Grade Success: Everything You Need to Know to Help Your Child Learn* (Hoboken, NJ: Wiley Jossey-Bass, 2005).

7. Brain Balance Information Centers (www.brainbalancecenters.com).

8. Brain Balance Information Centers (www.brainbalancecenters.com).

9. Ralph Marston, "Success Is Not a Secret," *The Daily Motivator*, November 9, 2013 (www.greatday.com).

6

Self-Success Leads to Self-Fulfillment and Better Self-Esteem

It is not what we get, but who we become, what we contribute . . . that gives meaning to our lives.

—Tony Robbins

EARLY PATTERNS OF SELF-ESTEEM

We have discovered that young children are already learning to judge themselves in relation to others. For the first time, they find that their goals are set not by an internal clock but rather by the outside world and school. Now this can be a rude awakening to them.

At age one, the child struggles to just walk, and then the shock of adult expectations meets students face-to-face in the classroom. We know that young children have not learned the difference between effort and ability. If they fail when trying to do something, they might decide they will never be able to do that task, which is very self-defeating.

The patterns of self-esteem start very early in the lives of children, who begin to learn that success happens with effort and persistence. Self-esteem is similar to self-worth, or how much a person values him- or herself. This can change from time to time, day to day, and even year to year. Overall, self-esteem tends to develop from infancy and keeps going until we are adults. However, like many traits, once people reach adulthood, it is harder to make changes in how they see themselves.

Since many children have trouble finding things to become successful at when they are very young, we need to help them choose tasks we know they *can* do. Helping around the house or classroom is a great way to start. It can help you, as it makes the child feel important and needed at the same time. Remember, when you offer a sincere compliment to your child, it gives him a reputation to live up to in a positive way. It encourages him to shine in your eyes, and it is a way of telling him you appreciate and love him.

When you offer compliments, not only do you make that child feel good, but you get to feel good as well. It is an immediate payback.

> The secret to success is to do common things uncommonly well.
>
> —John D. Rockefeller

There are many easy tasks that young children can do and love to do. In the classroom and at home, there are endless jobs that help teach responsibility. Being the light and hall monitors, office messengers, whiteboard cleaners, calendar teacher, line leader, and so on, may seem silly to us, but to a child these are powerful positions! All children love to feel selected as a leader, and this selection is even more important to those who are not succeeding as well at school. Everyone can do something well. We may just have to look harder.

Even at home, you may find that tasks such as setting the table, taking out the garbage, calling others for dinner, helping to clean out the garage, and feeding the pets may seem like "chores," but many children enjoy being chosen to do them. These leadership positions are a wonderful incentive for better behavior, which is great for the teacher, the parent, and the child.

The process of finding self-fulfillment and better self-esteem sometimes has to be done in reverse order. When a child has positive self-esteem, it leads to self-fulfillment, and then self-success comes more readily. This process has much to do with the way challenges are viewed and how one responds to them. We have heard people say that the "power of positive thinking" is huge when it comes to what we desire out of life.

Joel Osteen, pastor of Lakewood Church in Houston, Texas, said the following about our thoughts, choices, and imagination and the effect they will have on our destiny:

> It's so important that we create the right image in our minds because the way we see ourselves is what we move toward. Visualization is simply seeing yourself the way you want to be. It's creating a picture in your mind of accomplishing your goals, overcoming your obstacles, and fulfilling your God-given destiny. Our imagination is extremely powerful. The way we see ourselves in these pictures that we create, over time, will not only drop down into our spirit, but if we continue to dwell on them, they get into our subconscious mind.
>
> Once something is in the subconscious, it's just like gravity; it pulls us toward it. All these internal forces are released, and more often than not, we become just like we've imagined. If you'll create a picture in your imagination of something

you want, a dream coming to pass, a business succeeding, a picture of yourself healthy and whole; if you'll keep that image in front of you, that's what you'll move toward. What you see right in front of you, that's what will happen. Keep the right things in your mind and the right things in your life![1]

GOOD OR POOR SELF-ESTEEM?

We all have known people and children who are confident—who will try anything and love the challenge. Others fear the unknown, lack self-confidence, and are perfectly happy to never try anything new. Why is this? Is it in our genes or the way we are raised? Probably, a little of both. Usually the first type becomes more successful in life.

> Our words reveal our thoughts, manners reveal our self-esteem, actions reflect our character, and habits predict our future.
>
> —R. E. Shockley

Healthy self-esteem is like a child's suit of armor against the challenges and pitfalls he might have to face in the world. Boys who know their strengths and also their weaknesses and who feel good about themselves seem to have an easier time handling conflicts and resisting negative pressures in their environment. We see those children smiling more and enjoying life in general. They are more optimistic and fun to be around. They seem eager to try new things and are willing to try harder. Much of this can be attained by shared reading in the classroom or at home.

For example, through exposure to books with different points of view, children begin to develop the ability to make carefully considered choices. This is an important step toward *critical thinking* as they grow. Dealing effectively with different points of view is something that can be learned during the communication of reading discussions.

Another important point is that reading can encourage a child or student to explore other possibilities and take his imagination to distant corners of the world. This is a wonderfully natural way to learn about differences in cultures, languages, and beliefs—all critical for world peace to ever become possible. Reading helps us understand these cultural differences and opens up a whole world of experiences. Many will never get the chance to travel outside their own country, but they can certainly visit any place in the world through books.

In contrast, boys with low self-esteem can find challenges to be sources of anxiety and frustration on a daily basis. Those who think poorly of themselves have a harder time finding solutions to problems. If given to self-critical thoughts such as "I can't do anything right!" or "This is too hard," they may become withdrawn, passive, or depressed. Worse yet, some frustrated children can turn to aggressive behaviors.

When faced with a new or difficult challenge, they might say, "I can't do it" without even trying first. They are more pessimistic and not much fun to be around. They do not want to attempt new things or even want to try. Making friends for these boys can be more difficult. We need to impress on all children the following:

> Know and believe in yourself and what others think won't disturb you.
>
> —William Feather

Self-esteem can also be defined as feeling capable while also feeling loved. A child who is happy with an achievement but does not feel loved may eventually experience low self-esteem. Likewise, a child who feels loved but is hesitant about his own abilities can also develop low self-esteem. Healthy self-esteem is established when there is a *good balance of love and ability*.

It is very important to think about developing and promoting self-esteem during early childhood. Positive patterns begun early can last throughout life. All children will try and fail from time to time, but the goal is to finally succeed by not giving up. Children develop their own ideas about their capabilities. They are creating a self-concept based on interactions with other people or other children Therefore, parental involvement is the key to helping children form accurate, healthy self-perceptions.

Parents, teachers, and coaches can promote healthy self-esteem by showing encouragement and enjoyment in many areas. Do not focus on one specific area, such as writing, spelling, reading, or math. The child may think he is not good at something and therefore is only as valuable as his scores or ability. Worse yet is when a child has trouble with one subject and presumes he will have trouble with all other subjects.

If children would realize that one year is totally different from the next, many of their feelings of failure or lack of ability would dissipate. Adults need to realize this as well.

> A birthday is just the first day of another 365-day journey around the sun. Enjoy the trip!
>
> —Author unknown

Self-esteem changes as children grow. It is often fine-tuned or changed because it is affected by a child's experiences and new perceptions of self. Naturally, it is important to know the signs of both healthy and unhealthy self-esteem. Boys with low self-esteem may not want to try anything new and may speak negatively about themselves: You hear them saying, "I'm just dumb!," I will never learn how to do this right!," "Everyone else gets this but me," or "Why do I have to do this, anyway?"

Boys might show a *low tolerance for frustration* by giving up easily. Often they will wait for someone else to do it for them. These boys are overly critical of and easily disappointed in themselves. They see temporary setbacks as permanent and intolerable. Unfortunately, this negativity can put boys at risk for stress and mental health problems and makes it more difficult to solve the problems they face. With time, practice, and more patience, changes can be remarkable.

> Just as diamonds are formed under pressure over time, so strength and character is forged from hard work, struggle and failure.
>
> —R. E. Shockley

On the flip side, we have the lucky children with healthy self-esteem who tend to enjoy interacting with other children and adults. They are comfortable in social settings and enjoy group activities as well as independent tasks. When there is a challenge, they know how to work toward finding solutions. Fortunately in learning new things, the boy with self-confidence is not afraid to say, "I do not understand this." He is not afraid to ask for help so that he can be successful.

Boys with good self-esteem know their strengths and weaknesses and can accept them with optimism. Teachers and parents can make the difference for these boys by using the seven Es of teaching, and again, encouragement is the most important of those seven.

When a child feels encouraged by others in all that he does, he stays engaged and excited. With consistent enthusiasm, the final result will evolve into his success.

> The first requisite for success is your ability to apply your physical and mental energies to one problem incessantly without growing tired.
>
> —Charles Caleb Colton

SEVEN STEPS TO HELP BOYS BUILD SELF-ESTEEM

1. Be a positive role model.

When you as a teacher or parent are excessively harsh on children, with high expectations, or unrealistic about the child's abilities and limitations, that child will feel *inadequate*. Children need much more encouragement than adults. Any adults who point out the smallest success can change behavior for the better. Take the time to notice.

2. *Be very careful how you say things.*

Children are very sensitive to the words or advice of parents, teachers, and coaches. Remember to praise the child not only for a job well done but also for all the effort. You can be truthful but encouraging. If the child does not do well at something, such as soccer, you can say, "Well, you did not make the team, but I am really proud of the effort you put forth." Make certain you reward effort and completion rather than just outcome.

As discussed earlier, the task must be developmentally appropriate for that child. Helping boys overcome disappointments can help them learn what they are good at and what they are not so good at. As adults, it is good to point out the areas you had trouble with as a child. For example, say, "I could not kick a ball to save my life at your age!" If you can use warmth and humor, they soon learn more about their abilities and appreciate what makes them unique. In addition, they learn *acceptance of self*, which is so difficult with many boys in today's competitive society.

3. *Identify and redirect inaccurate beliefs.*

It is important for parents to identify children's beliefs about themselves, whether those beliefs are about perfection, attractiveness, ability, or anything else. We must help boys *set more accurate standards* and be more realistic in evaluating themselves. This will help them have a healthier self-concept. To do this correct identification, a parent, teacher, or coach will need to be observant of each and every child under his or her care and might make dated anecdotal notes in a booklet of the entire class.

Inaccurate perceptions of self can become reality to young children. A child who does very well in school but struggles with math may think that he cannot do math or that he is a bad student. Not only is this a false generalization, but it is also a belief that can set up a child for failure. Encourage children to see a situation in a more objective way. You could say, "You are a good student. You do great in school. Math is a subject that you need to spend more time on. Don't worry, as we can work on it together." We can make a real difference using the most important "E": *encouragement*.

4. *Be spontaneous and affectionate.*

Your love will help boost a child's self-esteem. Give hugs and tell children you are proud of them when you notice them putting effort toward something at which they previously failed. Put happy notes in your child's lunch sack or lunch box: "I think you are a terrific boy! Love, from Dad." (Mom may already be doing this.) Just imagine how extra special it would feel for a child to get a surprise note from Dad. It takes such a little time to make a special difference for a child—at school or anywhere.

Give compliments often and honestly but without overdoing it. Having an "inflated sense of self" can lead to other children putting them down. Bragging can become socially isolating. In addition, undeserved compliments can set up a child for failure when someone else is evaluating his ability. Eventually, we want children to feel good internally by doing what they know is the best choice to solving their own problems, without advice or praise from us. *The goal is for our children to become independent of our constant praise or advice and to do the right thing naturally.*

5. *Make sure you create a safe, loving home or classroom for all children.*

Children who do not feel safe and are bullied often are likely to develop very poor self-esteem. A boy who is exposed to parents who fight and argue repeatedly may feel he has no control over his circumstances and may often blame himself.

The child can also feel depressed and helpless. Watch for signs of abuse by others, problems in school, trouble with peers, and other things that might affect a child's self-esteem. Catching the problem early can make a lifetime difference for that child. *Encourage your children and students to talk to you or other trusted adults about solving problems that are bothering them.*

6. *Help children become involved in constructive experiences.*

Activities that encourage cooperation rather than competition are especially helpful in building self-esteem. The art of compromise is a valuable skill we must teach children early in life. The use of older children as tutors in all subjects is excellent for both the tutor and the child. Volunteering for and contributing to your local community, such as bringing items to a food bank, can have lasting effects on self-esteem for all involved. *We all feel great when we feel we are "needed" by others.*

Another important opportunity for a child is attending some type of camp. The variety of children's and teens' camp experiences can be overwhelming. From cooking to hockey and even art, there really is something for every child, including those with disabilities.

Camp may not be possible or even desirable for some. However, camp, whether part day, full day, or overnight, can have many benefits for children. Peter Scales of the American Camp Association, a well-known author and educator and senior fellow at the Search Institute, has stated, "Camps help young people discover and explore their talents, interests, and values. Most schools do not satisfy all these needs. Kids who have had these kinds of camping experiences end up being healthier and have fewer problems which concern us all."

Whether camps are responsible for happier kids or whether happier kids are able to attend camp is debatable. Regardless, the truth is that camps can have a tremendous impact on children and can create lasting fond memories. So whether your child attends camp or simply spends more time playing and picnicking out of doors with friends and family, there is much more fun to be experienced with hands-on activities.

7. *Find professional help early if necessary.*

When you suspect that your child or student has very low self-esteem, consider bringing in experts as soon as possible. Child therapists and counselors can help the child with coping strategies and to be able to deal with the problems at school or home in ways that help children feel better about their choices. We cannot think that low self-esteem will go away as the child gets older; it will usually become worse.[2]

Therapy might help boys learn to view themselves and the world more realistically as well as help with problem solving. Developing the confidence to understand when you can deal with a problem and when you should ask for help is vital to self-esteem. Taking responsibility and pride in who you are is a positive sign of better self-esteem. With so many years of growth and change, we know that children will pass in and out of how they view themselves; *our job is to encourage them on positively.*

RELEVANCE OF REWARDS

There is much controversy when it comes to using rewards with children for any behavior or action. Some feel that it sends the wrong message. These people believe that it is teaching children that by doing what is expected, they are still rewarded. They fear that it sets children up for disappointment when they become adults. Furthermore, they want the child to feel the reward internally and not by an external representation. However, children are still trying to learn what adults' expectations are. They need immediate encouragement so they will repeat the acceptable or desired behaviors.

Small weekly allowances can help with a child's incentive to do certain chores, such as making his bed, taking out the garbage, setting the table, cleaning his room, and so on. If you want it to be a learning activity at the same time, make sure he becomes familiar with the value of individual coins and dollar bills and the importance of saving. The monthly counting of what has been earned is valuable. The child's having a goal to save for helps him do subtraction and addition of how much is needed to accomplish the purchase. Besides, these are real-life skills, even if our money does lose value.

Sticker charts are fine if the task is not out of reach for the child. For boys at home or in a classroom, receiving a colorful sticker for staying on task, good behavior, helping others, bringing back papers, or returning a library book, is fine. When a child is very young, he needs *immediate gratification* for doing what is expected. Determining how society views certain behaviors is a learning process. The child has to learn little by little with reinforcement for the correct choice.

When that child can put up his own shiny star and count the ones he has accumulated, he sees the reward as a validation of success, sending a positive message to his brain. In addition, he is practicing math skills and comparative graphing.

Over the years, the child should develop his own self-pride and not need reinforcements, such as stickers. Verbal compliments can mean even more.

Posting scores or grades for all to see is *unacceptable*. Why do we even need grades in elementary school? Children soon know how to grade what they do when compared to their peers. The assessments given and recorded into their portfolio lets the correct people see how that child is doing; his strength and weaknesses are evident. However, the portfolio is private from other classmates and off-limits to snoopy eyes. Through daily observation and reviewing work in the portfolio, parents and teachers know how to change instruction to fit the needs of that unique child.

Children need to pace themselves according to their developmental age, not their chronological age. Good teachers know this and will reach out to children at whatever level they may be learning. This pace is almost impossible to predict beforehand. Some children come to kindergarten already reading, while others have trouble identifying letters or writing their names. Rewards are given for effort, not for being on grade level.

Surprisingly, by fourth grade some of the slowest readers have a spurt of learning, as do many with their size. Many students can even catch up in a few weeks or months in reading or math with the proper instruction and guidance. Tutors can be invaluable.

Rewards, as a "certificate of excellence," can do wonders for progress and self-esteem. Having the teacher and principal sign the award can make all the difference. Even the simple addition of a taped-on sugarless candy dresses up paper awards unbelievably. All children love to be recognized for a job well done.

ADVANTAGES OF CROSS-AGE TUTORING

Mixed grade levels help the boy who is either advanced or behind in his classroom. It provides a *perfect environment* for struggling boys as well as for those who are ahead of the others. In addition, many studies have shown that retention usually does not work to the child's advantage and can stifle him when it comes to self-esteem.

Struggling boys can even help the lower-grade children in reading and other skills. They then feel more competent at their own level and are encouraged to try harder to be selected for this important coaching assignment. Being asked to tutor other children can do much for a boy having trouble with basic skills and weak self-confidence. Number recognition, basic math skills, partner reading, learning new vocabulary words, spelling simple words, writing letters, writing their name, and practicing letter sounds are just a few things a struggler can do with a younger child.

This sharing of knowledge is wonderful for all involved. We often have seen that children learn better from other children. It appears that they "speak the same language of learning." Observing this is heartwarming.

Showing responsibility and good behavior can be just the added incentive needed for many children wanting to be the "teacher" or "coach" for another child. This privilege can be taken away when the child's behavior changes from positive to negative. Naturally, the child soon learns that he, not the teacher, is responsible for his own choices.

If the child loses the privilege of helping others, it is the choice he made by his unacceptable behavior. Point out to him that everyone can have a bad day, even adults. Remind him of the following:

> Every day may not be good but there is something *good* in everyday—
> I encourage you to find the *joy* in every day.
>
> —Rock Christopher

Major problems of self-worth often appear during the dreaded testing times so prevalent in schools now. Whether it is the weekly spelling list, a pop quiz, or state-mandated testing, a child who is aware of his weaknesses can really feel stressed out. The same can be true for a child of high achievement with fear of missing a question. This early intense pressure, felt as early as kindergarten, can set the tone for feelings about school and testing in the future. All children need to realize the following:

> Mistakes are the portals of discovery!
>
> —James Joyce

Some classes give spelling tests to children before they even can read. We all know that children can easily memorize words and spelling by sight, but is it retained for long? Why spend time learning how to spell words we have not yet learned to read? This requirement just proves again how backward and *developmentally inappropriate* much of our curriculum is in today's classroom.

Competition for boys is a huge part of them, and when they find out that they cannot compete because of size or ability, often it is easier for children to just give up. Peer group involvement is constant, and the students can soon see "survival of the fittest" at its worst. *Embarrassment can last a lifetime, and feeling inadequate, whether real or perceived, might last forever.* Children must remember what Ralph Waldo Emerson stated: "To be yourself in a world constantly trying to make you into something else is a great accomplishment!"

As teachers, parents, or coaches, it is important for us to compliment any small success and encourage children to try and try again. Give them stories of things that were hard for you and get the male role models involved as much as possible. A coach, brother, uncle, father, or grandfather needs to take a daily part in helping a son know he is wonderful as he is. Life changes ability and circumstances, so we all have to learn the word "perseverance."

To reiterate, often we confuse the number of years children have been in school with brain development. A boy who has been in preschool for several years still has a five-year-old brain on entering kindergarten. Starting reading, writing, and math earlier and earlier is only more frustrating to children who take a little longer to mature and learn basic skills. Sadly, our educational system continues to begin these skills earlier and earlier, with the hopes that children will compete well on mandated assessments.

We all learn differently, yet we all can learn with time and patience given by all who teach us. Keep saying that "patience is a virtue" to help during frustrating times.

UNDERACHIEVEMENT AND UNDERMOTIVATION

The absence of a goal is like aimlessly shooting to hit an unidentified target.

—Marcela Bennett

Marcela Bennett knows how important it is to have a goal and then focus one's efforts toward that attainable goal. *Children need to realize that goals are not something that happens through wishing and hoping; sincere effort must be involved daily.*

Parents, teachers, coaches, administrators, and even boys often attribute undermotivation to their low self-esteem. This makes sense. Parents and teachers will often remark that this low self-esteem is the cause of the under-motivation. Unfortunately, they seem to notice this later in the school years when in the early years it could be reversed. The undermotivation is not truly noticed until the upper grades in both elementary and middle schools when in fact this lack of motivation was building from much earlier. The important opportunity to help change their lack of motivation is missed.

> You are the only one who can use your ability. It is an awesome respon-sibility.
>
> —Zig Ziglar

This quote certainly lets us know that if we do not use our ability to its full-est potential, then we have lost the chance for success at its best.

When a boy has trouble performing required tasks in school, he deter-mines that it is his lack of ability. He sees that others do better than he does and starts to feel incompetent. Many times, it clouds his judgment of even trying or asking for help. Later in life, he realizes that reading is an educational tool and that, in order to complete schooling, he must be able to read textbooks, manuals, guides, and so on, and that the hardest part is in understanding them. As some boys get older, they feel like giving up this daunting challenge of reading.

Here is where cross-age tutors can change an undermotivated child or stu-dent by reading with them. Of course, teachers, parents, and peer tutors can show this child how to ask for help. By interacting with this child while read-ing, the activity will naturally lead to questions. This teaches children how to ask for help and how to give help; the exposure to reading enables children to better express their thoughts and ideas. *Reading together encourages self-expression, which is vital.*

More and more reading can foster independence as well. While reading together, even the youngest child will begin to feel independent because of the interaction as an equal with an adult or older tutor. Children feel more empowered by being a valuable part of the reading experience. *Independence is one of the greatest attributes a child can develop in life.* This independence will give him the courage to try new things.

For children who struggle continually, without the help needed to progress, school can become a daily nightmare. We need to help them think of mistakes as the continual opportunity to learn and change. Without mistakes, there would be no growth or reason to change. The tasks he is asked to do may be totally developmentally inappropriate for him. He may become unengaged and even a discipline problem due to his deep frustration. Compare this to an adult being put into a job for which he or she has no former training and being expected to do well. Imagine the frustration.

Naturally, there are many other reasons besides developmentally inappropriate lessons and tasks. Problems within the family can mark that child forever. The reason for the beginning of depression and underachievement can be attributed to almost anything traumatizing the development of the male brain during learning times. For instance, divorce can be a huge factor. Depression resulting from the divorce of a child's parents is likely to affect performance in social, academic, or athletic endeavors. If a parent or teacher notices undermotivation after a parental separation or divorce, it is important to get some *therapeutic interventions* as soon as possible.

Many times, it is difficult for the child to even talk about the hurt being experienced and often feels he might have caused the separation or divorce. We cannot even imagine the guilt a child would experience with this misconception. Here is where reading specific books can help tremendously. It would make sense, then, that through reading, we can find new ways to explain difficult concepts, such as divorce, death, sexual abuse, long illness, and so on, in ways that do not overwhelm our children.

Setting aside time to read to our students and children creates an emotional space for us to share feelings and thoughts. We can see that others have the same problems we have. Reading together and solving problems gives our children a start in developing the skills of teamwork, too. *This teamwork is one of the first indicators of success in school.*

No one likes to think about the physical, sexual, or emotional abuse of any child. Sadly, this abuse might happen more than we even know and can certainly scar the child forever. Again, as with divorce or separation, the child may even blame himself. If a child was abused in his younger years, he might be still having post-traumatic stress symptoms in the form of nightmares. This stress may continue into his late teens and adulthood. Talking about any type of abuse is difficult but can be therapeutic in the future.

Stress hormone levels do not decrease just because the unwanted sexual, emotional, or physical abuse has stopped. Not surprisingly, many boys who have been abused turn to alcohol, drugs, and high-risk behaviors as an escape. Learning in school can spiral farther away from any success.

Another symptom can be a lack of attachment. A child might use his failure to learn as an attention-getting device. If there is no grandparent, godparent, or other mentors available to the boy during early childhood and the parents are also gone from the home most of the time, the boy may suffer from insecurity. The lack of attachment can lead to supervision problems, latchkey risky behavior, early sexual activity, media addiction, and becoming unengaged in school.[3]

Sometimes the boy will overplay his experimentation in order to get attention from his caregiving adults. As we found in the classroom, any attention received, even if negative, is better than no attention. The child may believe that by doing these risky behaviors and/or underachieving in school, he is punishing his parents as well. The boy may hope that he will make his parents angry and disappointed enough to pay more attention to him. When parents are not available, the boy needs loving members of the extended family or mentors to become involved with him.

The companionship of a dog is one of the best remedies for lack of attachment, low self-esteem, and low self-confidence in general. We have all witnessed how much love and sharing a dog has to give to anyone who loves that dog. When we talk about a dog being man's best friend, there is no denying that truth. Even hardened criminals have made dramatic changes in their own behavior by being responsible for the care and life of a dog assigned to them. Dogs can seem to break down all barriers.

Sick and elderly patients perk up when a dog is brought into their depressing state of affairs. Dogs seem to be empathetic and comforting to anyone with a problem. Perhaps the same treatment should be considered with any boy at risk. Dogs love people unconditionally, are always upbeat, and are eager to wag their tails and lick one's face with unending love to give. Why wouldn't that behavior make anyone feel better?

Recently, the Internet showed a touching picture of a dog and a soldier at an airport. The soldier was still dressed in his fatigues. He looked totally exhausted from travel and was simply trying to catch a few minutes of sleep on the cold, hard floor of the airport during a layover. His canine partner, a German shepherd, was on guard and alert while lying on top of his master, devotedly watching out for anyone approaching who might harm his buddy. The caption above the photo was "I bet no one goes over and shakes him to awaken him! Sleep soundly soldier." There is no measure of loyalty greater than that shown in the photo. *"A worthy goal in life is to be as good a person as your dog thinks you are."* Whoever said that had an enormous sense of wisdom.

The following passage from *The Daily Motivator*, written by Ralph Marston, is great advice for every one of us: teachers, parents, coaches, administrators, and especially children, who sadly feel they want to give up. We must make that choice to "make it good!"

Make It Good

Even when you've had it bad, you can choose to make it good. With what you have from where you are, no matter where you have been, now you can make it good. The easy choices are to whine, to complain, to blame, or to simply do nothing. The best choice, however, is to make it good. Take the victories, the defeats, the frustrations, the successes, the joys and the disappointments, and with it all, make it good. Take this moment, this situation, this environment, this opportunity, this challenge, and make it good. There's nothing you can do to change what has already happened. What you can do now is make it good. Don't just talk about it, or plan to do it, or wonder if you can. Get busy, get going, get committed and make it good. This is your life and this is your opportunity to make a difference. This is your great chance to make it good, so do.[4]

Studies have shown that there is a huge relationship between underperformance and undermotivation in men who grew up in impoverished social conditions to the number of males in prison or institutions.[5] Many times, boys who are raised in poverty and who lack motivation to learn with words attend schools that teach by a verbal system. These boys must listen to lessons that hardly ever pertain to their daily lives. Teachers are often untrained in the way boys' minds work and unfamiliar with their lives. With so many more of today's children in poverty, additional training for teachers should be available.

HERE ARE SOME IMPORTANT FACTS

Did you know that children raised in poverty use fewer words than other children? Ruby Payne, author of a *Framework for Understanding Poverty*, points out some studies that were done in the 1990s. She found that children raised on welfare, on average, hear 616 words per hour. Children raised by working-class parents hear 1,251 words per hour. Children raised by professional-class parents hear 2,153 words per hour.[6] Are you now wondering who had to do the counting?

It would follow suit that the use of many words is crucial in today's educational structures. Impoverished children are not receiving that verbal stimulation equal to other children. *We have learned already that most boys in this group may use fewer words than girls and have a natural disadvantage at school.*

Malnutrition and dietary deficiencies are more common in homes of poverty than in working-class or professional-class homes. However, good nutrition in any home has a *direct relationship to how a brain learns*. Schools try to do their best in providing meals to these impoverished children. To start a good day of learning, we all need a good breakfast to get our engines running. We see that all the time in television commercials, but unfortunately many of the pushed products would not give much quality fuel to anyone. Too much sugar can almost be worse than no breakfast at all.

Dangerous social conditions, as with the constant threat of violence, can create a different hierarchy of survival needs than conditions in neighborhoods where violence is less common. When social survival requires the young boy to protect himself or his family, the constant pressure is stressful. This protection is usually done through gangs or other social networks.

Becoming unmotivated in school is natural for these boys. For many of them, performing well in school is not a worthwhile use of their time; in fact, as they get older, it might leave them or their families vulnerable to greater poverty or to death.[7]

Today, one out of four African-American males is in jail or under court supervision. This statistic should give great concern to any of us involved in helping boys. Each ethnic, racial, and socioeconomic group of males has its own type of need for help with personal motivation and with their social actions.[8]

Gifted children need to be challenged more in our schools. On the other hand, when gifted boys are undermotivated, it is helpful to remember that low interest and negative attitudes toward school causes low achievement, too. Their nonachievement and undermotivation result in other problems, such as the following:

- Low academic self-esteem
- Negative attitudes toward teachers
- Low motivation and self-motivation skills
- Negative attitudes toward school
- Negative attitude toward classroom involvement
- Low goal-setting and self-evaluation skills
- Refusal to complete homework or read at home

These are problems that we need to address sooner rather than later.

Sometimes boys act indifferently, as if they don't care, and it can be a vicious cycle. They may feel bored and decide there is no reason to learn what they are being taught. We might want to agree with them in some instances.

As these boys get older, they have not learned good study skills from average-ability peers, such as calendar keeping, outlining, note taking, and organizing materials in their desk or backpack. These gifted boys might skate by or even achieve a high level of performance and learning without having to be responsible for these important study skills. *Earlier reading with them might have helped them learn how to focus.* A fundamental skill of learning is how to focus, as we all have experienced on days we cannot concentrate.[9]

Shared reading time is all about focusing on the story being read, asking questions, and predicting outcomes. The child or student must learn to listen for important information. Learning to focus on important information helps children focus better in everyday life and at school. By letting our students and children interact with us during reading time, we are letting them know they are being heard and valued. There is no reason for them to withdraw or overact, so this shared reading can curb inappropriate emotions. This is important for teachers with students who act out often in class.

Skills need to be taught for children to find success at home or in school. Taking the time to make reminder lists of what the boy needs to do for his homework, items to bring back to school, papers to finish or have signed, and so on, are all valuable skills for boys to remember. The teacher or parent can help the child by making the list or, better yet, teaching the child how to make his own checkoff lists. As the check marks are accumulated, he feels some pride in what he has achieved.

By having a positive interaction with shared reading in school or at home, both teacher and parent will likely see an improvement in homework done. This reading can help ease the difficulties that may arise with homework. This shared reading time enables the children to openly ask questions. This can greatly improve their results not only on homework but also on upcoming quizzes or mandated tests.

With so much writing now expected of children in school and on tests, we know that proficient readers usually become good writers as well. *Reading will encourage self-expression, which improves one's writing skills at the same time.*

We will say this over and over: reading will improve performance in school and in life. Learning should be a lifelong activity first modeled at home by reading to the child as much as possible. Studies indicate that success in school can be predicted by a child's third-grade reading scores on achievement tests. This known fact is scary but true. Another reason we as parents, teachers, and administrators cannot wait is because the world is changing around us quickly. We cannot stay as we are and hope for different results with our current curriculum and educational system.

DADS CAN MAKE A HUGE DIFFERENCE

Since fathers are important role models for their children, they have the opportunity to give their children a head start on an active lifestyle and to participate with them in healthy activities that feel much more like play than a prescription. As it turns out, a prescription for healthy kids is much the same as is recommended for their grown dads. According to the American Academy of Pediatrics (AAP), exercise strengthens kids' hearts and lungs, which may help protect them from heart problems as they get older. Active kids are more likely to avoid obesity and the health problems that go with it.

We know that exercise is the most important foundation that men can build for themselves and their families to achieve and maintain optimal health. It is more powerful than any pill in preventing and treating many conditions, including diabetes, stroke, heart disease, colon cancer, and the thinning of bones. In today's increasingly overweight society, activity helps stop weight gain as men and children age. While dieting is necessary to lose weight, exercising regularly helps accelerate the weight loss and is critical to keeping it off.

When a child sees his dad being active, this active lifestyle can have a lifelong effect on the child's own life. Regular exercise is also proven to treat conditions such as high blood pressure, heart disease, asthma, and smoker's lung disease.

We see much talk about the relationship of depression and mental illness to violence today in our society. Becoming active early in life, a child can avoid diabetes, high cholesterol, mental health conditions, arthritis, and other diseases. More important in regard to education, this exercise can even increase brain activities, such as thinking, learning, judgment skills, and mood.

Best of all, we know that regular exercise helps men live longer lives with greater physical abilities, achieving an overall better quality of life. Too many children sit in front of the television or computer for hours at a time. Obesity is becoming the norm. This obesity can become another vicious cycle of eating more to end depression and feelings of low self-worth and low self-esteem.

Naturally, a boy's self-confidence is lowered as well if he is overweight. Teasing and bullying can become intolerable and lead to frustration and aggression. Children need to strive to tell themselves,

> A successful person is the one who can lay a *firm* foundation with the bricks others have thrown at him or her.

> —Author unknown

We know that this is much easier said than done with today's bullies and others who can say cruel things. Children must not let others determine how they should perceive themselves; parents and teachers can help tremendously in building self-esteem, leading to self-confidence.

WHAT IS THE BEST FITNESS PLAN FOR CHILDREN?

The AAP, which is dedicated to the wellness of all children, recommends at least sixty minutes of physical activity each day for children, and the current national guidelines for adults is a cumulative 150 minutes or more per week of moderate-intensity aerobic exercise. In addition, there should be two or more days of muscle-strengthening exercise. An excellent resource for any parent, teacher, or coach looking to find suggestions and answers about healthy living is www.aap.org.[10]

This can seem like a lot if your family isn't used to exercise, but doing it together is fun, and the overall benefits will far exceed the physiological advantages. The following seven tips from the AAP and other experts can help you and your children get moving together.

SEVEN STEPS TO MALE BONDING WHILE KEEPING FIT

1. *Encourage your child to join a team sport, such as baseball or soccer.*
   You can volunteer to coach the team if at all possible.
2. *Take your children to places where other children are playing, such as public parks and swimming pools.*
   Gyms are excellent when supervised.
3. *Keep sports equipment handy.*
   If you have some tennis rackets, jump ropes, hula hoops, or a softball and glove in the closet, you and your children can easily grab them and go. Roller skating is a great activity to share, but be sure to wear knee pads and helmets.
4. *Walk or bike your child to school.*
   Make sure both of you wear helmets every time and enjoy the extra time together while staying active.
5. *Have your children help around the house.*
   Washing the car, gardening, and vacuuming are all good habits that could double as exercise. Mom will also be forever grateful. Why not clean out the garage or, better yet, have your children clean out their room? Think of simple rewards as encouragement.
6. *Limit screen time.*
   Children sitting in front of a television or computer are just sitting. Challenge them to log at least as much active time as screen time. Here is another opportunity to work in some math skills, such as graphing the number of hours spent on the computer. At the very least, monitor what the child is doing on that computer so that he is making his screen time valuable.
7. *Put down this book and get going.*
   Additionally, you can leave now only if you promise to read more of this book soon. There is so much more for us to say.

By the way, if there is not a dad in the family, a big brother, uncle, family friend, coach, or mentor can fill in for doing activities with your son. Naturally, if Mom has the energy, she can do it as well. As we have found out, many moms have to do it all.

Since a mom is excellent at multitasking, she may love this additional time spent with her son, knowing how much it would help the entire family. But occasionally, it is beneficial for the son to interact with another male in outdoor exercise, learning activities, and guy conversations. *This is the perfect opportunity for a troubled child to open up.*

MORE QUALITY TIME WITH DAD IS IMPORTANT

Most fathers love to spend time with their children, but, unfortunately, it can be difficult for many dads to find enough time to be the coach, teacher, and companion to their children that they want to be. *Children need to see their dads showing compassion, emotion, and laughing.* Additionally, many dads (and some who have to be the mom as well) are familiar with the wonderful joys of parenting.

However, there is also the struggle to balance the other demands of life. Getting quality time with your children can be very difficult; there is nothing old-fashioned about sitting close to our sons and enjoying quality time while reading an excellent book. Besides, reading to your child establishes a positive routine for today's rushed family. Activities done with reading, such as drawing pictures, finding places on a map, or looking up related searches, can make reading much more interesting.

If single dads can put that child as their priority over work, both the dad and the child will gain much more than the valuable quality time spent together. After a long day at work, it may be very hard to give your child the time and attention he deserves. By finding the time, however, you will build a lasting bond and love with that child over the years.

Remember that life has no "do-overs," and no one wants to have regrets down the road. By thinking about what you will miss later in a close relationship with your son, you are reminded of what is truly important now. Many of the things that burden and overwhelm us are the very things that we might miss when they are gone. Laughing together can lighten our burdens, so humorous books are a welcome break from our hectic lives.

Believe it or not, there are men who have become actively involved in school Parent-Teacher Associations and even enjoy shopping and watching movies with their children. Your child can become your greatest joy, so try to make spending time with him as simple as playing catch often. Men may recognize that they cannot always be there, but they can still help prepare their children for life by providing support and guidance whenever possible. Everyone profits from the time made by a dad.

Try board games as a great source of quality time for children. When more learning is involved by providing task cards, you are killing two birds with one stone.

In addition to a game being lots of fun, children learn about sportsmanship and losing or winning graciously. These are hard skills for children to master. Scrabble, Monopoly, Chutes and Ladders, Candy Land, Clue, and even simple card games can teach children many skills. Why not make up your own task or answer cards reflecting skills they need to know. You probably even have dominoes in a drawer at home that you can play to polish up some math skills.

Having fun with our children should be a priority for every dad, but whether you are a stay-at-home dad or working overtime most weeks, meaningful connections with our children can be difficult, to say the least. It is important to have a little space in between activities, too. If you can learn to sit still with nothing going on, you'll find the comfort level to be relaxing. This quiet time is excellent for discussions to begin.

Some protected time needs to be set aside simply for doing activities with your children. While dads cannot always do an elaborate activity with their children every day, with a little effort, every day we can create special moments with children. *Simple things, such as taking time to help fix a bike or skateboard or involving your son in a repair or other project, is a great way to teach life skills and spend quality time together.*

Parents teaching children to help with the housework may not exactly seem like fun to the child, but it does teach them about responsibility and being part of the family. If these chores are started when a young child feels like they are fun, by the time that same child is older, he may think of it as part of his routine. Maybe a small bribe of allowance will be needed, but then he can learn "money skills," as mentioned before.

Any child loves to be read to—and even more so if he gets to choose the story read. Moms are generally the one to do this, which is great, but boys need to see real men reading and asking questions about the story afterward. Moms and teachers will love you for this., as will your child for a lifetime of loving memories of reading. *Boys usually do not see their dads reading, and it will make a lasting, positive impression.*

Dads should also take time to join their children in other activities of their children's choosing. Playing a video game with your son is a great way to check out what he is viewing and also have some fun. Having a meal or just enjoying quiet time together is an important kind of together time that can easily be overlooked.

Not all quality time involves quality activities. After a long day, consider watching a movie or television together. This can be a special way to wind down together and relax. Try to keep an eye open for worthwhile shows and entertainment options to explore topics that your child is to encounter soon. Public television is an excellent source for many genres of interest. A well-planned movie might provide a useful springboard for conversations or simply an opportunity for being together at the end of a hectic day at work or school.

A busy father may find it challenging to have as much patience left at the end of the day as our children need. Certainly, patience is critical right from birth and will continue being required for a very long time. It is important that dads have a plan for recharging their batteries or patience. Some strategies might include listening to relaxing music on your way home from work or allowing Mom to take over for a bit so you can catch up on the news. And if you promise to return, she may tell you to retreat into your man cave for a few minutes alone. We all should remember that when you spend a little time taking care of yourself physically, emotionally, and spiritually, you become a kinder person.

In conclusion, as parents, teachers, administrators, counselors, or anyone else trying to make a positive difference in children's lives, we give kudos to you for making the effort toward that goal. At the same time, the ultimate choice will be up to that child. *We are working toward pursuing the dream for all children, especially boys, to make the best choices possible for now and for their future lives.*

Although we can present the consequences for actions a boy makes, he ultimately will do what he wants. Hopefully, however, through our consistency in pointing out the power of a parent's passion to find the passion or interests of the child, the results will show. Working together as a team, we can all improve his self-esteem, self-fulfillment, self-confidence, and desire to pursue his own dreams for life and happiness to come.

School or homeschooling will become his tool to achieve the information needed to learn more about his passion. With the consistent guidance of parents, teachers, counselors, and coaches, boys will have a better chance at loving school because they see it as the road to their passion and finding out interesting facts along the way.

A parent or teacher can always try harder to wish children well and share in their happiness with them. In a predictable and reliable way, your mental enthusiasm translates into feelings of inner happiness for you and your child or student. *Never take it for granted that your child knows you are happy for him and yourself; make it obvious to him by displaying your joy on the outside. Joy can make life amazing.*

In our country, we are all fortunate that we have the power to choose. Many countries are not allowed free choice or even much freedom of thought. This special right of ours must be protected, never taken for granted, and used wisely. Ralph Marston alludes to this precious right:

The Power to Choose

The pains, disappointments and frustrations tug at you. And yet, you are infinitely more powerful than all of them put together.

With your very next thought, you can rise above any kind of negativity. With your next action, you can begin to put real distance between yourself and whatever was bringing you down.

You have the power to choose the way you see life, and the way you experience life. You can take whatever comes, and make something positive out of it. The more you make a conscious, intentional choice about how to live, the stronger you become at doing so. Over time, as you continue to exercise your power to choose, you add real richness and fulfillment to your life.

Look at this day, with all its problems and challenges, and see the positive possibilities. Look inside yourself, and find the dreams, goals and desires that have the strength to push you forward.

Choose to live a life of unique greatness, and to give that greatness to your world. In every moment you have the power to choose, so choose the very best.[11]

SPORTS CAN IMPROVE ACADEMIC SUCCESS AND SELF-ESTEEM

Boys are fortunate that they have other avenues available to feel successful besides education alone. While being great at sports does not ensure their futures, it certainly can help with their self-esteem while going through school. Some even think that sports can improve academic success.

> You already have every characteristic necessary for success if you recognize, claim, develop and use them.
>
> —Zig Ziglar

There have been studies that imply that there is a biological need for boys to express themselves through motion and to find an outlet for their competition. It is obvious that boys need movement, and becoming involved with any type of sport can have a secondary advantage in academic achievement. If we look at neurology, we see that the nervous system's connections to boys' brains are exclusively designed for motor function response.

Pollack and Shuster have suggested that we can use this movement function to help boys open up and express his feelings when words elude him.[12]

This is referred to as an "action talk." For instance, boys open up and talk while engaged in an active, hands-on task—another red flag showing that our too-structured classrooms need to change.

Action could occur in the context of a fast-paced game or a slower-paced activity, such as fishing, but many of our boys need movement of some sort to be able to express their feelings. To support the emphasis on movement in boys' lives, Sax has found that the optical systems of boys are far superior at tracking moving objects than similar-age girls. This optical tracking ability may be a major advantage in many common athletic endeavors.[13]

Boys have been interviewed time and time again, and they express the need for more movement in the school day. To think that recess is being cut back or eliminated is troubling. Among athletes, this movement was discussed as being a need to relieve their stress as well.

You might be thinking, "Why is this book spending so much time with sports? I thought it was more about boys liking school more. Sports can be a distraction!" But wait, there's more. Sports can have a positive impact on school learning, better behavior, and self-esteem—all necessary for success in school. In Project HIGH HOPES, allowing for movement was the key to all of the classroom instruction activities and a general improvement in behavior when movement was incorporated in the learning environment.[14]

Individuals are questioning the importance of competition in the twenty-first century and challenging its relevance to our modern society. However, for thousands of years throughout the world, boys have been competitive. They seem to "thrive" better when it is put into the activity. Of course, there are many girls as well as boys who become threatened by competition.

Recently, psychologists are questioning whether competition is actually an expectation of society learned by boys that might be better conditioned away. These psychologists propose that if we create noncompetitive environments, then boys will follow suit and lose interest in competition. However, the field of neurology has combated this idea, noting that the brain of the male fetus is bathed in testosterone that could contribute to a competitive drive.[15]

Another study done by Kindlon and Thompson note that competition is necessary to a boy's understanding of himself. In order for boys to under-stand their own abilities, the authors tested them in a series of competition to measure what they can do.

Kindlon and Thompson also say that teenage boys crave a competitive situation yet will shy away if they believe that the task is one in which they will not be successful. Subsequently, a function of competition is to give a boy a measure of what he can do and a knowledge that he does not have a developed set of skills and runs the chance of losing. It would appear, then, that competition forms a "tape measure" by which boys understand their abilities.[16]

Although boys can find outlets to express their needs for movement in competition other than organized sports, many will still choose to join an athletic team or club in the future. Athletics has many more benefits than simply allowing a boy to release his energy. Boys involved in athletics can express themselves competitively and physically while helping them find male mentors. *These positive mentors or coaches can encourage boys to succeed in other areas, especially academics.*

Sports can have a dramatic effect on some boys' belief in their own abilities to achieve in areas both on and off the field. The involvement in an athletic activity can help the boy believe in his capacity to accomplish specific tasks: his self-efficacy. This belief can be affected by the boy's cognitive perceptions as well as environmental influences, such as an instructor's method of teaching. Changing classroom instructional strategies to match a student's ability has resulted in improved self-esteem in students who struggle in a regular academic setting.[17]

It is important for boys to develop the ability to recover from and adapt to adversity—called his resiliency. Boys who have their resiliency nurtured in sports have been able to face crises, trauma, stress, and challenges to experience success in life. Boys who are faced with continual challenges in athletics can also face life problems and find success. Others have suggested that boys with active athletic lives are more adept to resist adversity in the form of gang-related delinquency.[18]

As boys grow older, the skill of self-regulation is of utmost importance. The ability to influence one's own motivation, through processes, emotional state, and controlling patterns of behavior, can be described as self-regulation and suggests that athletes use self-regulation and self-monitoring and build confidence in their ability to achieve specific tasks.[19]

Many athletes say that the motivation and awareness of their own behavior developed in their sport has proven to be highly beneficial to their academic success. Parents can use sports or activities as an incentive for better grades as well. A child soon learns that he has to "earn the right" to participate in favorite activities by being able to balance schoolwork with the time spent in the activity or sport.

Down the road, the student will see the effect of regulating his study times by improvement in his grades. If we must have grades, then let's use them as an incentive to help your child work harder in order to play harder at sports.

Perseverance is necessary for all children (as well as adults) to learn. In today's society, it might be called "stick-to-itiveness," or continuing to try until you succeed. It is not as simple as it might sound since it involves commitment, hard work, facing hardships, and having the patience to continue to do endless tasks on one's journey to excellence. We have often seen that participation in most sports requires perseverance in continued training and self-discipline. *A big factor in achieving success in sports is not giving up despite facing stiff opposition and perhaps overwhelming odds.* We have all witnessed games on TV that seem over but are not.

The ability to listen to and receive constructive feedback and then show a change in behavior due to that instruction is "coachability." This characteristic is so sought after that a search on the Internet returns a large number of business programs to access and develop coachability.[20]

Maybe young boys are not ready to go out into the workforce just yet, but at least being coachable provides them a valuable skill for their future. Instead of calling it "college prep," we can call it "workplace prep."

One of the most obvious valued skills developed playing sports is teamwork. *We see that teamwork is an important characteristic highly valued in the corporate world of today.* Team spirit and cooperation are vital in any workplace, and many boys will develop these characteristics through sports. The ability to work with others to complete a common goal is not only necessary to winning sporting championships but also the basis for much of one's success in life.[21]

Additionally, teamwork sometimes requires self-sacrifice and putting aside personal goals for the good of a team. Many children have difficulty sharing the limelight with others if not trained to do so at an early age. Applications of teamwork can be helpful when it comes to boys working with others to complete school projects.

This teacher loved it when she saw everyone getting along, sharing ideas, and coming to conclusions without much of the instructor's guidance or interference. The time spent is much more productive and peaceful. Additionally, if guided correctly, given the opportunity for children to work more together, we can see amazing results.

THE IMPORTANT ROLE OF A COACH IN A BOY'S LIFE

Whether you are in favor of sports for children or not, many boys who do not have a father in the home can retain many benefits received from a good coach. The coach has a unique influence on the development of boys. The coach may or may not be a lifelong mentor, but his or her impact is undeniable. A good coach evaluates each child by observation and tries to build on his strengths and help with his weaknesses. The coach instructs, directs, and challenges the children on a daily basis and hopefully, at the same time, works on boys' self-confidence and self-esteem.

Of course, how a coach motivates his team can make or break a young man's dedication to a sport. It makes perfect sense that the level of respect a coach develops in parents as well as his or her players is key to the relationships that are achieved. Successful coaches need several characteristics. They must have knowledge of the sport, enthusiasm and motivation, and the ability to communicate well, and, most important, they must know their players.

It seems self-evident that a coach should have knowledge of the sport he or she is coaching. The children would not accomplish half as much in skills and learning the sport if the coach were not the expert. The coach must keep up on new techniques and strategies to make the learning worthwhile.

In watching young children playing soccer, baseball, or any group sport, we often see that enthusiasm and motivation are contagious. When the players and parents see the coach being enthusiastic, this enthusiasm makes the children play harder and the parents cheer more—all becoming a contagious cycle. However, winning should not be the only thing of importance. "Life" shows boys that they cannot always win soon enough.

The younger the boy, the more vital is the skill of a coach in understanding each boy. Coaches must be able to understand what drives young boys to succeed and provide appropriate instruction based on their needs. The coach must keep the sport fulfilling and still be fun for everyone involved. Being a great coach is not easy for many.

Finally, one of the most needed characteristics for a coach is the ability to communicate effectively. Certainly it cannot be enough to be able to conceptualize a game plan; in addition, this plan has to be clearly communicated to the players. By concentrating on the correct drills and clear expectations, success will be more easily accomplished. No one wants to hear the coach saying, "What we have here is a failure to communicate."

SEVEN STEPS FOR A COACH TO HELP BOYS LOVE SPORTS

1. *Good sportsmanship must always be demonstrated—win or lose.*
   Give good feedback to every player after a win or loss regardless of how you might really feel. If a child learns to lose with dignity, knowing he gave it his best, then he will take that attitude to each game in the future. We once saw a sign in a coach's office that read, "Winning is not everything; it is the ONLY thing!" He thought it was funny, but unfortunately too many coaches seem to believe this when the pressure is on.
2. *Never, ever, use sarcasm or insults with young children—or their parents.*
   Children usually know their own shortcomings or weaknesses, and it will crush their spirits if you point them out to others. One-on-one talks are usually the most productive and a way to see how things are going for that child. Some children need a trusted adult to open up to.

3. *Make sure you organize your practice.*

Do you make appropriate time for stretching and conditioning? How much time is allotted to skill development? Does the practice run smoothly? And never forget to make all boys feel like they (and you) learned something important each time.

4. *Always make sure the goals are explained well to the players and parents.*

Depending on the age of the boy, communication about the goals of the team can vary. With younger boys, the coach should emphasize the fun of the game and the development of skills. Let them know that many skills are harder for some boys than others.

5. *The coach needs to demonstrate an understanding of boys' learning styles.*

He or she should be able to model some expected skills. The coach should also have realistic expectations of the boys' attention spans and be able to explain the game to them. As mentioned earlier, an observation book that dates noted behaviors, strengths, or weakness will help determine the proper course of positive action for that child.

6. *The coach must have fair expectations for all players.*

Especially among young boys, skill levels are going to vary widely. The coach needs to work effectively with all of the players and must show that all players are valued as part of the team.

7. *A good coach must handle negative situations calmly on and off the field.*

When a parent or player gets out of line and insults another player or even the referee, the coach must "stay cool" and diffuse the situation quickly and calmly. Children notice how adults "behaving badly" can be embarrassing to everyone. We see that everywhere. Besides, when the child looks to you as a role model, being out of control definitely sends the wrong message. You may see that child mirroring your bad behavior.

Whether it is martial arts, tennis, golf, skiing, swimming, track, horseback riding, or anything else, there are arguably many life skills learned, and it might even be the child's passion for many years to come. The additional benefit of staying in shape or getting back into shape is becoming more and more relevant in our overweight society.

Recently, we heard about a fabulous and caring coach of a high school football team. We wish all children could experience, at some time of their life, such a stellar coach as Doug Johnson. The following article shows what one coach's team did to make their community near Denver, Colorado, better:

Longmont High School's football players have made it a tradition to spend a day during summer camp focusing on improving the community instead of their own athletic skills. Their efforts recently garnered the attention of NFL Films, which documented this year's "day of service" for a possible television spot on NBC during Sunday's Broncos game. NFL Films also is planning a compilation showcasing football teams from across the country to air before or during the Super Bowl.

It's great to really come together as a team and focus on the community and helping out people who really need it," said senior Logan Green, a Trojans linebacker. "As football players, we're pretty blessed to do what we do, and we should always think about giving back to those who are less fortunate."

On Friday morning, the team also is expected to be recognized on NBC's *Today* show through a live feed from Sports Authority Field at Mile High. Plus, the team has been invited to watch Sunday's Broncos game.

Football coach Doug Johnson said he started the day of service in 2007 because he found community service through mission trips "life changing" when he was in high school. "Generally, the guys love doing it," he said. "They really get into it and all pitch in when they go out to work. It's become a tradition, one we can be pretty proud of."

The team this year worked in groups to complete six community projects. The projects included knocking out a driveway with a jackhammer and raising a concrete slab at Mountain States Children's Home in Longmont. Another team cleared out rocks, raked, laid sod, mulched and installed a sprinkler system for a flood victim's yard in Lyons. Other projects included helping residents with yard work and hanging a fence for the ColorRODans of Longmont's hot rod weekend display.

Senior Ethan Hitchcock, who plays safety, helped remove the concrete patio at the Children's Home. He said the community service day is one of his favorite parts of the summer camp.

"You're getting work done, but you're having fun at the same time," Ethan said. "The community comes to support you at your games and cheer for you, so you should go out to support your community." Senior Barrett Ingvaldsen, who also plays safety, was on the "cleanup crew," loading up whatever needed to be thrown away from the various projects. "It's such a neat experience working with your team to help the community," he said. Barrett said he is "super excited" for both the *Today* show appearance and Sunday's Broncos game. "It's a way to create stronger bonds with your teammates." (permission to use given by Kevin Kaufman of the *Daily Camera*)[22]

What an excellent idea—and one that should be duplicated around the country. Just imagine how much character development would be instilled in the players who participated in such valuable community involvement. Besides, it is still an active activity.

THE MAGIC OF MUSIC FOR CHILDREN

How sad that many schools have been cutting back on their music instruction in grade school. For young children, rhythm, singing, clapping, and active movement are ways to creatively release energy and for many becomes their passion in life.

When we see marching bands in parades and football games, it is exciting for them as well as their audiences. The beat of the drums, the sounds of the horns, and all the instruments combine to create music of sorts inside of everyone. You can see people's positive engagement with tapping toes, clapping hands, and smiles on their faces.

Just think how it must affect young children at home or in school. All that enthusiasm is contagious and, in a way, feeds the soul.

The combined talent in the band represents hours of dedication, practice, and patience—all skills necessary for any jobs they may pursue in the future. *Teamwork is critical.*

Whether music is being eliminated because of financial woes or a lack of time due to more time spent reading and writing, either reason is a big mistake in the end. Thousands of children will never have the opportunity to play a musical instrument in a band, but they could at least experience the joy of music during class.

The link between musical sound and learning is wired into our brains, but we often do not realize it. Music is what neuroscientists call a whole-brain activity. It engages both the left and the right hemisphere at the same time.[23] You can use this whole-brain stimulation in many ways, such as connecting academic learning to areas of the arts, such as music. In preschools, music is often compared to being a child's second language. Music is a daily "event" for small children.

Hopefully, our preschools are playing lots of recorded music and providing opportunities for children to create their own music with rhythm, melody, and words. When they get to make their own instruments, the learning is twofold and creative.

Since male brains by nature produce fewer words, the linking of words in lyrics to music is helpful. Sounds made in nature have been found to be calming as well.

Listening to the wind, rain, or leaves rustling is considered "nature therapy" for the male brain. Listening to water flow over rocks releases chemicals in the brain that calm the brain. Why not try putting a type of water fountain in your home or classroom to help spread "calm" for energetic boys during study time?

Schools should invite parents, other teachers, or anyone they know who is comfortable playing an instrument to visit often. Children are not critical, and it makes them understand that it takes time and dedication to become proficient at anything.

During reading time, it is wonderful to put on quiet music while you do writing, reading, math, or science. We call it "thinking music" for better creativity and problem solving. Both the teacher and the child relax more, and even playing classical music can extend their learning of the arts.

For students with behavioral or learning issues, music can make the difference between success and failure. Some teachers use rain sticks (a traditional Australian instrument that can be made with a narrow tube filled with rice). Children who have frustrations or behavioral issues can use a rain stick to calm their brains.

Since we have learned that music helps children enhance their verbal skills, musical activity can activate music centers of the brain. Getting your son into piano, guitar, flute, drum, saxophone, or any other music lesson program is definitely more effective than the passive activity of simply listening to music. In addition, reading notes left to right can increase reading skills.

A study at the Chinese University of Hong Kong found that children, specifically boys, who were given as little as one year of musical training tested better in verbal memory than children who had no musical training. This musical training, even a year later after the lessons had stopped, stayed with the child in verbal memories better than those of the nonmusical children.[24]

Inexpensive karaoke machines can be a hoot for the entire family or even at school, and in addition it can help with a child's self-confidence. Whether the child sings well is unimportant, and reading the song's lines is a form of reading they will certainly enjoy. Just make sure they have a supportive audience. "Listening etiquette" has to be established beforehand. After they have learned how to sing along with its musical background, you can ask them to tell stories or read their writings or own books.

Karaoke machines are similar to music lessons in that they not only use music–verbal connections but also have the added advantage of directly helping boys with their self-confidence in using words and expanding sentences. Being the "lucky one" to come up front can help monitor boys' behaviors as well. We are all "hams at heart," and talent has nothing to do with it, fortunately.

The other subject areas, such as math and science, can be incorporated into this fun change of routine. They will never call this a "boring activity." While exposing boys to music, whether it be recorded music, live music, pop music, classical music, or music he performs himself, building math skills is involved. Many parts of the brain that build math skills are the same as those that react to music. *Studies show that music can "wake up" the brain for math learning and keep it awake, so leave the music playing for math homework time.*

Over and over, research has shown that music often correlates directly with math success. The foundation of music is built on a mathematical framework of scales, chords with prescribed intervals, timing, rhythm, cadence, and beat. So if your son learns an instrument and practices it daily (the hardest part, of course), this simple activity can lead to improved math performance. You may have to get some earplugs as well for your sanity. Hopefully, your son does not settle on becoming a drummer or cymbal player.

On a related note, this teacher and author played the squeaky clarinet for several years, much to my parents' chagrin. They are so glad it was not my passion.

In conclusion, self-esteem is the collection of beliefs or feelings that we have about ourselves. Self-esteem can also influence our motivation, attitudes, and behaviors. Some studies have shown a connection between self-esteem and emotional adjustment. Paluska and Schwenk found that sport participation had a direct effect on individual self-esteem that transferred to other areas of the athlete's life. Participation in sports develops a boy's sense of success.

The long hours put into sports practice, music lessons, or any structured learning and then seeing gradual improvement gives boys a positive sense that they can succeed in a variety of tasks. This positive sense of self can sustain them through many challenges and confrontations, whether they are sport-oriented or musically inclined or even in the academic arena. Music for many is their passion, and as Rock Christopher has noted, *"Purpose is the reason I journey. Passion is the fire that lights my way."* In bringing this chapter to a close, we would like you to hear what an experienced educator has to say.

Julie Kemp, an excellent administrator and teacher for over thirty years, gave us some words of wisdom about what she has observed over her many years being involved with children of all ages. She points out that there are still various negative factors affecting our children in school districts even today. These easy-to-fix obstacles can keep much learning from ever happening as early as kindergarten.

Until we all take more time to observe our children more carefully and to determine what they may need, we will see the same lackluster results in their ability to learn. The basic needs of all struggling children must be met first for learning to occur.

Kemp says, "As a retired elementary school teacher (14 years) and vice principal (16 years) for the Hillsborough County Public School System, I know firsthand about the importance of helping boys make a successful journey through the education system. Whether the child was in kindergarten or 12th grade, it just didn't matter. I found that these following factors influence success in school: nutrition, adequate sleep, appropriate clothing, stress, support, and interest level." She continues with the following:

1. *Nutrition is paramount.*

   Just like a car needs gas to run, boys must have proper nutrition to function in school. In my at-risk schools, students would often beat me to school in order to get breakfast. For many low-income students, the only nutritious meals they would get would be at school. When boys are hungry, their minds will not be on their studies but rather where their next meal will come from. During key testing times we always had extra food on hand. Remember the old adage, "If you feed them, they will come!"

2. *Adequate, uninterrupted sleep.*

   Sleep is also a key factor in having success during the school day. When boys are not given appropriate sleep times, when boys must share rooms with multiple family members, when boys are awakened by sounds of gunshots or fighting parents, they cannot function in school. I kept a mat, pillow, and blanket in my classroom and office just so a child could rest. It is amazing how therapeutic sleep is.

3. *Educators must be on the lookout for inappropriate clothing.*

   One of my jobs as a vice principal was breakfast duty. This was my chance to see who came to school in inappropriate clothing. When boys are cold, wet, wearing clothes or shoes that are too small or too large, I would send them to the clinic for a quick change. When boys are wearing hats, scarves, and so on, these could be indicative of gang affiliations.

   Often students, especially in low-income schools, get themselves up and dressed for school. Inappropriate clothing distracts the student from their studies. So many fights occur over clothes. So much bullying takes place over what someone is or isn't wearing. Observant and helpful educators are the key here.

4. *When boys are stressed, they often act out in aggressive or withdrawn ways.*

   I have often said that when a child is acting out, it is their silent cry for help. The same is true if a child becomes silent. Educators and parents must determine the true meaning of the aggression or the silence before doling out the consequences. Listening is the key. Reading between the lines, making those phone calls to the home, and getting a real history of the family can be instrumental in determining the proper course of action.

5. *Everyone needs support whether you are 8 or 80.*

Boys must find a support base, be it friends, a family member, a teacher, sports teams, the clergy, and so on. Educators are extremely busy, but they must give some one-on-one time to each student every day. Can you imagine how you would feel if no one talked to you in a positive way all day?

6. *Finally, boys must find something of interest to them in order for success to take place.*

If you are disinterested, you will tune out. If you are bored, you will find something to do in an inappropriate manner. Educators and parents must provide stimulation to young boys and see what sparks an interest. Not all students learn in the same manner. Smart educators use all of the senses to help boys learn. Smart educators know that giftedness isn't just in the academics of science and math and reading but also in the arts and music and in the physical realm of athletics.

You have read the headlines. You have heard the stories. We are losing our boys to suicide, gangs, and drugs or alcohol. Boys are now arming themselves and taking out their anger and frustration by going on shooting rampages.

Enough is enough. We can't let even one more child fall through the cracks. Wise educators, parents, and legislators must heed all of the warning signs. We can't lose even one more boy.

7. *Working together, we can alter a boy's life so that he will become successful in school and, in turn, become a hardworking productive member of society.*[25]

Now, hopefully, with more understanding of the big obstacles our children, teachers, coaches, administrators, and parents still have to face in our country today, we can "charge on" to the final chapter, all the while thinking about the following:

> Don't limit yourself. Many people limit themselves to what they think they can do. You can go as far as your mind lets you. What you believe, remember, you can achieve.
>
> —Mary Kay Ash

NOTES

1. Joel Osteen, "Power of Imagination."

2. Peg Tyre, *The Trouble with Boys: A Surprising Report Card on Our Sons, Their Problems at School, and What Parents and Educators Must Do* (New York: Crown Publishing, 2008).

3. Terry W. Neu and Rich H. Weinfield, *Helping Boys Succeed in School: A Practical Guide for Parents and Teachers* (Waco, TX: Prufrock Press, 2007).

4. Ralph Marston, "Make It Good," *The Daily Motivator*, May 25, 2013 (www .greatday.com).

5. Michael Gurian, *The Minds of Boys: Saving Our Sons from Falling behind in School and Life* (San Francisco: Jossey-Bass, 2005).

6. Ruby Payne, A *Framework for Understanding Poverty: A Cognitive Approach*, 4th ed. (Highlands, TX: Aha! Process, Inc., 2005).

7. Ruby Payne.

8. Terry Husband, R*ead and Succeed: Practices to Support Reading Skills in African-American Boys*. Rowman & Littlefield Education: Lanham, MD, 2014.

9. Peg Tyre.

10. American Academy of Pediatrics, "Healthy Dads," www.aap.org.

11. Ralph Marston, "Power to Choose," *The Daily Motivator*, April 12, 2014 (www.greatday.com).

12. William Pollack and Todd Shuster, *Real Boys' Voices* (New York: Random House, 2000).

13. Leonard Sax, *Why Gender Matters: What Parents and Teachers Need to Know about the Emerging Science of Sex Differences* (New York: Doubleday, 2005).

14. Susan Baum, Terry W. Neu, Carolyn R. Cooper, and S. V. Owen, Evaluation of Project HIGH HOPES (Project R206A30159-95) (Washington, DC: U.S. Department of Education, 1997).

15. Neu and Weinfield, *Helping Boys Succeed in School*.

16. Dan Kindlon and Michael Thompson, *Raising Cain: Protecting the Emotional Life of Boys* (New York: Ballantine, 2000).

17. Neu and Weinfield, *Helping Boys Succeed in School*.

18. Neu and Weinfield, *Helping Boys Succeed in School*.

19. Neu and Weinfield, *Helping Boys Succeed in School*.

20. Scott A. Paluska and Thomas L. Schwenk, "Physical Activity and Mental Health: Current Concepts," *Sports Medicine* 29 (2000): 167–80.

21. Paluska and Schwenk.

22. Amy Bounds, *Camera* staff writer, September 4, 2014.

23. Daniel Amen, "Music and the Brain," Brainplace (www.brainplace.com/bp/music/default.asp).

24. Paluska and Schwenk.

25. Julie Kemp, retired administrator and teacher from Florida.

7

Changing the Love of Power to the Power of Love for Learning and Life

Kindness is the language which the deaf can hear and the blind can see.

—Mark Twain

Can boys even be "taught" to focus less on power and concentrate instead on the power of love for learning? Can they learn to love and respect other human beings as they grow into prideful young men? Can boys and men be taught to compromise more? Compromise would seem to be a "lost art" when boys or men have to work with others who look, act, or think differently than they do.

However, first, to clarify, not all boys have trouble with power, and many can accomplish their goals without abusing power. These boys are not afraid to show love of learning with compassion for everyone. They certainly need to be role models for other boys.

It is possible for the "others" to succeed as well, but only through "change" implemented at home, in our schools, and in our communities. The positive change must be started somewhere, sometime. Why not here? And then it will hopefully spread throughout the world by future generations. This change will not happen in a year or even several, but it can happen.

If parents are our first teachers, then schoolteachers, administrators, and children's caregivers together share an important role in making this change for the good of everyone. *School and homeschooling lessons must change to teach more than simply skills and facts for literacy, math, and science.* Our precious young children need to have their belief system formed early on, learning that we are all created equal, with the same opportunities, if we work hard and believe. It is certainly true that some have more disadvantages, obstacles, and frustrations, but blaming others is not the answer.

THOSE WHO HAVE MADE A DIFFERENCE

This chapter concentrates on individuals who have made a difference for positive change. Many are well-known people still living today, others are simply average citizens, and some are from historical times of long ago. Much of what they said is still often quoted today because it is so meaningful. More importantly, a majority of these well-known men were once frustrated young boys. Others were women, such as the wonderful and greatly missed Mother Teresa, who wisely said: "We ourselves feel that what we are doing is just a drop in the ocean. But the ocean would be less because of that missing drop."

Additionally, they might have come from disadvantaged homes or communities. Even some were boys who hated school and dropped out, and others simply learned on their own. Several were homeschooled, but all had a passion for life and living in the way "their passions" led them.

In Dr. Wayne W. Dyer's "The Power of Intention" public television discussions, there is much truth for us to consider. His idea that we should see ourselves surrounded by the things we want to see or be . . . is positive. Think how powerful this concept could be if used for the betterment of schools, homes, humankind, and our planet Earth.

Boys love competition, and how valuable competition could be when used to help others. They could challenge children to join in collaborative thinking, sharing what they learn and discover for the good of all. Team effort works for sports, so why not for all learning?

Dyer goes on to emphasize that there is no such thing as hopes too high:

If you believe in shortage, you are surrounding yourself in shortage. However, we all must be in harmony with our intention, spending our lives in cooperation, not in conflict. One can never resolve problems by the shame of others, but we should rather be in a state of gratitude and appreciation. Through time spent daily in meditation, we can all connect ourselves with our source of energy.[1]

Naturally, many of us do not meditate, but all of us do think daily, and it is possible to train our brain not to be so critical of others; especially of ourselves. Parents, teachers, coaches, counselors, administrators, and certainly children need to think before saying critical or mean things to others. Once something is said, it can never be deleted. Many times, it would be a blessing, if that "delete button" were available to our speech processes, especially with young children. *Hurtful words can last a lifetime, and they determine how we perceive our possibilities.*

Additionally, we know that attitude can change our daily efforts to a large degree. Boys can make their lives much more difficult by the way they face their problems. When we take on the attitude that things won't change or get better, we are probably right. And when we have a positive attitude toward obstacles, those obstacles seem to dissipate.

A positive attitude by parents, teachers, coaches, counselors, administrators, and children can spread when it is consistently applied to learning as well as how we treat others. *Happiness is something you decide ahead of time, and when you change the way you look at struggles in life, things do change.*

This retired teacher can attest to the importance of being positive when dealing with the negativity; often faced by other teachers inside the schools. Several would blame everyone and everything for any problems they might encounter. We might have felt frustrated, too, but by having a smile for everyone, combined with a "can-do," humorous attitude, everything changed. Those problems would become resolved one way or another. If they could not be solved, then valuable time was wasted by complaining.

And one of the best side effects was becoming less stressed about those things that could not immediately be changed anyway. *Negative energy* is a waste of time. There is much to be said about the "power of positive thinking." Positive thinking not only helps ease the situation but also helps all involved feel better. We can all make good and bad choices, as Ralph Marston wisely points out:

With Every Choice

Every choice you make makes a difference. Remember always to use that power wisely. Every moment you live provides you with opportunity.

Transform that opportunity into meaningful value in your own unique way. You have immense power over the quality of your life and the shape of your world.

That power is exercised in the choices you make. When you live with positive purpose, a positive attitude and positive expectations, you'll make positive, life enriching choices. Those choices will reliably create a life of great fulfillment.

What you think, what you feel, what you say and what you do all matter very much. In every moment, with every choice, you move your life in a specific direction.

Make the commitment to always make that direction a good and meaningful one. Choose wisely, and live magnificently.[2]

THE POWER OF YOUR POSITIVE ACTIONS

Having gone through another Christmas season, we might wonder more about "peace on Earth" and "power of purpose" combined with "goodwill." Many seem to be praying for these positive events to happen and are singing their virtues. If all men, women, and children would focus more on goodwill and peace, especially in our schools and homes today, bullies could not flourish. These positive actions would certainly help our boys' frustrations be averted. Aggressive behaviors might be lessened or, best of all, become a thing of the past.

> Love never fails, character never quits; and with patience and persistence; dreams do come true.

> —Pete Maravich

If humankind could change with hearts pure and seek the same goals for a better world, it might be hard to even imagine what we could accomplish as a whole human race. However, starting with young, impressionable children seems most logical. Is this simply another "Pollyanna approach," jumping on another new bandwagon?

Studies have shown that the *act of kindness* releases a higher level of serotonin in the brain. Serotonin is the chemical released in the brain that makes us happy. But the interesting fact discovered is how this release of serotonin affects all those involved with the kindness. The person receiving the kindness, the person giving the kindness, and the person watching the kindness— all three have their levels of this happiness endorphin raised. Acts of kindness are basic to every moral code and are probably so for a good reason.

Recent research suggests that kindness may improve resiliency by promoting feelings of happiness and peace and supporting immunity. Cultivating happiness and peace is a key to resiliency because it bolsters one's ability to stay grounded during difficult times. It also keeps the body healthy and helps ward off disease. Additionally, by improving interpersonal relationships, kindness can help build support systems so crucial during crises.

According to Talya Steinberg, "Over the past several years the subject of kindness has been receiving increased attention in the scientific community. *Numerous studies have shown that receiving, giving, or even witnessing acts of kindness increases immunity and the production of serotonin, a neurotransmitter that regulates mood in the brain.* A recent study at the University of British Columbia showed that even toddlers may show psychological benefits from giving."[3]

Researchers compared toddlers' displays of happiness after giving their own cracker or one handed to them by a researcher to a puppet and found that toddlers displayed greater happiness when they shared their own crackers than when they gave away a cracker provided by the researcher. These findings suggest that humans, as innately social beings, may even be biologically predisposed toward acts of kindness.

Kindness may foster community and sharing of resources, which ensures resiliency and survival. Additionally, kindness may nourish one's sense of purpose and meaning and reduce tension accumulated through interpersonal conflict. *To quote the Dalai Lama, "When we feel love and kindness toward others, it not only makes others feel loved and cared for, but it helps us also to develop inner happiness and peace."*

Surprisingly, serotonin is released in the brain for the person who witnessed that act just as much. Furthermore, the act of kindness not only helps all involved feel happier but also strengthens one's immune system.

There are many small tasks that would make a difference to someone else. Here is a thoroughly noncomprehensive *list of random acts of kindness*:

- Write about the "perfect surprise" you would do for someone special.
- Hold the door for a stranger.
- Send a random "hello" e-mail or text to a family member or friend you hardly ever see.
- Give a compliment to someone at work or school.
- Create a handmade card.
- Bring donuts or bagels to work.
- Smile to everyone.
- Help an elder with his or her groceries.
- Wave to children at the park.
- Say "I love you" to everyone you love.
- Do a chore for someone who needs help.
- Donate.
- Volunteer.
- Listen to a friend.

Keep in mind that kindness has an additive effect and it's really the little things that add up. So no matter how big or how small, each act of kindness makes an impact for us all.[4]

In the perfect world, humans could focus on the "we" and not just the "me." Kindness and compassion would flourish. There would be more accomplishments. Additionally, if we would do for everyone and not only oneself, think of the miracles that could certainly happen in schools, homes, and communities.

Schools and neighborhoods would be free of bullies, thugs, and frightening violence everywhere. Children, parents, and teachers would feel safer at school, leading to better attendance. Gangs could not take over a boy's chance for a fulfilling life. Those less fortunate, who have the most disadvantages, would feel encouraged to get an education to improve their lives and their futures.

Worldwide, scientists would be working collectively toward a cure for cancer and for every other debilitating disease. Everyone would be working together to make our planet environmentally friendly, and each person would be nurturing to the plants and animals living there. *Wars would not exist, as there would be no need to fight, making it "one world" working for the betterment of all people everywhere.*

Earth would become a place our grandchildren could truly enjoy and be proud to pass along to their children. Then many of our children might want to learn more about how to make the world a better place by becoming scientists, teachers, or coaches or by joining the millions of other professions or trades, providing services for the happiness and health of the entire world. Good role models must begin in homes, schools, churches, and communities; that cannot be stated enough.

So here it is, another year gone by, and will anything really change for the better? We probably will all promote peace on Earth, better schools, more conservation, more kindness to others, and so on, but speaking about it and doing something about it are two different things. As a yearly tradition, we write or say our New Year's resolutions, hoping to stick to them.

Meanwhile, we are afraid that the upcoming year will see more school shootings or stabbings, more bullying, more physical abuse of wives, more intentional fires, more drunk-driving deaths, more bombings, more murders, and more of anything else that can be considered "newsworthy." We will think about these tragedies with disgust. We will listen to the shocking events, over and over, until we become numb, with many proclaiming, "So, what can I do about it?"

You can change things. It must happen little by little and consistently every day. This quote from W. Mitchell discusses this issue:

> What I focus on in life is what I get. And if I concentrate on how bad I am, or how wrong I am, or how inadequate I am; if I concentrate on what I can't do and how there's not enough time in which to do it, isn't that what I get every time?
>
> And when I think about how powerful I am, and when I think about what I have left to contribute, and when I think about the difference I can make on this planet, then that's what I get. You see, I recognize that it's not what happens to you; it's what you do about it![5]

YOUR CHILD MIGHT DEVELOP INTO
ONE PERSON WHO MAKES A DIFFERENCE

We need to remember what Myra Janco Daniels said: *"Every private citizen has a public responsibility."* For young children, many of their attitudes are taught by their grandparents, parents, siblings, teachers, coaches, and peers. Perhaps if we *refused to accept the sensationalism* of our daily news and instead demanded more positive news, with schools learning about the "true heroes of our world," things could change.

People from the past and those still living today represent so much good worldwide. Role models such as Oprah Winfrey, Mahatma Gandhi, Martin Luther King Jr., Mother Teresa, the pope, Princess Diana, Maya Angelou, and others should be shared with our children. Their hard work throughout their lives should be celebrated more. *Remember, you can't change any circumstance or relationship or your life without the substance of love. Caring about others instead of dwelling on the past leads the way to positive change.*

Joel Osteen, pastor of Lakewood Church in Houston, Texas, gave this insight, which is relevant to many boys today who have been bullied in the past; bullying that still affects their self-esteem:

> There was a report about children who had been bullied in school. It talked about how years later, those negative words were still having an effect on many of them. They interviewed this one man.
>
> He was in his 40s. He looked to be a bright, intelligent man, but he had not been able to hold down a good job, struggled in his relationships, and couldn't seem to get on course. He said as a child, he was overweight. He was chubby, and some of the other children made fun of him and called him names like "loser" and "failure." He made the mistake of letting those words take root. Now they were keeping him in mediocrity.
>
> When somebody calls you something, either good or bad, that seed is planted in your soil. Now you get to determine whether or not that seed takes root and grows. When you dwell on what was said, you are watering the seed. You're giving it a right to become a reality. That's why it's so important that we're disciplined in our thoughts. It's great when people tell you, "You're blessed. You're talented. You're going to do great things." Meditate on those throughout the day. Water those seeds and watch this truth become your reality![6]

There are many encouraging stories out there of unknown people doing unendingly good deeds. These unsung heroes are volunteering and trying to make a positive difference locally and abroad. The things we take for granted in our lives, such as shelter, pure water, food, and medical assistance, are given freely by these volunteers to those less fortunate. Now and then, we hear about it but not nearly often enough.

Not long ago, there was an amazing effort by many in the almost crash and disaster of the U.S. Airways flight in Hudson Bay. Whether it was a miracle of God or simply a much-needed miracle of hope, the story filled us with new encouragement. The united effort of humanity gave many a wonderful feeling of hope for humankind. We would be amazed at how much good is really happening in our world. But even with all that goodness happening, we too should try to make a difference in our schools, communities, and world. *If we*

concentrated more on what we can do, not what we cannot do, this realiza-
tion of change might happen.

Every once in a while, we see something in a human kindness story, think-ing, "Wow, what a giving person, what a true hero, and why don't we hear more of these uplifting stories on the news?" But then I guess it is because the other stories are more shocking and get our attention immediately. Once again, are we giving in to unnecessary sensationalism? It would seem that media watchdogs are certainly needed now more than ever.

Maybe now we have to be the media watchdogs to start change happening faster. *Each and every one of us should demand better and engaging educa-tional television. Less violence in computer games and more movies with super-heroes for children to emulate or try to relate to more would be exciting.* By the way, those superheroes need to be portrayed as good readers, good writers, and good students so that boys will see literacy and school as a positive endeavor to pursue. Just demonstrating super strength does not make a hero!

Let's cut back on all the sensationalism and violence. We should celebrate the heroes everywhere and use a boy's natural competitive spirit, by hav-ing healthy contests of competition to reach the needed productive goals in school or in the community. How about classes with the cleanest desks, cleanest room, or cleanest cafeteria table?

Why not point out classes with the best behavior, the least trips to the principal, or the best attendance for the week and awards for those students observed helping others in any way? Perhaps these positive actions would encourage others to do the same. Good competition can lead to better results everywhere. The positive energy produced by good competition could be-come contagious.

THE SMALLEST EFFORT CAN HELP OTHERS

More important, we must realize that we can do something no matter how small the effort. *Any action causes a reaction that can help make this a better world, especially if done by thousands of individuals worldwide—performed not only one day but day after day, month after month, and year after year.* We certainly have witnessed what can happen with Facebook and YouTube, where great ideas can be easily shared all over the world now through the Internet. Bad ideas should be monitored, of course, which sadly might be easier said than done.

Remember the song "Accentuate the Positive" by Johnny Mercer? "You've got to accentuate the positive, eliminate the negative, latch on to the affirma-tive; and don't mess with Mister In Between." What a great song that was.

Someone once said that all the arms we need are for hugging, not wars and killing. As Jill Jackson Miller and Sy Miller sang in their song "Let There Be Peace on Earth," "Let there be peace on earth, and let it begin with me."

Additionally, Norman Vincent Peale perceptively said, "Christmas waves a magic wand over this world, and behold, everything is softer and more beautiful!" And why can't Christmas be year-round?

Year-round Christmas is easy to accomplish with our daily actions of love and caring. Another example of all ages and genders learning to give to others happened in my own classroom. Each Christmas, we would organize a donation of sorts done by children wanting to help. We collected nonperishable food, new socks, books, puzzles, and toys. The children got to wrap up the items, and, if necessary, they marked whether their "gift of love and caring" was for a boy or girl. They loved signing their names the most, giving them the added feeling of importance once again. Next, their gift was placed under the tree for pickup. Often many of those gifts stayed at our own school and community for families needing the most help. Many skills of literacy were used in reading, writing, and discussion of what they had brought for others. What a great way to add to self-esteem we discovered.

We explained to the class that there were many other children in our community who *might not* have a Christmas if we did not do something. By learning the following poem, which was illustrated on visual aide cards, even our underprivileged and bilingual students understood the importance and true meaning of giving:

Sharing at Christmas

Some children have no toys at all; others have so many
So I will share the ones I have, with those who haven't any.
Christmas is the time to share,
to show someone you really care!

Kindergarten students were excited to give gently used toys to those less fortunate. Those who usually gave the most, surprisingly, were children on the lower end of the socioeconomic scale. *Was this because they could empathize with how those less fortunate children might feel?* Some children who had more at home seemed to think they did not have much to give away, or enough to share with someone else.

Giving and sharing should be experienced not only at Christmastime but also during the entire year. Our country has lonely, stressed soldiers all over the world now. Throughout the months, our class also sent letters to the troops and raised many pennies, nickels, and dimes for different causes over the years. You will be amazed how most children really want to help. They enjoy feeling like they, too, are worthy of making a difference in the world. Think of the joy a card or letter would bring to any soldier away from home.

Sometimes we would even get a letter back as a reward. We also experienced a secondary benefit: those same students learned to look at maps and world globes, saw where peoples lived, and learned about habitats that need our protection. *Natural learning and curiosity was progressing by simple acts of kindness.*

One of the best things we did—and an action that needs to happen more— is having the children visit the hospitals and rest homes in their areas . . . again, not only at Christmastime but also during the entire year. The interaction between the very young and very old is incredibly sweet and much appreciated by the elderly. We have witnessed the importance firsthand and often. The children loved singing songs, reciting poems, reading a story, playing music, and dancing for the elderly. The involvement of literacy, music, poetry, dance, and creativity was very entertaining when shared in hospitals and rest homes in our community.

Our older generations need a reason to live, as do the sick, young and old alike, in both hospitals and nursing homes. The children spent much time writing cards, drawing pictures, and bringing gifts or flowers to cheer up the elderly and sick. Writing skills came easily and naturally to those students since we allowed "inventive" spelling. Never once did a sick child or old person say, "Hey, you misspelled that word."

The children's new friends were read to and read with on most visits. What a terrific type of field trip, promoting understanding of our stages of life while establishing a foundation of better compassion for their own parents and grandparents. Often these elderly are hidden away, and children have no idea how valuable they are to us. In reality, these older people are our tie to history which can be lost when they die. Many of the elderly pass away with no one even caring. When we become more aware of them, see their struggles, realize the gifts they hold, share their unending love and spirit . . . life takes on new meaning for all involved.

We had some of the children interview the brighter elderly for great stories to learn about. Then everyone got to hear various stories again and again. The children would write their new friend's story, and illustrate it at school for the anticipated return visit. To see many proud children with the loving elderly relating together so well was truly wonderful. Our media need to find more of those feel-good happenings, so that others decide to get involved as well.

The elderly and sick are right in our own backyard; it is easy for any of us to take the time to visit. Many times at assisted care facilities, we have seen very old and feeble people sadly sitting in their wheelchairs, hoping to have a visitor. Who would want to be in that depressive state when they, too, become the elderly? What happened to the elderly being revered as in days gone by? *They are our link to history and can connect us with their struggles to even survive. Truths need to be told about what they had to give up for their own children.*

Our classes learned about how acts of kindness can heal everyone involved. Here is a meaningful quote by Maya Angelou: "If you find it in your heart to care for somebody else, you will have succeeded." Many of our students and children might be hospitalized one day, and these visits took away the fear of the unknown for them.

Why can't we better utilize our retired people who want to stay active and productive? Sadly, a few years ago when a very bright, older mom offered her free services at a nearby elementary school, she was never even contacted later. Since she had worked off and on in our classroom for years, she was more than qualified. There were times when she could take over the class if needed, but by law that could have never happened.

The school never called her back, and she had gone there in person to show a sincere desire. This retired mother, hoping to volunteer, even had stellar references—ours included. It boggles the mind how any school could turn down quality help that was free to them. This is where our communities need more organization in how to use any and all volunteers, especially our vast retired population—if nothing else but to help a child with reading, writing, or math or even just companionship. *Our children need to respect the elderly and feel their love. It may be hard to believe, but we will all be elderly one day.*

We know that both the old and the sick will always need our help; therefore, getting involved with them now is something any of us can easily do. Set a time when you as a parent or teacher could visit each week or month. If we could all practice kindness, caring, compassion, empathy, and giving, the world would be a better place. In doing so, we would all discover that, as E. Joseph Cossman said, "love is a friendship set to music." Love being related to friendship is valuable for all human beings, but being set to music gives the word "love" something special, as does this excellent passage by Ralph Marston:

Love Always

Give love away . . . and you will have even more. Love like nothing else matters, for without love, it doesn't.

When you act solely out of self interest, you end up making yourself that much smaller. When your actions are sincerely guided by love for others, you are lifted up as much as they.

When love is attacked, it grows stronger. When love is denied, it becomes even more compelling. Love endures through the most difficult of times and the most hopeless of situations. By yielding, love overcomes, setting up a dynamic that cannot be defeated.

Think of your life as it was ten or twenty years ago. The details in your memory have likely faded, yet the love you experienced is stronger than ever.

Is there any truth that is greater than this? Love is, and will always be.[7]

Not much needs to be added to those poignant thoughts.

The next section discusses volunteers as a real asset to children and saving time for the overworked teacher. We deal with the valuable resources that are available and free to every classroom teacher. Allowing these volunteers to come into the classroom environment and share their best talents with the teacher and children can be amazing.

VOLUNTEERS CAN OFTEN SAVE YOUR LIFE

When burdened daily with so much to accomplish at school, most teachers should encourage anyone who knows how to simply smile to help in their classes. *There is a lasting bond formed between the students and volunteers, resulting in a definite "win/win" situation for everyone.* All parents need to visit their child's classroom and help in any way possible. The teacher and parent need to work as a team for the benefit of the child.

Even our limited-English-speaking parents enjoyed coming to help. Naturally, this took some convincing since some are very shy. Once that barrier was broken down, they loved visiting and seeing what a great help they were, much to their surprise. These parents additionally learned better ways to help their child at home with homework simply by observing our daily class routine and seeing techniques used in teaching.

Bilingual parents are usually shy, but by showing them how you want your students to learn about different languages and cultures throughout the world, they begin feeling important. "We would help them with their English, if they would help us with their language," we would tell them with a smile. Children love to learn new languages, even if it is pig Latin! Luckily for them, their brains can pick up a new language quicker than we can and are not afraid to try.

We know that using these volunteers is an uplifting experience for everyone participating. The weekly interaction with the volunteers, the teacher, but especially the students makes this experience great for all. Naturally, they get so excited when they see a familiar face coming to help them, especially if that familiar face belongs to their mom or dad, big brother, grandmother, grandfather, or mentor.

Spend time with people who love you the way you are, support your dreams and believe in you. It is the fuel that propels you forward!

—Rock Christopher

Many children never know the love of a grandparent. Each volunteer, young or old, had certain strengths valuable to our students. Many seemingly simple tasks, done by the volunteers can save the teacher hours of work at home. *Best of all, this additional help leaves more time for important lesson planning, observation, and individualizing those lessons for unique students—and they are all unique.*

Once we have a great teacher, qualified volunteers, and children eager to move into an exciting journey of learning and exploring, the topic of competition needs to be addressed. For most girls, competition has its place and is not usually at the top of their priority list. However, when it comes to boys, as early as in preschool, the behavior shown in competing with others is obvious to those watching.

Some competition is invaluable to make a game or task more fun to boys, but it needs to be monitored, or soon that *innocent competition* can quickly change to bullying behavior. If we as parents, teachers, caregivers, and coaches can make the competition healthy, it can serve any child as a positive trait. We do not need to encourage "survival of the fittest" in school or at home.

IMPORTANCE OF HEALTHY COMPETITION

We are prideful people—many of us are driven and very hardworking. Most of us have been proud living in a time of such advancement in technology and cannot imagine living during any other time in history. *On the other hand, we can also see things changing in a negative way and want that widespread sense of pride back for our incredible nation.* Lately, we have seen huge changes in other countries; not only academically, but also competitively in technological innovations. This type of expansive building is evident in many faraway countries.

After watching the Summer Olympics in Beijing in 2012, we saw this heartfelt pride in many of the games. Competition fuels people, as most of us know well. *Competition, used correctly, can accomplish miracles.* For all of the medal winners, it was obvious that the athletes had worked tremendously hard to obtain their recognition. They gave it their all, and the years of practice were evident; the effort finally paid off.

When comparing Western nations and their "star athletes" to other countries, most of our athletes have not been training since age three or pulled from their homes and parents for the purpose of Olympic preparation, as is often done in other nations. They were free to come and go as they pleased in pursuing their Olympic dreams. Even their parents remarked that they did not want to push their children, yet those same children set their own high goals for what they wanted to accomplish. *Could this focus come from the passion that this book keeps referring to?*

What we realized in comparing other countries to the West was that pride, passion, and competition can do wonders, but these traits must be combined with *freedom*. Unfortunately, that right we all should have does not exist in all countries. More important, that pride, passion, and competition should not be combined with power to be used for aggression or bullying.

China, as the host of the Olympics, was spectacular, and the amazing accomplishments they achieved were evident. Reaching their goals within only a few years was incredible. The building of so much Western culture was evident in their stores, structures, styles, attitudes, and so on, yet they still did not have the freedom we have in the West. Their people love McDonald's, Starbucks, Disneyland, Pepsi, Coke, and thousands of our businesses and products we choose from daily without a thought.

What people loved the most at the Olympics was the "One World" theme, resonating throughout the Olympics and referenced to in this book. We all must respect and allow people and governments to grow—as long as they are not trying to take our freedom away. There appears to be a fine line between the interpretations of what we should allow or not allow. Unfortunately, many governments encourage the wrong type of power and conflict. Worse yet, some countries will even begin wars by trying to control others far away and of different cultures.

General Omar Bradley stated, "The world has achieved brilliance without wisdom, power without conscience. Ours is a world of nuclear giants and ethical infants. We know more about war than we know about peace, more about killing than we know about living." These "nuclear giants and ethical infants" seem to thrive on war and destruction in many cases. We need more wisdom and conscience working in tandem to help solve the issues we face today and certainly with more of them in the future. Much could be alleviated by more open communication before conflicts even begin.

The word "compromise" needs to be revisited when talking with other nations. *If we do not learn to value others' cultures and their differences and let people choose for themselves, we are no better than they are.* What is good for one country may not be the best for another, especially those living under different circumstances.

SUBSTITUTING MILITARY MONEY FOR
BETTER EDUCATIONAL CHANGES

Often we hear people saying how much more we could do for our country and its growing problems with the money that is now spent on wars outside of our borders. We have so many homeless and unemployed people, and this vast amount of military money could make a difference in our educational system as well. Vera Brittain pointed out in 1964, "The pacifist's task today is to find a method of helping and healing which provides a revolutionary constructive substitute for war."

Some nations are getting the reputation of becoming the world's bullies, trying to force their beliefs and values onto others all over the world. Oddly, these conflicts usually begin in places with an abundance of valuable oil or other natural resources that everyone needs. Maybe the bullying that starts in the classroom and in our communities leads to what is happening around the world today, or is it vice versa?

What does this pushy behavior say to our children? *Does it say that the biggest and strongest should be feared because they are more powerful?* This sounds like some children we often see who bully others on the playground.

Have you ever wondered what would happen if we just spent all that military money on our own nation's problems, specifically on schools, teachers' salaries, and better living conditions for all children, while still helping others around the planet with their needs? Would those military cutbacks leave us open to attacks, or would it make the world take more notice of our generosity? We might then become that "kinder, gentler nation" we should strive to be. Millions or billions of dollars are spent daily on unnecessary projects.

Certainly we are getting nowhere with the bullying tactics, and it seems to be unifying the other nations against us, which cannot possibly secure our future. Now many little boys want to become soldiers without knowing the sacrifices those soldiers must make every day for their country. We do think of our military as heroes, and they are—but at what cost? The price is way too high. We have lost too many men and women, not to mention all those caught in the crossfire of war.

The following is a scary observation. A German proverb says that a great war leaves the country with three armies—an army of cripples, an army of mourners, and an army of thieves. And here is an even more poignant quote from the Albert Einstein: "The release of atom power has changed everything except our way of thinking . . . the solution to this problem lies in the heart of mankind. If only I had known, I would have become a watchmaker."

On the other hand, unfortunately, foreign countries do not seem to really notice all the generous and loving actions many nations try to do for them.

By giving financial aid, medical help, and volunteer services during hor-
rific disasters overseas, millions of lives are saved and made better. Perhaps
that nation's bullying behavior overshadows the good it does in other, more
worthwhile challenges.

So, after watching the Summer Olympics, we had a renewed sense that all
was well with the world. Everyone participating in the events was headed
toward the right goals with competition in a healthy environment, win or lose.
Seeing the athletes being so proud to represent so many different countries—
young men and women excited to share the spotlight with the other eager
participants—certainly did our hearts good.

Witnessing the great sportsmanship of those winners as well as losers was
tremendous. In reality, we had to stop and admit that there were no losers.
These athletes were included in the small select group of individuals chosen
to go to the Olympics in the first place. To be invited to the games is an honor
for any athlete.

Then two weeks later, reality hit, and in watching the nightly news rather
than the uplifting Olympics, we were suddenly brought back to the same
realization that we had escaped during the Olympics. *The murders, rapes,*
school shootings, kidnappings, robberies, and so on, had not stopped for the
Olympics, only for those people watching the competition daily. The channels
covering the Olympics were free of the violence and negativity. We were the
lucky ones who had immersed ourselves into an exciting diversion. Unfortunately, it was only temporary.

WE MUST STOP THE BLAME GAME AND TAKE RESPONSIBILITY

Do you recall that this book alluded to the "Band-Aid approach" in attempt-
ing to fix schools. The intent of the No Child Left Behind Act (NCLB) was
an honest one, making all teachers, schools, and students more accountable.[8]
However, this act, passed in 2001, has become a nightmare in many ways.
Schools and teachers did not feel that NCLB was funded enough to begin
with. The failures of certain schools were punished further by having to jump
through new hoops to get more money the next year when they were already
struggling. These failing schools and their scores were posted for all to see.
The stress on teachers, principals, administrators, and parents was known to
everyone involved. Worst of all, the children hated having to spend so much
time on testing and having to do so much writing. You can guess who hated
it more and who showed the worst performance in most cases: the boys.

To make matters worse, below-grade-level children were not tested for
improvement or growth; making many students feel like failures from the
start. *Children who show any growth need to be celebrated and rewarded*
for their efforts.

As mentioned before, the intent of NCLB was to be helpful, yet when many tell why it is mostly a failure, not much change happens. Again, they hope for the scenario that schools will learn how to teach better and earlier and fit the children into the system. *Why not stop what is not working and begin fitting the school to what we now know about boys' brains and brain research in general?* Sure, responsibility has to start at home, in the schools, and in our communities, but funding mandated programs has to be there for any of it to work properly.

Unfortunately for all of us, "People are always making rules for themselves, and then finding loopholes!" What a truthful line by William Rotsler. Along this same subject, "The trouble with the future is that it usually arrives before we're ready for it." This truthful quote is by Arnold S. Glasow. Isn't that the same sad realization, when it comes to real estate busts, economic woes, failing educational systems, and especially wars? History seems to repeat itself.

What should scare us more is an opinion piece from the *Columbian* newspaper (February 6, 2008, as submitted by James T. Johnson): In comparing "Apathy" to much of what we see in our world so often, but especially when it comes to boys in school, this is a real danger! James T. Johnson sees the future we are hoping to avoid . . . with our most valuable resource . . . our children!

APATHY IS OUR GREATEST DANGER

Today we see so many apathetic students in high school, with no real direction, and students not really caring to even be in a classroom there. How many more have to drop out before we decide it is not just because they are "being boys," who never liked school anyway?

According to most boys, they feel reading, writing, and poetry, is really for girls anyway. Maybe this is not so far-fetched when looking at the structure of so many schools. We appear to make the boy fit the school, rather than the school fitting most boys. Why is that? Because we do not believe the studies that show how boys need a different type of curriculum than the girls? Or is it because it is just easier to keep what we have, and too difficult to do a revamping of our educational system? Neither are acceptable answers, however.

Many of us want the newest technology, more material items and fancier homes, too. Unfortunately, most of us were raised to believe we should have these things. Most parents agree that they want the best for their children; their child's happiness is a primary focus. Our credit cards are already stretched to their limit. We want things now, rather than wait until we can afford them. Some of our children observe our drinking and self-medicating; and may possibly follow our lead. We are becoming a society of wanting that magic pill to feel good. Our "must haves," are purchased earlier and earlier;

by parents, children, and even by our broke government. So now even our own government never has the money needed, having to borrow or put expenditures on credit. These actions are not economically sound for the United States. Now many families have more dependence on our already stretched government, socially, mentally, and academically.

WE NEED A TEAMWORK APPROACH

The key has to be a teamwork approach, using more compromise, while trying to cut back somewhat in our reckless spending and poor care of the planet everywhere. The Native Americans and the animals can teach us much about being conservationists. Hopefully, it is not too late for big changes in the care of our planet. Many groups are working tirelessly to save our environment, while many more are not caring, leaving the mess and changes for future generations to worry about and clean up.

Many want to blame the schools for not educating their children correctly, yet some of those complaining are not home enough to reinforce study habits. In addition, little time is left to teach the social skills necessary for their children to be successful. Others try to blame the parents for not volunteering or participating at school in any way.

Having been an elementary school teacher for so long, I have witnessed firsthand many parents never taking time to come to a conference, a play, or a sporting event or becoming involved with the school. *Children never forget who showed up, especially if they were not their parents. Why, then, would the child value education?*

Do not get the wrong idea; there are plenty of parents or caregivers who are your best classroom helpers and advocates. Those super people keep the schools running through organizations such as the Parent-Teacher Association and volunteering in the classroom and in school sports. They are the ones who keep the "need for change" communication going.

This constant communication with the school and teacher better prepares the child to be the best he can possibly be. Our country's future depends on these children, their parents, and their positive attitudes toward a successful future in their seemingly shrinking world called Earth. Who knows what planet might be next for them if we cannot even protect this one?

In the final analysis, we need millions more to help us accomplish real positive change. This retired baby-boomer teacher does not have the answers, only some suggestions and maybe helpful solutions to our current problems. She questions where our country is headed and the legacy we will leave, and hopefully her concern for educational change has been conveyed in this book.

Passion fuels men and women, so maybe this book will lead others to not only question more, but also find solutions closer to home. The dream or vision is for changing the "love of power" to the "power of love for learning and life." This statement could also be applied to how we should be teaching children in the early years, so that they can experiment with and pursue their own interests. And we wish, with proper guidance, these "nurtured passions" will be for the benefit of all humankind.

Hopefully, this book's strategies for struggling boys and girls make sense to you as well. The desire expressed throughout this book tried to sum up how our beloved United States should begin these necessary changes through correct funding of projects, while providing better school programs for our unique children. We need everyone's support in helping to establish more meaningful laws to stop the unending violence in schools, in our cities, and local communities not only here but abroad. *As concerned citizens, we must contact our representatives in our cities and states to begin this change.* We have seen that power, when misused, can lead to war. This is not the power we want.

SEVEN HOPEFUL THOUGHTS

1. What this planet needs is more mistletoe and less missile-talk. (Author unknown)
2. Sometime they'll give a war and nobody will come! (Carl Sandburg)
3. War will exist until that distant day when the conscientious objector enjoys the same reputations and prestige that the warrior does today. (John F. Kennedy)
4. The man with a new idea is a crank, until the new idea succeeds. (Mark Twain)
5. In order to fulfill your destiny, you have to make a plan and stay focused. Wake up each day knowing where you are headed, which direction you are taking and what you are going to accomplish . . . then stick with it! (Author unknown)
6. No matter how many weaknesses you may think you have today; no matter how many mistakes you make, you have to stay confident that with time, persistence, practice, and perseverance you will have the ability needed to succeed. (Linda M. Gilliam)

And finally, the most hopeful dream of all is by Eve Merriam:

7. "I dream of giving birth to a child who will ask, 'Mother, what was WAR?'"

The imbalance of school success between girls and boys is not only our problem. *Everywhere in the industrialized world where boys and girls have equal access to education, the underperformance of boys is a huge problem and getting worse.*

Long ago, the British government made the problem of boys in schools a top priority, as it should be. "We should not simply accept with a shrug of our shoulders that boys will be boys," said Stephen Byers, the school standards minister, when he announced a new national boys' initiative. "Failure to raise the educational achievement of boys will mean that thousands of young men will face a bleak future in which a lack of qualifications and basic skills will mean unemployment and little hope of finding work."[9]

Other governments have recognized the huge economic, social, and cultural problems that will result from letting the recent gender gap grow even larger. Government officials in New Zealand, Australia, Canada, and Jamaica all came to the same conclusion: helping boys in school is a matter of grave importance to the future of their respective countries. *Anyone who downplays the problem with boys is ignoring our changing world.*[10]

Girls are rushing into college, and boys are lagging further and further behind. People without college degrees have less chance in the job market—unless they have superior special skills, as with technology. Long ago, the economy was based on a solid agricultural and manufacturing base. This base depended on enormous numbers of unskilled or semiskilled workers. The times have since changed drastically.

This past economy has shifted greatly and are now primarily service-based industries, needing workers with more than a high school diploma. We all have seen how many of our jobs here are going overseas. Again the "almighty dollar" wins out for the cheaper costs available for all. We put our own workers out of work.

Many low-skilled jobs, as in manufacturing, textiles, and auto parts, are now done by boys who don't do well in school, who are not engaged in learning, and who as a result fail to reach their potential. They not only have poor self-esteem and poor self-confidence, but also will probably have to face a life of financial and emotional insecurity. No wonder so many people today are stressed—or depressed. Many are on the treadmill of working long hours to pay the bills that only become larger.

Again, our intent is not to spread more "doom and gloom" but to shake up our leaders to listen to others more. No one has all the answers, but certainly some have valuable suggestions.

Our perfectly insightful summary quote is again by Ralph Marston:

The Opportunity of This Day

Today, life will give you the opportunity to be honest. Take that opportunity, and keep yourself aligned with the power of truth. Today, life will give you the opportunity to be compassionate. Take that opportunity, and feel the priceless satisfaction that comes from making a difference in the lives of others.

Today, life will give you the opportunity to act with discipline and focus. Take that opportunity, and enjoy the fruits of being highly effective in whatever you do. Your life today will give you the opportunity to learn, to achieve, to enjoy, to reflect, to share, to listen, to understand and to love. Embrace each opportunity that comes your way with gratitude, enthusiasm and a sense of positive purpose.

On this day, life will give you the opportunity to be your best, to live and to act true to the unique and beautiful person you know you are. Take that opportunity, and run with it. If you've been wishing and waiting for a perfect opportunity, it is here and now! This day will be what you make of it, and there's no opportunity better than that.[11]

What most everyone knows deep in their heart is that we need to shake things up in our public schools, and that opportunity is now. We are also aware that your child's or student's issues are unique to your particular family, school, and community. This book can only supply strategies that are exciting, engaging, and better for boys, with suggestions of how they can enjoy learning more than they do currently.

In order to help young men struggling in school or at home, it is logical to start with young boys first. Why wait until they are too far behind to want to even come to school? Whether the boys are bored because they are more advanced than the other children, or hate school because everything is too hard for their level of ability . . . both are still struggling, just in different ways. We need to figure out what the changes must be, and then make the opportunities available to provide the necessary action our leaders can follow. *More and more talking about this huge problem helps for increased awareness but does nothing for the changes needed.*

As you can see, this book is really about all types of passion, as well as methods, techniques, and lessons that have been tried and proven to be successful in the classroom.

Hopefully, this book will help parents, teachers, coaches, children, and mostly administrators address the much-needed changes in our educational system. You might notice that the primary focus is on helping boys, especially those boys who struggle the most. These boys pull at our heartstrings daily in the classroom. In reality, however, our main goal is success for all children in their journey of learning, which should lead to better self-esteem with less frustration along the way. Therefore, girls benefit from most of these strategies, too.

Maybe you are saying, "Well, if she can write a book, I can write a better one, full of better ideas!" We encourage all of you to get more involved and, as Nike says, "Just Do It!" At least that would be an effort in the right direction; the conversation of needed change would have begun.

This book also tried to suggest many problems needing solutions for people to ponder, so that they might become involved in providing those solutions to classrooms and communities everywhere. We need to do what we can and not wait for others to do it.

In conclusion, we as educators and parents need to provide the best age-appropriate knowledge available to drive our schools' improvement. At the same time, we must give these children every tool necessary to facilitate better outcomes for our unique children.

Hopefully, this book gave you interesting information, new strategies with fun techniques to try, combined with the inspiration to believe that *by imple-memting the appropriate changes in educating our children, all boys can learn; boys can learn to love school or at least like it.* And during this happy discovery, boys will become successful, self-confident, and fulfilled students, leading to less frustration for everyone.

Finally, and more important, all children must *thrive*, not simply *survive* school.

NOTES

1. Wayne W. Dyer, "Power of Intention," Oregon Public Television, aired often in 2014.

2. Ralph Marston, "With Every Choice," *The Daily Motivator*, April 19, 2014 (www.greatday.com).

3. Talya Steinberg, guest blogger, "The Resiliency of Caregiving: A Look at Parents and Caregivers of Individuals with Intellectual Disabilities," *Psychology Today*: "In the Face of Adversity: The Importance of Resiliency," by Ron Breazeale, July 9, 2014 (www.psychologytoday.com/blog/in-the-face-adversity/201407/the-resiliency -caregiving).

4. Talya Steinberg, guest blogger, retrieved on July 9, 2014.

5. W. Mitchell, "What I Focus On" (www.wmitchell.com/freeresources.html).

6. Joel Osteen, "Bullies."

7. Ralph Marston, "Love Always," February 14, 2004.

8. No Child Left Behind Act of 2001, US Department of Education (www2 .ed.gov/legislationlESEA02).

9. Peg Tyre and Stephen Beyers.

10. Peg Tyre.

11. Ralph Marston, "Opportunity of This Day," June 17, 2014.

Bibliography

Albert, R. S., and M. A. Runco. "Independence and the Creative Potential of Gifted and Exceptionally Gifted Boys." *Journal of Youth and Adolescence* 18 (1998): 221–30.

Amen, Daniel. *Change Your Brain, Change Your Life.* New York: Three Rivers Press, 1999.

———. "Music and the Brain." www.brainplace.com/bp/music/default.asp.

American Academy of Pediatrics. "Healthy Dads." www.aap.org.

Armstrong, Thomas. *Multiple Intelligences in the Classroom.* 2nd ed. Alexandria, VA: Association for Supervision and Curriculum Development, 2009.

Bailey, Keith, Patrice Moulton, and Michael Moulton. "Athletics as a Predictor of Self-Esteem and Approval Motivation." *The Sport Journal* 2, no. 2 (1999): 1–5.

Baron-Cohen, Simon. *The Essential Difference: The Truth about the Male and Female Brain.* New York: Perseus, 2003.

Baroody, Allison E., and Jennifer Dobbs-Oates. "Child and Parent Characteristics, Parental Expectations and Child Behaviors Related to Preschool Children's Interest in Literacy." *Early Child Development and Care* 181, no. 3 (2011): 345–59.

Barry, Dave. *Dave Barry's Complete Guide to Guys.* New York: Random House, 1995.

Baum, Susan M., Terry W. Neu, Carolyn R. Cooper, and S. V. Owen. *Evaluation of Project HIGH HOPES* (Project R206A30159-95). Washington, DC: U.S. Department of Education, 1997.

Baum, Susan M., Julie Viens, and Barbara Slatin. *Multiple Intelligences in the Classroom: A Teacher's Toolkit.* New York: Teachers College Press, 2005.

Big Brothers, Big Sisters. "Our Impact." www.bbbs.org/site/c.diJKKYPLJvH/b.1632631/k.3195/Our_Impact.htm.

Bishop, Katherine M., and David Wahlsten. "Sex Differences in the Human Corpus Callosum: Myth or Reality?" *Neuroscience and Biobehavioural Reviews* 21 (1997): 581–601.

Borba, Michele. *Nobody Likes Me, Everybody Hates Me.* San Francisco: Jossey-Bass, 2005.

Bronzo, Bill. "Boys Will Read When Their Interest Is Piqued." *Reading Today* 27, no. 6 (2010): 7.

Centers for Disease Control. "ADHD: A Public Health Perspective Conference." www.cdc.gov/ncbddd/adhd/dadabepi.htm.

———. "Suicide Trends among Youths and Young Adults Aged 10–24 Years, United States, 1990–2004." www.edc.gov/mmwr/preview/mmwrhtml/mm5635a2.htm.

Coangelo, Nicholas, Susan Assouline, and Mirica Gross. *A Nation Deceived: How Schools Hold Back America's Brightest Students.* Iowa City: University of Iowa, 2004.

Council for Environmental Education. *Project WILD Aquatic: K–12 Curriculum and Activity Guide.* Houston: Project WILD, 2003.

Cramond, Bonnie. "Attention Deficit Hyperactivity Disorder and Creativity: What Is the Connection?" *Journal of Creative Behavior* 28 (1994): 193–210.

Dixon, John P. *The Spatial Child.* Springfield, IL: Charles C. Thomas, 1983.

Dobson, James. *Bringing Up Boys.* Wheaton, IL: Tyndale House, 2001.

Drake, J. A., James H. Price, and Susan K. Telljohann. "The Nature and Extent of Bullying at School." *Journal of School Health* 73 (2003): 173–80.

Elkind, David. *The Hurried Child: Growing Up Too Fast, Too Soon!* New York: Perseus, 1989.

Fox, Robert A., and Nina K. Buchanan. *Proud to Be Different: Ethnocentric Niche Charter Schools in America.* Lanham, MD: Rowman & Littlefield Education, 2014.

Gaines, Lawrence. *A Teacher's Guide to Multisensory Learning: Improving Literacy by Engaging the Senses.* Alexandria, VA: Association for Supervision and Curriculum Development, 2008.

Gambrell, Linda B. 2011. "Seven Rules of Engagement: What's More Important to Know about Motivation to Read?" *The Reading Teacher* 65, no. 3 (2003): 172–78.

Gardner, Howard. *Intelligences Refrained: Multiple Intelligences for the 21st Century.* New York: Basic Books, 1999.

Gentry, Marcia, and Terry W. Neu. "Project High Hopes Summer Institute: Curriculum for Developing Talent in Students with Spatial Needs." *Roper Review* 20 (1998): 291–95.

Ghiso, Marlo Paula. "Writing That Matters: Collaborative Inquiry and Authoring Practices in a First Grade Class." *Language Arts* 88, no. 5 (2011): 346–55.

Gilliam, Walter S. "Prekindergarteners Left Behind: Expulsion Rates in State Prekindergarten Systems." Yale University Child Study Center, 2005.

Goldberg, Gail L., and Barbara S. Rosswell. *Reading, Writing and Gender.* New York: Eye on Education, 2002.

Gopnick, Allison. *The Philosophical Baby: What Children's Minds Tell Us about Truth, Love, and the Meaning of Life.* New York: Farrar, Straus & Giroux, 1998.

Graham, Steve, and Michael Hebert. "Writing to Read: A Meta-Analysis of the Impact of Writing and Writing Instruction on Reading." *Harvard Educational Review* 81, no. 4 (2011): 710–44.

Green, Jay P., and Marcus A. Winters. "The Boys Left Behind." www.nationalreview.com/comment/green_winters200604190558.asp.

Gurian, Michael. *Boys and Girls Learn Differently! A Guide for Teachers and Parents*. San Francisco: Jossey-Bass, 2001.

——. *The Minds of Boys: Saving Our Sons from Falling behind in School and Life*. San Francisco: Jossey-Bass, 2005.

Halpern, Diane. "A Cognitive-Process Taxonomy for Sex Difference in Cognitive Abilities," *Current Directions in Psychological Science* 13, no. 4 (2004): 135–39.

Harris, Theresa L., and George Taylor. *Raising African-American Males: Strategies and Interventions for Successful Outcomes*. Lanham, MD: Rowman & Littlefield Education, 2012.

Hirsh-Pasek, Kathy, et al. *Einstein Never Used Flashcards*. London: Rodale, 2003.

Husband, Terry. *Read and Succeed: Practices to Support Reading Skills in African-American Boys*. Lanham, MD: Rowman & Littlefield Education, 2014.

James, Amy. *First Grade Success: Everything You Need to Know to Help Your Child Learn*. Hoboken, NJ: Wiley Jossey-Bass, 2005.

Karnes, Frances, and Tracey Riley. *Competitions for Talented Kids*. Waco, TX: Prufrock Press. 2005.

Kelly, Joan. "Moms across America." www.momsacrossamerica.com.

Kerr, Barbara A., and Stanford J. Cohn. *Smart Boys: Talent, Manhood, and the Search for Meaning*. Scottsdale, AZ: Great Potential Press, 2001.

Kimura, Doreen. "Sex Differences in the Brain." *Scientific American* 267 (1992): 119–25.

Kindlon, Dan, and Michael Thompson. *Raising Cain: Protecting the Emotional Life of Boys*. New York: Ballantine, 2001.

King, Kelly, and Michael Gurian. "Teaching to the Minds of Boys." *Educational Leadership* 64, no. 1 (2006): 56–61.

Ladner, Joyce, and Theresa Foy DiGeronimo. *A Mind at a Time*. New York: Simon & Schuster, 2002.

Levine, Madeline. *The Myth of Laziness*. New York: Simon & Schuster. 2003.

Litner, Timothy. "Using Exceptional Children's Literature to Promote Character Education in Elementary Social Studies Classrooms." *Social Studies* 102, no. 5 (2011): 200–203.

Logan, Sarah, and Rhona Johnson. "Investigating Gender Differences in Reading." *Educational Review* 62, no. 2 (2010): 462–505.

Marcon, Rebecca. "Moving Up the Grades: Relationship between Preschool Model and Later Success at School." *Early Childhood Research and Practice* 4, no. 1 (2002): 358–75.

Marston, Ralph. *The Daily Motivator*. www.greatday.com.

McCartney, Sarah J. "The Impact of No Child Left Behind on Teachers' Writing Instruction." *Written Communication* 25, no. 4 (2008): 175–87.

Meyer, Heinz-Dieter, and Brian Rowan. *The New Institutionalism in Education*. Albany: State University of New York Press, 2006.

Miller, Donalyn. 2012. "Creating a Classroom Where Readers Flourish." *Reading Teacher* 66, no. 2 (2012): 88–92.

Mooney, Jonathan, and David Cole. *Learning outside the Lines.* New York: Basic Books, 2000.

Mortenson, Tom. "What's Still Wrong with the Guys?" www.postsecondary.org/last12/152guys.pdf.

National Center for Educational Statistics. *National Assessment of Educational Progress.* Washington, DC: U.S. Department of Education, 2011.

National PTA. "Recess Is at Risk, New Campaign Comes to the Rescue." www.pta.org/ne_press_release_detail_1142028998890.html.

Neu, Terry W., and Rich H. Weinfield. *Helping Boys Succeed in School: A Practical Guide for Parents and Teachers.* Waco, TX: Prufrock Press, 2007.

Neuman, Susan B. *Literature in the Television Age: The Myth of the TV Effect.* Westport, CT: Greenwood Publishing Group, 1991.

Newkirk, Thomas. *Misreading Masculinity: Boys, Literacy, and Popular Culture.* Portsmouth, NH: Heinemann, 2002.

Newman, T. "Coaches' Roles in the Academic Success of Male Student Athletes." *The Sport Journal* 8, no. 2 (2005): 13\–18.

No Child Left Behind Act. 20 U.S.C. 6301 (2001).

Paluska, Scott A., and Thomas L. Schwenk. "Physical Activity and Mental Health: Current Concepts. *Sports Medicine* 29 (2000): 167–80.

Payne, Ruby. *A Framework for Understanding Poverty: A Cognitive Approach.* 4th ed. Highlands, TX: Aha! Process, Inc., 2005.

Perlstein, Linda. "School Pushes Reading, Writing, Reform." *Washington Post*, May 31, 2004, A1.

Pollack, William, and Kathleen Cushman. *Real Boys' Workbook.* New York: Villard Books, 2001

Pollack, William, and Todd Shuster. *Real Boys' Voices.* New York: Random House, 2000.

Protacio, Maria Selena. "Reading Motivation: A Focus on English Learners." *The Reading Teacher* 66, no. 1 (2012): 69–77.

Ravitch, Diane. *The Death and Life of the Great American School System: How Testing and Choice Are Undermining Education.* New York: Basic Books, 2010.

———. *The Language Police: How Pressure Groups Restrict What Children Learn.* New York: Knopf, 2003.

Rigby, Ken. *New Perspectives on Bullying.* Philadelphia: Jessica Kingsley, 2002.

Sax, Leonard. *Why Gender Matters: What Parents and Teachers Need to Know about the Emerging Science of Sex Differences.* New York: Doubleday, 2005.

Senn, Nicole. "Effective Approaches to Motivate and Engage Reluctant Boys in Literacy." *The Reading Teacher* 66, no. 3 (2012): 211–20.

Stahl, Lesley. "The Gender Gap: Boys Lagging." www.cbsnews.com/stories/2002/10/31/60minutes/main527678.shtml.

Stauffer, Suzanne M. "Developing Children's Interest in Reading." *Library Trends* 56, no. 2 (2007): 402–22.

Stein, David B. *Ritalin Is Not the Answer: A Drug-Free, Practical Program for Children Diagnosed with ADD or ADHD.* San Francisco: Jossey-Bass, 1999.

Suckling, A., and C. Temple. *Bullying: A Whole-School Approach.* Philadelphia: Jessica Kingsley, 2001.

Taylor, Shelly E., Lauren C. Klein, Brian P. Lewis, Tara L. Gruenewald, Regan A. Gurung, and John A. Updegraff. "Biobehavioral Responses to Stress in Females: Tend-and-Befriend, Not Fight-or-Flight." *Psychological Review* 107 (200): 411–29.

Time-Life Books. *A Child's First Library of Learning—Things to Do.* 3rd printing. Alexandria, VA: Robert H. Smith, Publisher, 1992.

Tyre, Peg. "The Trouble with Boys." *Newsweek,* January 30, 2003, 44–52.

———. *The Trouble with Boys: A Surprising Report Card on Our Sons, Their Problems at School, and What Parents and Educators Must Do.* New York: Crown, 2008.

USA Today Staff. "Boys Academic Slide Call for Accelerated Attention." *USA Today,* December 22, 2003, A17.

U.S. Department of Education, National Center for Education Statistics. *The Nation's Report Card: Reading Highlights.* Washington, DC: U.S. Department of Education, 2013.

Weinfeld, Rich, Linda Barnes-Robinson, Sue Jeweler, and Betty R. Shevitz. *Smart Kids with Obstacles and Realizing Potential.* Waco, TX: Prufrock Press, 2006.

Younger, Mike, and Molly Warrington. "Raising Boys' Achievement." Research Report No. 636. London: Department of Education and Skills, 2005.

About the Author

Linda Marie Gilliam has taught for over forty years and currently lives in Portland, OR. She is passionate about helping all children, boys in particular, enjoy learning and school. Her dream is to convince parents, teachers, coaches, caregivers, librarians, and administrators to try these successful strategies that are developmentally appropriate, fun, active, exciting, hands-on, and easy to do at home or in the classroom. Ms. Gilliam received Teacher of the Year for her efforts in Vancouver, WA.